THE MOURNING HANDBOOK

*The Most Comprehensive
Resource Offering Practical
and Compassionate Advice
on Coping with All Aspects
of Death and Dying*

HELEN FITZGERALD

A FIRESIDE BOOK
PUBLISHED BY SIMON & SCHUSTER
New York London Toronto Sydney Tokyo Singapore

F

FIRESIDE
Rockefeller Center
1230 Avenue of the Americas
New York, New York 10020

First Fireside Edition 1995

Fireside and colophon are registered
trademarks of Simon & Schuster Inc.

Designed by Hyun Joo Kim
Manufactured in the United States of America

1 0

Library of Congress Cataloging-in-Publication Data

Fitzgerald, Helen.
The mourning handbook : the most comprehensive resource offering
practical and compassionate advice on coping with all aspects of death
and dying/ Helen Fitzgerald.
p.   cm.
Includes bibliographical references and index.
1. Grief. 2. Bereavement—Psychological aspects. 3. Death—Psychological aspects. 4. Counseling. I Title.
BF575.G7F57 1994
155.9'37—dc20
94-4833
CIP
ISBN: 0-671-86972-8
ISBN: 0-684-80161-2 (Pbk)

Where case studies appear, names, professions, locations,
and other biographical details about the people have been
changed to preserve their privacy and anonymity.

This book is dedicated to my father, John Cihak, Jr., who introduced me to learning, not just from books but from observing the world around me. And it is dedicated as well to all the people who trusted me enough to share their stories with me.

Acknowledgments

Communicating with others takes many forms. In my case, it began with the spoken word; I was a lecturer before I was a writer. Through the years my lecturing has turned into magazine articles and now books, thanks in part to the help and loving support I have received from my second husband, Richard Olson, who has encouraged me to put my words on paper and helped me to do so through editorial suggestions and advice. It was he who gave me the concept for this book and persuaded me to write it.

Starting a book is never an easy task, but starting this one was made easier by our friends Bill and Barbara Chapp, who offered my husband and me the use of their lake home for two weeks. It was a very productive time that produced the first outline and a rough draft of the first chapter or two.

As the project progressed I was encouraged once again by my gifted agent, Anne Edelstein. She supported the book and convinced me that my editor at the time, Sheridan Hay at Simon & Schuster, would respond favorably, which she did. Later I had valuable support from Sheila Curry, who did the final editing of the book.

All this while my work was continuing at the Mount Vernon Center for Community Mental Health, part of the social services of Fairfax County, Virginia. I want to thank particularly my supervisor, Dr. Maria Mancusi, director of the Springfield

Outpatient Unit at the center, who has always supported my program and has the vision to allow me to try new and innovative ways to help grieving people.

And finally, I want to thank my friends at the Haven of Northern Virginia, an outreach program for the dying and the bereaved, for their continuing support over the many years we have worked together.

Contents

Foreword

Life is fragile. We know it but we live our lives as if nothing really bad could ever happen to us and as if all those we love will live out normal lives. What else can we do? We have to make the most of what life offers; dwelling on the prospect of pain, suffering, and death is hardly the way to live a full life.

When tragedy strikes, however, we are brought face to face with the fragility of life and of the persons and things we love. Very often this collision with reality finds us unprepared, shaken to the core. It is at such times that we find the need for help, often from people we don't even know. This book is a splendid example of help that is becoming available today through the new profession of death education and counseling.

With this book Helen Fitzgerald, a certified professional death educator, has expanded the literature available to grieving people in a very significant way, assembling a comprehensive handbook on the subject of grief and mourning. There is nothing else available to the lay reader that comes close to its breadth.

If you are mourning the death of a loved one, you are likely to find in this book the stories of people like you who have suffered similar losses. If you are wondering what kind of future you can have following some personal tragedy, you are likely to find new hope in the experiences of the people who were able to rebuild their lives with Ms. Fitzgerald's help.

What makes a good therapist? A psychiatrist once wrote that for a therapist the important thing—the really crucial thing—is not a medical degree, or any degree at all, but rather *empathy*. I have known Helen Fitzgerald for many years, and if there is one quality that stands out in her, it is empathy. This book is a reflection of her empathy: her concern for and identification with others.

I recommend *The Mourning Handbook* to any reader in search of a path out of the wilderness of despair. It is a compass, pointing the way to recovery.

—Earl A. Grollman,
author of *Living When a Loved
One Has Died*
Belmont, Massachusetts
October 1993

Before You Begin This Book

Grief and mourning are not subjects people usually want to read about. Few people other than professionals want to become experts in the subject. *The Mourning Handbook* is not intended to make you an expert, either, but rather to give you a source of ready information to help you in time of need.

Of course, this is a book that you can read like any other book, but basically it is a handbook to help you find answers to specific questions that may be troubling you. You can decide, based on your need for information and your ability to absorb it, how you want to approach the book.

If you are mourning the death of a loved one, it may be impossible to concentrate long enough to read the entire book, much less comprehend what you have read. For this reason, the book is arranged in a manner that will enable you to go directly to those topics of greatest importance to you. If you are mourning the accidental death of a husband, the unexplained death of a small child, the suicide death of a mother, the murder of a daughter, or the loss of several loved ones at once, you may need immediate help in dealing with your intense pain. Arranged as it is by topics, subtopics, and many cross-references, this book has been planned to give you help *now* in your search for solace and comfort. It is filled with stories of people like you who have had to rebuild their lives after a wide range of personal tragedies. Just knowing that others have experienced similar losses and survived can give you some measure of hope.

Chapter 1 contains basic information about grief and explains why it lasts longer for some people than others.

Grieving often begins before a death, when a loved one is suffering from a terminal illness. Chapter 2 talks about preparing for a death, visiting the dying, and saying good-bye. Whenever death occurs you have to decide about a funeral, burial, and other practical things. Chapter 3 deals with these matters and why they are important. Chapter 4 explores the emotional responses to grief—guilt, anger, depression—and is full of ideas on how you can help yourself deal with these emotions. Chapter 5 focuses on the many continuing reminders you will have of your loss and gives special attention to coping with holidays and anniversaries. Chapter 6 examines the relationship you had with your loved one and how this can affect the length of your grief. If the grief you feel has been complicated by unusual circumstances, making it difficult even to mourn your loss, Chapter 7 offers special help to you. Chapter 8 is directed to the adult who had a difficult death-related experience as a child and is still affected by it. It offers you ways to determine whether you are carrying such emotional residue. Chapter 9 gives you some methods to measure whether you are healing. Chapter 10 goes beyond the immediate family of the deceased to give advice to friends, or even professional caregivers, who want to help someone coping with grief.

As you read about people who have lived through painful ordeals perhaps similar to your own, you may become aware of new possibilities for yourself: things you can do to get on with your own life. If you need professional help, you will learn how to go about finding it. If you feel you could benefit from joining a self-help group, there is a resource list in the back of the book that can steer you to the right one. If you want to read more about the grieving process, there is a bibliography with many excellent books you can obtain to expand your knowledge and give you hope for the future.

Finally, let me say a word about myself. Motivated by the

death by cancer of my first husband and inspired by a personal meeting with Dr. Elisabeth Kübler-Ross, author of the pioneering book *On Death and Dying*,[1] I entered this field two decades ago as a volunteer helping terminally ill cancer patients. From 1977 to the present I have been the director of the grief program of the Mount Vernon Center for Community Mental Health in Alexandria, Virginia, the only such program in the nation operating from a mental health center. During the intervening years I have helped several thousand people deal with their grief, many of them suffering from excruciating losses. I organized the nation's third chapter of the self-help group for terminally ill patients, Make Today Count, and I have organized many other self-help groups to meet the special needs of people. These include groups for suicide survivors, AIDS patients and their families, the mentally retarded, and people whose unmarried mates have died. I regularly conduct seminars for widows and widowers, and I currently have four groups of grieving children I work with regularly to address the grief they feel following the death of parents and other close relatives.

Through the years I have had occasion to give many lectures and write many magazine articles. I have been an active member of the Association for Death Education and Counseling, and I am now a member of its Board of Directors. I am a Certified Professional Death Educator. This is my second book; the first one was *The Grieving Child: A Parent's Guide*.[2]

None of this guarantees that what I have to say will help you, but I believe it can. Having worked with so many suffering people for as long as I have, I know that there is hope for you, too. Let this book be the start of your recovery.

---

[1]Kübler-Ross, Elisabeth. *On Death and Dying*. New York: Macmillan, 1969.
[2]Fitzgerald, Helen. *The Grieving Child: A Parent's Guide*. New York: Simon & Schuster, 1992.

Introduction

If you are bereaved and are wondering what life can possibly offer you after your great loss, I bring you *hope* based on my own experiences and the experiences of thousands of people who have come to me through the years seeking help. When my first husband died in 1974, I was a widow with four young children, feeling empty, angry, guilty, and confused just as you may be feeling today. While I don't know your personal situation, I have listened to so many sad stories, so many heart-rending accounts of personal tragedy, that I have come to recognize certain common feelings, concerns, and anxieties that most people experience when a loved one dies.

In warfare, business, or football, victory depends on knowing one's adversary. The same is true in the struggle to recover from grief. Facts about grief are not usually included in one's education, yet knowing something about this most painful of all human emotions is essential if you are going to loosen its grip on you. This book is intended to provide you that knowledge.

Intellectually we know that we are mortal. After all, we have funeral homes, cemeteries, and obituary sections in our newspapers. We know that death will happen someday, not only to ourselves but to those we love, and we know it's going to hurt when we lose loved ones. But we don't think about death a lot, do we? Nor should we. Instead, we go about the business of living, making plans, falling in love, getting married, having children, beginning careers, acquiring real estate, building homes, accumulating all sorts of possessions—in short, making the most of what life has to offer, and not dwelling too much on its ending.

It takes only a fraction of a second to shatter that sense of well-being—a brief moment when we have an accident, or an instant when a blood clot forms in a loved one's aorta. When such an event happens, the *world we knew* suddenly seems to vanish, and suddenly we see ourselves as the vulnerable creatures we always knew we were but somehow never fully acknowledged. Much as we may have prepared ourselves for that moment, when it does arrive we are going to feel emotional pain.

One young woman I know recently marked the first anniversary of a tragic event that shattered her life. I am happy to say that she is getting on with her life even though only a year ago a car accident took the lives of her husband and her two sons. One day she was a wife and mother; the next day, single and childless. Nevertheless, she has been able to begin building a new life for herself, even while pursuing the prosecution of the drunk driver who caused this calamity.

I also worked with an older man who came to me after the unexpected death of his wife of forty-two years. He is living an active, outgoing life today, but he was in shock when I first saw him. What caused the shock was the suddenness of her death. They had thought she had several years to live with a seemingly slow-growing cancer. They had planned to travel and make the most of the time they had left together, but it all ended abruptly when she died "ahead of schedule" with a heart attack.

A young woman who shared an interest in rock climbing with her fiancé was badly shaken when I first saw her following her boyfriend's fatal fall while he was climbing alone. She is doing well today, but his accident brought an end to their plans for a future together. I mention these real people because their experiences may resemble your own. But even if they do not, there is a message here: Hard as it may seem now, you too can make a new life for yourself.

What is the common thread in these real-life stories? Life for any of us can change suddenly, unalterably, and there is little we can do to prevent it. To the survivor—the wife or husband or lover, mother or father, child or grandchild, brother or sister or close friend—life will seem to have lost its luster and the future, its promise. But there are things we can do to express our grief and to make the most of what life has left for us. The death of a loved one is always going to be painful, but when this loss occurs we are also faced with unexpected decisions about our own lives.

If you are experiencing such grief, you know that it is a volcanic eruption of emotion. It is extremely powerful. It can become a commanding presence—the centering point of our whole existence. The feelings triggered when a loved one dies often manifest themselves in ways that we least expect.

Because these feelings are so hard to control, you may find yourself wishing that you didn't have to deal with them and that you could just put them away in a closet somewhere, never to be felt again. I have been asked, "Why must I have these feelings? Why can't I just ignore them? Won't they just fade away?" Sad to say, they won't just fade away, any more than the memory of your loved one will fade away. No matter how difficult, it is best to deal with your grief and not ignore it.

We must recognize that grief is part of being human. What kind of person would not grieve the death of a loved one? When we say we would like our feelings of grief to fade away, what we really mean is that we would like to be relieved of our terrible sense of loss. Surely more than any other of nature's creatures, human beings have the capacity not only to remember—a mixed blessing—but also to express and discharge their feelings in nondestructive ways. And that is the greatest blessing of all. Grief that is expressed is grief that we can live with; grief that is suppressed is grief that will rise up to haunt us, surprise us, and shape our lives in ways we cannot control.

This book is offered as a guide and companion for you as you suffer the intense emotions we call grief. It attempts to answer the questions you may have about your grief and to share with you what is known about this little-understood human experience.

To you, the bereaved person who has turned to this book in search of relief from the pain of grief, I offer my love and understanding. I have been there.

—Helen Fitzgerald

THE

MOURNING

HANDBOOK

FACTS
ABOUT
GRIEF

Let's begin by providing you with some basic information that you need to have about this little-understood human experience.

. . .

1.1 Definitions

Grief

If you are grieving, you are familiar with the feeling, but what is grief exactly? *Webster's New World Dictionary* gives as its primary definition "intense emotional suffering caused by loss, disaster, misfortune, etc.; acute sorrow; deep sadness."

Grief is the emotion experienced by Darlene, a young client of mine who had flown home for a surprise visit on her mother's birthday, only to learn at the airport that her mother had died a few hours earlier. Darlene's sudden feelings of disbelief, panic, and anger are part of what we call grief, and it is what you may be experiencing right now.

Mourning

Mourning, on the other hand, is defined by the same dictionary as "the actions or feelings of someone who mourns; specifically, the expression of grief at someone's death." The key words here are *actions* and *expression*. When an uncle told Darlene of her mother's death, she fell into his arms, weeping hysterically. She was *mourning* her mother's death. Her mourning continued as she *cried* with her family, *expressed* her anger, *discharged* her feelings of regret for not coming sooner, and *took part* in the wake and funeral. When you are expressing your grief, you are mourning.

Although grief is most commonly associated with the death of a loved one, it can be experienced whenever there is an important loss in one's life, such as the loss of eyesight or hearing, a sharp decline in one's health, marital separation and divorce, or the loss of one's job. In all these cases mourning is an appropriate and often necessary response. If you have suffered a particularly severe loss, you may need to mourn just as much as someone who has lost a loved one. While this book focuses on the grief following a death, it can be helpful in dealing with other losses as well.

1.2 When Does Grief Begin?

Grief can begin whenever there is a loss or a perception of impending loss, but the three most common occasions are:

a. the time of diagnosis of a terminal illness,
b. the time of death, and
c. the time of learning about the death of a loved one.

When the doctor says, "I'm sorry, but your husband has brain cancer and it is inoperable," the hope for a cure changes to the prospect of impending death for the loved one, and the emotions of grief are likely to begin.

Sometimes grief begins at the time of death. At the moment that one's wife slumps over in her chair, has no pulse, and fails to respond to resuscitation, the realization that she is dead triggers the emotion of grief.

Grief may also begin at the time one learns about a loved one's death, whenever that might be. A young man whose mother was estranged from the family had rare, treasured contacts with her. Because of his mother's life-style of moving frequently, there wasn't an address or telephone where he could reach her, and he had to depend on her contacting him. When she died in an auto accident, it was several weeks before the family was notified of her death. His grief began when he got the belated news.

1.3 How Long Does Grief Last?

Since grief is painful, you undoubtedly want to know how long you will have to endure this powerful emotion. Pain is generally more tolerable if we know it's going to end sometime.

A shorthand answer concerning the duration of grief is that it will take as long as it needs to take. It will take longer for some people than others, depending on the nature of their relationship to the deceased, the circumstances of the death, their support systems, how they cope with adversity, what else is going on in their lives, and the resources they have available to them.

A young man called me one day to say that he was worried about his mother. His father had died and he was wondering just how long his mother would be acting so upset. I asked him how long his father had been dead and he replied, "Two weeks." When I responded, "That's not very long," he asked, "Well, will she be better in two months?" Once again I had to say, "That's not a very long time." He seemed disappointed that grief can't be put on a fast track.

You may encounter loving and well-meaning friends who hate to see you hurt and want to see your mourning end. They may not understand that the worst thing you can do is to try to shut off or deny these powerful feelings. Often these are people who have never experienced the death of a loved one and don't yet comprehend the function and importance of mourning. If you have friends pushing you in this direction, simply tell them that you can recover from your grief but that you need time to work it out; when you have done so, you expect to be back on track again. (See Chapter 10, "A Friend in Need.")

Although your grief can be expected to last a relatively long time—from a few months to several years—it won't always be the all-encompassing feeling of despair that you are feeling now. Commonly grief is sporadic. You will have good days as well as bad days. You may catch yourself laughing, perhaps guiltily, at a friend's joke, and then, moments later, bursting into tears when you hear a nostalgic song that reminds you of your loved one.

At some point your grief will end, but this doesn't mean that there will ever be an end to your sense of loss. A father whose son had died a quarter century earlier said, "If I were an actor on stage and needed to produce tears, I would only have to think of my son to cry." This father is a happy man leading a full and productive life, but the memory of his son and of the pain of his death will always be with him. You can expect your grief to pass, but this won't mean forgetting your loved one.

"Time will heal" is a common saying. Part of it is true, and part is myth. Time will aid in recovery from grief, but it is time that needs to be used well. Time spent frantically running from grief—traveling, perhaps, or visiting relatives, keeping ever busy with never a moment to think about one's loss—will not help. Eventually, you will run out of places to go or things to do, and at that point you will have to face the void created by the death of your loved one. On the other hand, if you use your time to *mourn* your loss, to adjust to a different kind of life, and to get acquainted with your now somewhat altered (maybe greatly altered) identity, healing will occur faster.

You may feel that your grief is unique. You are right, it *is* unique; the circumstances of your life will make it so. There is no standard recipe for grief that will apply to your situation. However, there are factors that will influence the length of your grief, and you can gain some reassurance from knowing what they are. (See Chapter 6, "Differences That Matter.")

Age of the Deceased

The younger the person is who died the more difficult it is likely to be to mourn that death. It seems unnatural in the scheme of life for a child to die, just as it seems unfair for a young adult to die just when life's adventure is about to begin. On the other hand, when an elderly person dies, one may feel some comfort in knowing that the person had lived a long and productive life. (See section 6.1 for discussion on old age, 6.7 on grandparents, and 6.14 on children.)

Cause of Death

When loved ones know in advance that death is approaching, they may experience much of their grief long before the actual death. Thus, they may actually feel a somewhat guilty sense of relief when the death occurs, and what grief remains may be of short duration. Alternatively, the more sudden or violent the death, such as an unexpected fatal heart attack, car accident, or suicide, the longer one may expect grief to last. Not only will the bereaved person have had no time to prepare for the death or to say good-bye, but the suddenness and possible violence of the death will add to the burden of grief. (See sections 6.1 through 6.5 on different kinds of death situations.)

Nature of Relationship

Was your relationship with the deceased a loving, fulfilling one? Has it left you with a sense of completeness, filled with memories to be treasured? Or was your relationship with the deceased stormy and volatile? The emotions generated by those relationships will play a part in determining the length and intensity of your grief. (See section 7.17 on conflicted relationships.)

Other Events in One's Life

Life following the death of a loved one doesn't always cooperate to allow one to work through one's grief. A very common story goes like this: "Not only do I have to deal with my dad's death, but now my favorite aunt has died, my car has broken down, work is not going well, and I don't know what will happen next or which to deal with first."

Other events in one's life sometimes dictate what must be handled first, making it necessary to put grief on hold. When this happens, the need to mourn is still there and will emerge at a later date, perhaps weeks or months later. Such complications will lengthen your grief and mourning period. (See section 7.1 on other changes in one's life.)

Support Systems

The support and understanding you have around you will make a big difference in how you experience and handle your grief.

Do you have a family that has rallied to your needs, or do you feel isolated and abandoned? Do you have care and understanding at your workplace, or are you expected to be 100 percent productive immediately? How about your friends? Are they loving and supportive, or are they making comments such as, "Come on now, put this behind you"? The more support you have, the quicker your recovery from grief will be, but you will still need time to reflect on your loss, to mourn, and to become comfortable with the changes in your life.

Resources One Can Command

Communities are becoming more aware of the needs of the bereaved and are developing more resources to help people like you recover from their grief. If you feel the need of such help but don't have the energy to do the research, ask a friend to seek out the resources that are available to you. Check your library or local bookstore for appropriate books. Watch for announcements of lectures that may be informative. Search out any support groups that would apply to your needs by checking with your local newspaper, mental health center, library bulletin board, library reference desk, church, temple, or local hospice. Support groups are informal gatherings of people who are dealing with similar situations in their lives. It is often very comforting to be with others who can "really understand" how you feel. (For more help, see the Bibliography and Resources at the back of this book.)

One's Coping Skills

As you wrestle with your grief, it may be helpful to reflect on how you have coped with other situations in your life. At times of crisis what was your response? Did you seek out information and help, or did you simply try to ignore what was happening and hope that it would pass? Did you get activated in solving the problem, or did you bury yourself in your work? "Know thyself" is a good rule to apply at times like this. Refining your coping skills can help shorten your grief.

Sexual Differences

"Vive la différence," said the Frenchman about the sexes. But the differences are not as great as some would have us believe. Popular culture allows women to show their emotions and seek support but requires men to be "strong," which is defined as not showing any emotion. Men are expected to make the tough decisions, take on the unpleasant jobs, and never cry. This need not be so. In fact, it is unhealthy for anyone to lock up his emotions; they need to be expressed.

Of course, crying is not the only outlet for one's feelings. Chopping wood, physical exercise, or building a guest room on the house are outlets that may be more comfortable to a man. Years ago the father of two dead sons poured his sorrow into creating a beautiful azalea garden in Washington, D.C., which is visited every year by thousands of admirers.

Also, it is now quite common for men to attend support groups to help them deal with their grief. There they find other men to talk to who share their feelings of anger and remorse. If you are a man struggling with grief, don't let imagined taboos prevent you from mourning your loss; you have just as much right to express your feelings as any woman suffering a similar loss.

1.4 Does Grief End?

Keeping in mind the definition of grief as "intense emotional suffering," you can look forward, at some point, to an end to these overwhelming emotions. This does not mean that you will cease feeling sad or wistful, nor does it mean that you will forget your loved one. However, it does mean that the intense emotional conflicts which you may be experiencing today can be brought to an end as you integrate this loss into your changed life. (See the introduction to Chapter 9 and sections 9.1 and 9.2 on helping yourself and on getting better.)

1.5 Why Must You Express Your Grief?

"Why must I express my grief? Why can't I just ignore it and get on with my life?" are questions you may be asking yourself as you suffer the pain of grief. The answers lie, not in theory, but in observed human experience. People who try to ignore the powerful, deep-seated emotions of grief usually see them reappear later in disturbing forms: physical responses such as rheumatoid arthritis, stomach ulcers, colitis, hiatal hernias, nervous tics, weight loss (or gain), chills, insomnia, back pains, or incessant headaches; or psychological responses such as depression, fits of unexplained anger, interpersonal problems, preoccupation with one's own death, anxiety, or new, unpleasant personality traits. There are no more powerful feelings than those arising from grief—ignore them at your peril. However, by learning to identify these feelings you can learn how to express them and thus avoid all those unpleasant alternatives.

Understanding the Grief Process

There is more to grief than what you may be feeling right now. While writers have approached the subject in different ways, there is general agreement that grieving is a *process* and that grieving people can help themselves by better understanding what is happening to them.

Writers on the subject of grief have attempted to identify different aspects of the process. In 1969 Elisabeth Kübler-Ross wrote about the five stages of dying. Her book *On Death and Dying*,[3] although written for the dying person, is really a book on grieving, helpful not only to the dying but to the bereaved as well. Her five stages consisted of the following:

(1) denial and isolation
(2) anger
(3) bargaining
(4) depression
(5) acceptance

In the denial and isolation stage, the grieving person refuses to accept the harsh reality confronting him or her. In the anger phase the person is continuing to resist reality and to ask, "Why me? Why not that old woman down the street?" In the bargaining phase the person tries to reverse that reality in various irrational ways, as in "bargaining with God," promising to do certain good works, perhaps, if God will spare your loved one. For example, I promised God I would say a rosary a day if He allowed my husband to live. The depression stage reflects the person's recognition of reality. In the acceptance stage the person no longer denies reality, no longer feels angry about it, no longer tries to bargain it away, no longer feels depressed about it, but contemplates his death with quiet expectation.

The basic problem with this analysis, as the author herself has pointed out, is the expectation some people have that each of these stages will proceed, in that precise order, and then pass. This expectation has proven frustrating to those who want the grief process to be clear cut and orderly. A young man whose mother was terminally ill told me, "Mother was depressed a

---

[3]Kübler-Ross, Elisabeth, M.D. *On Death and Dying*. New York: Macmillan, 1969.

week ago, and now she's depressed again. What's wrong with her?" A woman told me, "Janet shouldn't have died yet; she never got to acceptance." Nonetheless, Kübler-Ross's analysis can be helpful if you keep in mind that your case, like all others, is unique.

In his 1982 book, *Grief Counseling and Grief Therapy*,[4] J. William Worden wrote about "the four tasks of mourning":

1. to accept the reality of the loss
2. to experience the pain of grief
3. to adjust to an environment in which the deceased is missing
4. to withdraw emotional energy and reinvest it in another relationship

The first task recognizes that the death must become real before you can work through the process of grief. The second addresses the need to do specific things to express those emotions generated by the death. The third stresses the importance of analyzing the different roles the deceased played in one's life and to make those adjustments which will enable the person to build a new life. The last focuses on the possibility of personal growth.

Therese Rando in her 1993 book, *Treatment of Complicated Mourning*,[5] writes about the six "R's" as she takes yet a different look at the process of grief. Her "R's" include:

1. Recognize the loss.
2. React to the separation.
3. Recollect and reexperience the deceased and the relationship.

---

[4]Worden, J. William, Ph.D. *Grief Counseling and Grief Therapy: A Handbook for the Mental Health Practitioner*. New York: Springer Publishing Co., 1982.

[5]Rando, Therese A., Ph.D. *Treatment of Complicated Mourning*. Champaign, IL: Research Press, 1993.

4. Relinquish the old attachments to the deceased and the old assumptive world.
5. Readjust to move adaptively into the new world without forgetting the old.
6. Reinvest.

While these analyses vary in approach, each is based on the perception that grief is not static but rather a *process* leading toward a resolution of the kind of intense emotional conflict you may be suffering at this moment. Once you recognize this, you will be on the path, however slow and winding, to recovery.

Chapter 2

PREPARING

FOR A

DEATH

Things One Can Do When There Is

Time to Prepare for the Death of a

Loved One

It was mid-December, 1971. My husband, Jerry, had just undergone surgery to remove a tumor from his brain. At first the operation seemed to be a success, but a few days later the picture changed dramatically. I was visiting Jerry when a medical resident walked into the room. After checking my husband, who was sleeping, the young doctor commented that Jerry had only six months to live. Six months to live? I was devastated, but the resident, suddenly realizing that I had not been told, said any more information would have to come from our surgeon. I waited and waited, my heart pounding and my hands shaking, for the surgeon to arrive. Finally, I told a nurse that I *had* to talk to the surgeon, and she had him paged. When he came, he arrived with a group of residents who were on their rounds. The surgeon took me out into the hall, where I asked him to confirm what I had heard. He said it was true: Jerry's tumor had been a number four on a four-point scale—as advanced as it could get. He said Jerry had six months to live.

Having given me this shattering news, the doctor then left me standing in the hall as he continued his rounds. There was not another person present who knew what I had just been told. The cleaning woman bumped into me and asked me to move so she could continue her sweeping. A nurse, busy and preoccupied, hurried by, not giving me a second glance. No one had the time to look at my face and see my shock and despair. Not knowing what to do, not knowing what to say, I took a deep breath, put a smile on my lips, and returned to the room of my unsuspecting husband. Looking back on that moment and the three years of playacting that followed, I know that no one can tell me that I could not be an actress. From that moment on, I played a role that required more strength and more finesse than anything I had ever done or likely will ever do again.

At the heart of this playacting was the awful secret I knew and Jerry didn't: namely, that he had terminal cancer. When I asked the doctor whether I should tell Jerry, he gave me this advice: "We" should not say anything to Jerry yet about this prognosis. I believe he felt that, if Jerry knew, he would become depressed and give up on life, but if he didn't know, he would be able to enjoy what life he had left. The doctor never altered this advice; Jerry died not knowing that his tumor had been malignant or that his ensuing disabilities were caused by the spread of cancer.

This secret soon became a barrier between my husband and me and, far from helping Jerry enjoy his remaining days, inhibited our ability to enjoy the time we had left. While Jerry was making long-range plans, I was wondering how our children and I could survive without him. Like any guilty secret between a husband and wife, the withholding of this devastating information grew like the cancer in Jerry's body to destroy much of the tissue of our marriage.

Based on my own experience and that of so many people I have helped through similar tragedies, I strongly advise you not to go down that same path. I don't know how you might have received such news, but the ideal way would be for the doctor to present a prognosis of this kind ever so gently to the patient and his or her family all at the same time. The doctor should be available, at least for a few minutes, to let this news sink in and to answer questions. This way, everyone receives the same information and can rely on the memory of others to verify what the doctor may or may not have said.

On the other hand, you may have gotten such news in some other way. Although attitudes have changed a lot since 1971, you too may have been told to withhold information from a stricken loved one. My experience tells me that secrets like that will do nothing to help your loved one and can erode the relationship between you.

If you are still wrestling with how to share this kind of news, you would do well to discuss it with your doctor and arrange for a time when he or she can meet with you and your loved one and explain fully what is happening. This could be the source of great relief for everyone concerned.

2.1 The Diagnosis

Things have changed since I received that devastating news in 1971. Most doctors today are sensitive to the impact of a serious diagnosis on their patients and their families. However, there are still times when the diagnosis of a terminal illness is given only to the family and not to the patient. This may occur when the patient is still in the recovery room after surgery and the doctor is compelled to say that there is nothing he or she can do to save this person's life. If this should happen to you, you could find yourself alone, having to listen very carefully to what is said while trying to remain calm in the face of this terrible news. In such circumstances, your first task would be to call family or friends to let them know what has happened. If they should want to come to be with you and to comfort you, let them. You will need their support and love, and they need to know that they can be of help to you.

Your next task would be to face your loved one, who by now might be back in his or her hospital room waiting to see you and to hear how the surgery went. Take a few minutes to think of what you want to say. You will know best what words will work with this person with whom you share a unique relationship. I suggest that you use the correct language: If it's cancer, call it cancer, and be as honest as you can. Think about other circumstances in your relationship with this person and how they were handled. What worked in your communications and what didn't? How have you offered support to each other in the past? These unique aspects of your relationship will be present now but need not control how you handle this. If you have handled previous crises well, it will be easier for you to get through this one. If you haven't, look on this as an opportunity to change the way you communicate with each other. Sharing good news is easy; sharing bad news is much more difficult but can create a new bond between you.

I find some of the following can be helpful when delivering bad news.

- Try not to be overly bubbly. People will see through that facade very quickly.
- Give yourself permission to cry. Crying is a sign that you care.

- Sit down in a chair to look more relaxed and let your loved one know that you intend to stay for a while, not just drop the news and leave. More important, if your loved one is lying in bed, sitting in a chair will put you at the same level as the patient, not towering over him or her and making the news even more threatening.

- Use the correct language. You want your loved one to trust you and to know that you are not going to keep any secrets. Energy won't be wasted in trying to figure out what you *really* are saying. When you first see your loved one, you may want to let him or her take the lead and ask those difficult questions. If this happens, answer each question as best you can and defer others to the nurse or doctor. These questions may be asked again later as your loved one recovers from the lingering effects of the anesthesia. Or you may decide the time is right to offer the information the doctor has given you. As gently as you can, start with something like this: "Honey, you were in surgery for less time than we thought you were going to be. The doctor did as he said he was going to; he went in and looked at your liver and discovered what we suspected was right. However, the cancer was more advanced than he thought. He decided not to remove it because that wouldn't help. So he closed you up and he will be in to answer any questions we have and to talk to us about what treatments we have available to us [if that's the case]. We have a big fight ahead of us. I am going to fight this with you."

- Touching your loved one can be very reassuring. It is a simple, elemental way of communicating your concern and love.

- If saying these difficult words is particularly hard for you, you may have to look for other ways of "talking" openly and honestly with your loved one. One way might be to have a third person there, such as your doctor, a friend, a minister, or a therapist, who can say for you the words that are sticking in your throat. This may seem silly and awkward to you, but believe me, it is so much better than nothing and it can be the beginning of a better line of communication between you and your loved one.

- Try to offer hope and support. Almost always, there will be some form of treatment that can be tried, either to put the disease in remission or to ease the pain. You and your loved one need to know that the doctors are not giving up and that you have some choices with which to fight the illness. True, it may be a losing battle, but a battle nonetheless. Your loved one needs to know that you are going to see this illness as "our illness" and that you, the patient, and your doctors are going to see it through together.

- Ask your loved one what you can do that will be most helpful. You need him or her to guide you and to teach you about his or her needs. I remember that when my husband was first diagnosed, I treated him too much as a patient, doing too much for him, robbing him of all his independence, probably making him feel as if he were worse off than he may have been feeling. Let your loved one guide you through these new roles of caregiver and patient. However, you also need to let your loved one know when you are scared or tired, or when he or she is making too many demands on you, or when you feel there are tasks that he or she could really be doing for himself or herself. Communication can, at times, be painful, but honesty is needed if resentment is to be avoided. Honest communication can lead to more emotional growth and closeness.

Only the Beginning

This is only the beginning, but it is a good strong beginning that will aid you throughout the months to follow. You may want to talk about many things: legal matters such as wills, power of attorney, living wills, life without you, people to see and places to visit, and funeral arrangements. While you have the groundwork laid, it is never too late to improve communication with your loved one. (See section 10.5 on emotional help and 10.6 on things to avoid.) If you don't know where to start, never hesitate to find a professional who can help you. Or read the chapter on basic communication skills to enhance your personal relationship.

2.2 Visiting the Dying

The first time you visit someone who is dying is always anxiety provoking. I know because, even after all the times I have made such visits, I still feel somewhat anxious when doing so for the first time. You are not sure what emotions you will feel or how you will handle them. You don't know what you will find when you enter that room: how that person will look or how he or she may be reacting to these changed circumstances. You may not even know how much that person knows about his or her condition and prognosis. Then, too, you may be worried that he or she will talk about the prospect of death, and you won't know how to handle that. These and other unknowns can create the anxiety you might be experiencing now. Following are some thoughts that can make this visit less upsetting and more meaningful.

- If you are not an immediate family member, check to see if you are welcome. At times people who are dying prefer not to have visitors, and their wishes should be respected. This could be because the dying person is uncomfortable being seen in such a demeaning situation. Perhaps the dying person is trying to disconnect from this world and is preparing for whatever he or she believes is next. Perhaps the person is too weak for visitors or is afraid of contracting some infection that would add to his or her miseries.

- Some preparation should be made before your visit. Check with the nurses or family and friends about the person's condition. Be sure to ask what physical changes have occurred, such as weight loss, swelling, hair loss, circles under the eyes, or odors. How is the person taking all this? Is he or she depressed, hopeful, angry, guilty? Does he or she enjoy visitors? How long should you stay? Does he or she tire easily? Does he or she doze off while talking? Is the person in pain? Perhaps getting a general idea of what the room looks like will be helpful to you. Where is it located? What equipment is present? I find that such basic information can remove some of the unknowns that often add to our anxieties.

- Decide if you want to go alone or if it would be helpful to have another person with you—another family member or even the nurse who is caring for the dying person.

- I find taking a gift is a good idea. It can be a diversion, giving you something to focus on during those first few moments of your visit. Take some time to think about what would be appropriate, keeping in mind the patient's limitations. For example, a book will be of no use to a person with failing eyesight, unless you read it aloud. However, books on tape are very popular because they don't have to be either held or read but will keep the person's mind stimulated during otherwise long, boring hours in bed. They will also give you something to talk about during future visits. Flowers and plants are nice but require care; you will want to make sure they get watered. Silk flowers are an alternative. Pretty nighties or pajamas, colognes, combs (unless there has be a great deal of hair loss), lotions, and hair ribbons may not always be practical or even usable yet help bolster the person's sense of sexuality, which often suffers when one is sick. Think about what was important when he or she was well and what is likely to have meaning still to that person. I once painted a dying patient's fingernails just hours before she died.

There are many gift ideas to draw from: lap blankets for sitting up or in a wheel chair, soft pillows, calendars with large numbers that one can read in bed, bed jackets to keep warm and to look pretty, favorite juices, fruits, photographs of people and places, possibly videotapes of carefully selected movies, stationery, certain games that can be played alone or with another person, appropriate craft materials, or yarn for crocheting.

- Before starting your trip to the hospital or home, telephone first to see if this would be a good time to visit. If so, go immediately. If you wait a day or sometimes even a few hours, the dying person may be too tired or his or her illness may have made a turn for the worse. I know there are many situations when some time will elapse because of the travel time necessary to get there. You may live forty-five minutes away, or you may live in another city, requiring hours or even a day to get there. Whatever your circumstance, do the best you can. Just be aware that conditions may have changed when you do arrive and be prepared to wait in the hope that the patient's condition will improve.

- Short but frequent visits are better than long, awkward ones. Short visits allow the ill person to rest and give you a chance for a break to get some fresh air, run errands, and take care of your own personal needs. Visiting a dying friend or loved one has several purposes. It is a way of conveying your love and support. It is also a way to say good-bye, something that is important to both of you. It can comfort your loved one and aid you in your grief. It is a time to put closure on the relationship you have with that person. When and how to say good-bye are questions you may be asking yourself. My advice is just this: You don't have to wait until your loved one is breathing his or her last breath to say good-bye. It can be done whenever it feels right. You will feel more peaceful having done so. When my father, who lived in another state, was in the advanced stages of Parkinson's disease, he had several hospital admissions, which made me very anxious. Fearing that he would die without my having said good-bye to him, I decided to visit him. On the way I pondered how I could actually say what I wanted to say, since my family ordinarily doesn't talk about such things. When I arrived, I spent time with Dad talking about our life together, our horses, our rodeo appearances, the Studebaker convertible he gave me in high school, the dreams we shared for our lives. It was through this meaningful talk that I came to realize that I was, indeed, telling him good-bye. On returning to my own home, I found I was more relaxed about my father's condition and about the possibility that he would soon die. Thus, saying good-bye doesn't have to be, "Good-bye, I won't be seeing you again." Putting closure on the life you had with your dying loved one may simply involve reminiscing, talking about the good times you had together, looking through photographs, or even running some old family movies, and ending your visit or visits with hugs, hand holding, and kisses.

• Learn to be a good listener. Silence really is golden at times like this. You may feel pressure to carry on an animated conversation, but this may not be what your loved one wants or needs. Relax and observe him or her. There are occasions when I have found it helpful to have some knitting with me, allowing me to keep occupied while sitting quietly by the bedside. Bringing a book to read might also be a good idea.

Not all families are comfortable talking about serious things. This may be a skill that you and your loved one haven't developed. Here are some suggestions that may be helpful.

- Ask questions that require more than a "yes or no" answer.
- Use conversation "encouragers" such as: "Tell me more," "I see," "um-hum," "and then," and "yes-s-s."
- Avoid conversation stoppers like interrupting the person, standing up, changing the subject, finishing the sentence for the speaker, and looking bored.
- Look for ways to respond to difficult questions, such as "Am I going to die?" by turning them into questions of your own, such as, "What do you think?" This is an invitation to your loved one to say what he or she is thinking about.
- Look for topics to talk about that have a common interest for both of you, such as football, a particular book or movie, old photographs, an item in the news, or a hobby.
- Take special note of your body language. Are you sitting comfortably in a chair, or are you perched on the edge of it ready to run? Are you not sitting at all but pacing around the room looking for an escape? Are you looking directly at your loved one, maintaining eye contact, or are your eyes darting around the room making it difficult for anyone to talk to you? Think about what your facial expressions must be. Do you look interested in what is being said, or are you wearing a bored, anxious, or angry look? Your body language can either help or hinder the communication between the two of you.
- Touching is very soothing. I like to be touched and have often told my present husband that I could tolerate dying if he could be running his fingers through my hair. However, not everyone is accustomed to touching and

may find the stroking of one's arm awkward. If you are a person who likes to touch or hug but are not sure whether the ill person feels the same way, you might try a test run. First of all find out if touching is going to be painful in any way; with some illnesses even a light touch hurts. Then reach out and lightly touch the person's arm and look for a response. If the person pulls away, you can assume he or she doesn't want to be touched. However, the opposite is more commonly the case, and touching will enrich the experience for both of you.

- Give the patient some control of your visit. Often a patient is trapped in his or her bed, unable to get up and leave, and is subject to long, tiring visits and boring conversations. Call first and ask if the person is feeling up for a visit; ask if you can bring him or her something from the "outside world." Ask how long of a visit your loved one or friend would like to avoid getting tired. (The visit can always be extended if the patient wishes it.) When you arrive, ask again if the person is up for a visit, as he or she might have tired in the meantime. Also, keep a close eye on the person's body language: Is he or she in pain? Is the person restless, signalling that he or she may be anxious for you to leave? I remember a dying patient who gave me a cue to leave when he asked me to dial the phone for him and then proceeded to talk to a friend on the phone—a direct clue that our visit was over. By observing the person you can better decide when to leave. (For more on emotional help see section 10.5.)

2.3 Anticipatory Grief

I first heard this phrase when I was attending a lecture years ago by Dr. Elisabeth Kübler-Ross, the pioneer in death education, introducing me to the idea that grief can begin *before* death has occurred. Among other things, it made me aware that I was experiencing anticipatory grief because of my first husband's terminal illness.

The American Heritage Dictionary of the English Language defines *anticipate* as follows: "to feel or realize beforehand: foresee. To look forward to; expect. To act in advance so as to prevent; preclude; forestall. To foresee and fulfill in advance."

When I think back to my experience with my dying husband, I remember that the hardest time for me was *before* he died. I felt the most pain then. Because of his long hospital stay, I had the task of running the household without him, paying the bills, raising the children, making the decisions, dealing with the loneliness and many of the emotions of grief. When he finally died, I actually felt a sense of relief.

If you should have a similar experience, you may feel guilty for feeling relieved. It may seem as if you don't care that the person died. Even though I had been introduced to the concept of anticipatory grief, I too felt guilty for feeling this way. Only later did I come to accept that I had no reason to feel guilty. The grief you experience before a loved one's death helps prepare you for the loss when your loved one dies.

How Anticipatory Grief Can Be Helpful

I used the time during my husband's dying to express and feel my grief. I had a chance to live a life without him even though he was still alive and, most important, I had a chance to say goodbye and put closure on our relationship. I also had the opportunity to begin rebuilding my life without him before he died.

Allowing yourself to mourn before your loved one dies is possible only if you accept the doctor's prognosis and acknowledge what is happening. There are those who imagine that talking or planning for the death will somehow cause it to happen. Or they may be so frightened by the prospect that they go from doctor to doctor, from cure to cure, in a desperate search for something that will save their loved one. Or they may imagine that if they pray hard enough, God will perform a miracle of some sort. As a therapist I worked with such a family. The husband and father was dying of cancer. Whenever I had occasion to speak with his family, they would tell me that they were praying to God for his recovery, that God would cure him, and that they didn't need my help. However, one day the dying man asked me to help him with his family. "You know," he said, "God does answer our prayers but not always the way we tell Him. He may answer mine by sending me to heaven." After this dying man told his wife and children what he had told me, they were able to cry together and to begin to mourn their impending loss.

When Is Anticipatory Grief Not Helpful?

I remember a family in which the wife and mother was dying. In this family, communication was good and the entire family was involved as one would want them to be. However, there came a time when the wife said to me, "I feel I need to apologize for still being here." So much grief had been expressed that everyone in the family, including the dying woman, was ready for her death—but it wasn't happening. I remember her trying hard to concentrate on her death to help it happen. "I close my eyes and think, okay, this is it," she told me, "and then I open them and I'm still here." Impatience with the process of dying is not uncommon.

I found that even though I was experiencing grief before my husband's death, there was still a side of me hoping for a miracle. It is hard to give up hope even if you are preparing yourself for the worst. After all, dying is not predictable, like the unwinding of a clock. There will be times when death appears close, only to be followed by some improvement.

Life with a dying loved one is like a roller coaster ride, pushing you to the limits of your endurance. You may be physically and emotionally drained, praying for death to come. If you find this happening, know that you are not alone with these feelings and thoughts. There are support groups and organizations to help you. To find out what resources are available you could call your local hospital, community mental health center, church, your local community hot line, and/or the national office of an organization fighting a particular disease. (See the Resources at the back of this book for names and numbers.)

2.4 When Death Comes

When my husband was dying, I recall that there was a part of me that wanted to be with him when he died and a part of me that was afraid that would happen. I know now that if I had a loved one dying, I would want to be with that person at the time of death. You may feel differently, and that is all right. You should not feel guilty if you are not there when death comes. Nancy wanted to be with her mom when she departed from this world and was disappointed when her mother died while Nancy was asleep in a chair beside the bed. Nancy was worried that her mother might have opened her eyes and discovered that she was, indeed, alone as death came. Nancy was relieved when I said, "What more comfort could a mother get than gazing at her sleeping child as she died?"

When Death Occurs in a Hospital

If your loved one is not at home, there are some considerations to think through.

- Do you want to be called so you can be with your loved one when death comes?
- If you were not with your loved one at the time of death, you may still want to spend some time with the body of your loved one at the hospital or funeral home, perhaps to validate to yourself that he or she is really dead or perhaps to touch, kiss, or say good-bye one

more time. There is nothing wrong with doing so.

- You should find out the procedures of this particular hospital. You may want to know what will be done with the body and when the funeral home will be notified.
- You may receive the final belongings of your loved one in a brown paper bag. No matter how prepared you are, this is bound to come as a shock as the reality of the death hits you.
- You may feel the need to return to the hospital to see if your loved one is really dead and is really gone from that room. You may even want to talk to the nurses. This is all right to do if it helps you confirm that death has occurred.

When Death Occurs at Home

Not every terminally ill patient chooses to die in a hospital. Some elect to die at home in familiar surroundings and among loved ones. Yet death may come without warning or time for preparation. It may occur when it is least expected. When a person dies at home, there are these considerations to be aware of.

- How do you know the person is dead?
- Should you try CPR (cardiopulmonary resuscitation)?
- Call the emergency number 911. The medical team that responds will give you instructions over the phone on how to check for a pulse. If you don't know how, a team member can also give you instructions on how to do CPR. Once the emergency team arrives, it will continue to try to revive the stricken person, who then will be taken to the hospital, either to be revived or pronounced dead. In sudden, unexpected deaths autopsies are usually mandatory.

Chapter 3

FUNERAL
PREPARATIONS

You Have More Choices Than

You May Be Aware Of

As you turn to this book for help with your grief, you may need to face the necessity of making funeral arrangements for your loved one. You may dread this, yet attending to such matters is a way to mourn, to express your grief and your love for this person who has meant so much to you.

The first thing to keep in mind is that, if you are the person to decide these matters, you have control of this event. You don't have to put on an elaborate funeral. If you decide on cremation, you don't even have to choose a cemetery; you can have the ashes scattered in some meaningful place. You have the freedom to do whatever you wish, as long as you comply with state laws concerning death certificates and burial. So don't panic.

Now, knowing that you are in control, you can decide what you really want to do. However, you may want to consult other family members to find out what they would prefer. This is true especially for those closest to the deceased—parents, children, sisters, brothers, and special friends—for whom this event can have great meaning. (In your grief try to remind yourself that others are mourning, too.) You could have a private funeral if you wish, but a public funeral will provide the deceased's friends and relatives with an opportunity to say good-bye—and to comfort you as well. Except in unusual circumstances a public funeral is generally the best approach, but it's up to you.

3.1 Why Have a Funeral?

Contrary to what you may be thinking, a funeral is really for the living. The deceased will never know what transpires here, but it can be a source of comfort to you and the deceased's relatives and friends. It can be your first step on the road to recovery from your grief. After all, involvement in a funeral is a form of mourning. It provides special opportunities to mourn the loss of your loved one in the presence of others who also will be mourning. It gives you a time when family and friends can share stories about the deceased—even funny ones that may make you feel guilty for laughing. In talking with friends before or after the ceremonies, or at a reception later, you are likely to learn new things you never knew about this person who was so important to you.

When friends or loved ones part in daily life, they usually say good-bye. If they part without saying good-bye, an uncomfortable feeling usually ensues. Saying good-bye is a way of saying, "I care about you." Funerals are occasions for saying good-bye to someone who has died and are occasions for saying, "I care about you" or "I love you," or maybe "I'm sorry."

A funeral is also likely to be the last thing that you can do for your loved one, and no matter how painful your grief is, you may want to plan and carry it out as he or she would have wanted. However, what is most important is not some sense of obligation to the deceased but rather what will be most helpful and meaningful to you and others.

Finally, funerals help with the reality of death. The death of a loved one needs to become real before you can begin to work through your grief. Even in an expected death, the reality that your loved one is really gone is hard to comprehend. For those whose religious practices permit, viewing the body provides a confirmation of death. Yet acceptance of this harsh reality does not come easily. I know of a widow, for example, who saw her husband's body, planned and participated in a funeral, and saw his casket lowered into the ground—then returned to the hospital to see if he was "really" gone from his hospital room. Having a funeral will provide you with an anchor for such flights from reality.

3.2 Planning the Funeral

Did your loved one make funeral arrangements in advance? If so, some of the planning will be easier for you. Funeral directors promote the idea of preplanning, and it's not a bad idea. During times of intense grief, even simple decisions like selecting clothes to wear become difficult; decisions about caskets, cemeteries, funerals, and cremation may seem almost too much to bear. If your loved one made arrangements in advance, perhaps even paying for them, your burden will be much lighter. On the other hand, if death has not yet occurred and you have the opportunity, you may want to discuss these matters with your loved one to guide you when the need arises and to reduce some of the anxiety you otherwise are likely to feel.

A few years ago I returned to my hometown in rural Minnesota to visit my parents. We took our usual drive around town and ended up in the old cemetery. I was shown the plot that my parents had bought for themselves and the monument that they had already erected. It was helpful to me to know that they had made definite plans for their final rites and resting place.

Normally, of course, it is difficult to bring up the subject of someone's death, and this could be the case with your loved one. If so, you may want to approach the subject very gingerly. You might say, "I've decided that when I die, I want to have the organist play Bach's 'When Sheep Gently Graze' at my funeral. I love that piece." This might prompt your loved one to talk about his or her own funeral preferences. Or, you could begin by asking, "If you should die, what sort of funeral would you want to have?"

Sometimes it is the relatives who don't want to discuss this delicate subject. A young man who was diagnosed as being HIV-positive once handed me a large envelope, stating in front of his parents that the envelope contained his wishes for a funeral service. He felt his parents weren't ready to discuss this with him, and they readily agreed. However, by handing me the envelope, he was able to let them know that he had some plans he would like them to consider when the time came.

On another occasion, a woman who was battling cancer asked me to accompany her to the funeral home to make the arrangements for her funeral. It was important to her that she do this. She wanted an impressive funeral, and money was not an object. The arrangements were going well until we visited the casket room and she found two very lovely, very expensive caskets to choose from. One was the rich red of mahogany and the other a beautiful walnut. Not being able to decide, she finally decided to flip a coin, whereupon the funeral director, unaccustomed to such casualness, left the room for a moment to compose himself.

I would like to add that if you or your loved one have made

some funeral arrangements, write them down and give them to significant people in your life. They shouldn't be put in one's will or even in a safety deposit box because these things will not be touched until some time after the burial.

However, life is not always so predictable, and as many times as you have a chance to prepare for a death, there are times when death comes without warning and without advance preparations. If that is your situation, you might begin your planning by thinking about the rituals and customs that have been practiced in your family and your religion. These could include:

- Placing a black wreath on the door of your home.
- Wearing black clothing or a bit of black ribbon to let people know that you are in mourning.
- Having a viewing or wake, where friends and relatives can be present with the deceased and, more important, comfort each other and you. This could be in a church, funeral home, or even your own home.
- For members of the Jewish religion, "sitting shiva."

There are other customs, often stemming from ancient superstition, that might be part of your family tradition. An example that originated in Ireland involves turning all mirrors to the wall to avoid seeing evil spirits.

Perhaps you will want to arrange for flowers to surround the casket and to identify a favorite charity to which friends can make contributions.

Still another matter to consider is having pictures taken of your loved one's body in the casket. This has become a custom in my own family, and most family members are comfortable with it. I suppose it started as a way of sharing such important events with family members who could not be present. When an uncle of mine died recently, I was pleased to receive in the mail several pictures of him, his casket, and the many bouquets of flowers he had received.

If you feel uncomfortable about having pictures taken, don't do it. However, I remember a young widow who, though initially horrified that a relative had taken pictures of her deceased husband, later found them a source of great comfort. Remembering the pain he experienced in his last days, she can look at those pictures and see him free of pain and looking peaceful.

Another time I attended the viewing of a young man who had died from AIDS. His illness had been a long and slow process, leaving him very thin and tense with pain. As I was standing with his mother at the casket, she said, "How nice he looks." I was wondering if I dared to suggest that she have a picture taken of him in this peaceful state. When I did bring it up, I was pleased to learn that she already had done so.

If you decide this is something you would like to do, but are uncomfortable about taking the pictures yourself, you might ask someone else, such as the funeral director, to do it for you.

When Cost Is a Factor

Funerals can be expensive, but you can have a very nice, meaningful funeral without buying the most expensive casket and services a funeral home has to offer. You might ask a friend, your pastor, or rabbi to explore funeral costs for you before you begin making funeral arrangements. Having that person go with you can help you keep within your budget. I think it is a good idea to shop around as much as you have time and energy for, as prices vary for the services provided.

Making the Funeral Meaningful

You may want a "standard" funeral, leaving much of the planning up to the funeral director, other relatives and your pastor or rabbi, and that is okay. Or you may want to be more active and to participate in the planning of some of the following:

- Choosing the clothing the deceased is to be buried in.
- Selecting special music or poetry to be read. Perhaps a

soloist may be asked to sing a favorite song. Might you want to do this yourself?

- Writing a note to the deceased and tucking it into a pocket or placing it into his or her hands. (See section 7.18 on unfinished business.)
- Placing a picture of yourself or others in the pocket of the deceased's jacket.
- Placing certain meaningful possessions in the casket. I remember once that the classmates of a dead child were invited to place "things" in the casket to be buried with the child. The things included pictures, crayons and inexpensive toys. However, be careful not to put anything of great value in the casket, such as expensive jewelry or irreplaceable photographs.
- Arranging to speak at the service, recounting the life and contributions of your loved one. If this would be too difficult for you, you might write what you want said and have someone else read it. If you have a pastor or rabbi speak, he or she will want to meet with you and others to frame appropriate remarks. When my mother-in-law died, my present husband elected to say a few words. It was so beautiful to hear him talk about his mother and all the important memories he had. I hope I will have the courage to do so at the funerals of my loved ones.
- Having a special funeral service for children. This is something to consider if there are enough children involved to make it meaningful. Such a service would be one that was scaled down to meet their needs, one in which they could participate. (For more information on children's funerals see the reference to my earlier book, *The Grieving Child*, in the Bibliography.)
- Videotaping or recording the funeral. If you decide to videotape the service, have someone do this for you; don't try to do it yourself. Of course, it needs to be done as discreetly as possible. When the funeral is over,

you may find it hard to view at first, but it could become a treasure later on. It could be a useful tool to offer people who were unable to attend, but don't force it on anyone, as some may find it too painful to endure.

If you choose to do any of these things, let your funeral director, pastor, or rabbi know what you are planning. This will help ensure that events go as smoothly as possible.

3.3 Selecting a Cemetery

If you decide to bury your loved one in a cemetery, choosing the right one may involve deciding how important it is to have the burial plot near family members. Do you choose a cemetery near you, or do you bury your loved one some distance away in a family plot? You might even have the choice of burying this person in a national cemetery with military honors. Are you likely to visit the grave often? Are others? You decide what's best for you.

There are some considerations you may want to weigh. There are very formal cemeteries with strict requirements in the selection of headstones, placing of flowers, and other details. There are sculpture gardens. There are memorial gardens with no monuments at all—only plaques that lie flat to the ground. And, of course, there are old-fashioned cemeteries with different shapes and sizes of headstones and flowers of all sorts planted on or near the graves. Some cemeteries require a vault, which is a concrete liner for the casket to fit into, providing further protection from the elements; others do not. In some rural communities, you may be expected to keep up the ground you have purchased by planting the grass, weeding and mowing it. Most cemeteries now have something called "perpetual care," which is included in the initial cost.

Other things to know about cemeteries: If you own a plot of ground in a cemetery but want to use a different cemetery, your plot can be sold. I have even seen classified advertisements for cemetery lots in the newspapers, but most cemeteries will help you with this. You can also change the location of your plot within the same cemetery with the help of the management.

3.4 Burial

Unless you decide on cremation you will have to arrange for your loved one's remains to be buried somewhere. At first, it may be hard to think of this person's body being buried in the ground because this sets off the fear we all have of not being able to breathe. Even as an adult, you may have to remind yourself that your loved one no longer needs to breathe, see, or receive nourishment. Reflecting on this is a sobering reminder of the finality of death.

Normally, burial usually follows the funeral, but this need not be the case. If you have elected cremation, the body will be taken to a crematorium, and you can do whatever you wish with the ashes after that. Also, if you happen to live in such a cold place that graves can't be opened during the winter, it may be necessary to keep the body in a refrigerated vault until spring. More commonly, the casket is placed in a hearse after the funeral, and family and friends follow the hearse to the cemetery, turning their lights on to alert other motorists that this is a funeral procession. Sometimes the procession will have a police escort to stop traffic at intersections. This will be arranged by the funeral director.

As in all these matters, you can do whatever you wish with regard to a graveside ceremony. If you practice a certain religion, this may help you decide on what to do. Generally, you probably want to keep it fairly short. You can go with a more or less standard ritual that is arranged by your funeral director or religious adviser, or you can add some personal touches. These might include special songs or readings, taking certain flowers off the casket and giving them to special people, or electing to stay until the casket is lowered into the ground, perhaps taking part by placing a handful of soil in the grave. These are plans that should be made ahead of time and shared with everyone who needs to know.

Finally, keep in mind that the burial need not be in a conventional cemetery. If you live on a farm, it could be placed in a family burial plot on the farm, or, if you elect cremation, you could arrange to have the ashes buried or scattered in your churchyard or even in your own backyard. If any of this appeals to you, you might ask your funeral director for guidance in deciding what to do. In certain cases state laws may apply.

What Happens to the Body After Burial?

No matter how emancipated you may be, no matter how educated, no matter how worldly wise, you are likely to dwell just a bit on what will be happening to the body of your loved one after burial. In working with the bereaved, I find this subject cautiously broached but always troublesome. When my first husband died, I found myself wondering about these things, too. Finally I approached a funeral director friend and asked him about the natural decay of the body. What he told me was very comforting to me at the time, and now, a long time later, this sort of thing no longer bothers me. What he told me was that with embalming the process is very slow, the body taking years to decompose. The embalming fluid dries the body out and will make the skin very leathery. Caskets and vaults are now available that are sealed against the natural elements, slowing this process even more. Eventually the process of "dust to dust" will end.

Visiting the Grave

I usually suggest that you visit the grave at least one time after the burial. The reason for this is to see whether it helps with your grief. You may feel nothing. You may feel that your loved one isn't there anyway and that this does nothing for you. Or you may feel a closeness to your loved one. You may find yourself silently or even audibly talking to him or her. If this is the case, you may want to return to the grave from time to time.

I know of one woman who takes a lawn chair with her to sit on while visiting her husband's grave. Her children bring dry bread to feed the ducks at a nearby pond. Their visits are very pleasant.

If your loved one has been buried in a cemetery, you may not have made that first visit. Perhaps it is frightening to you. If this is the case, you might explore what part of the visit is most frightening, as this can help you overcome that fear. I remember having a conversation with one woman who had not yet visited the grave. When I asked what she was most afraid of, she replied, "I'm afraid I'll fall apart." I then asked her what her definition was of "falling apart." I asked her if "falling apart" meant that her arms and ears would fall off. As she laughed, she said, "I'm afraid I'll cry." "Is that so bad?" I asked her. Is crying really "falling apart"? Crying, I said, is an essential part of the mourning process.

If the first visit to the gravesite is frightening, consider taking a friend with you and perhaps some flowers or a note that could be left there. Your visit can be short. Five minutes is enough. Even a brief visit from the security of your car is sufficient if you can park where you see the grave. (See section 5.5 on visiting the cemetery.)

How Often Should You Visit the Grave?

Once a week? Once a month? Every day? My advice is not to think of cemetery visits as obligatory. Their purpose is to help you with your grief—period. If they are interfering with the process of getting on with your life, then you should reduce their frequency or end them altogether. If not, then probably what you are doing is all right. (See also section 5.5 on cemetery visits.)

Thoughts Pertaining to the Headstone

The selection of the headstone will vary with the cemetery. You may be limited to a flat granite or bronze plate, or you may be able to purchase an upright one with room for a special comment. In military cemeteries you may not have any choice but to go with what is regulated. Headstones can be purchased at any time; the cost will vary.

Whatever headstone or monument you select, be prepared for a shock when you see it in place for the first time. Seeing your loved one's name engraved on a monument or plaque, including the dates of birth and death, can be overwhelming—a further confirmation of the finality of death. Taking a friend with you for this first viewing of the monument would be helpful.

3.5 Cremation

Cremation of the body, once banned by some religions, is becoming more common in this country and is widely used abroad where land for cemeteries is scarce or expensive. It is also preferred by those who are uncomfortable with the idea of gradual decomposition discussed above. Yet misconceptions about cremation have kept many from considering it.

A friend told me recently of the reaction of her children when she told them she would like her body to be cremated. They were opposed to the idea. They said they did not want their mother's body put into a fire and burned. Only after she explained what happens during cremation did they come to accept the idea.

In certain countries like India bodies *are* burned as part of religious rites, but cremation as generally practiced in this country is not burning; it consists of putting the body into a huge brick-lined kiln. Intense heat, with short bursts of spontaneous combustion, reduce the body to ashes. The ashes are medium-gray in color and very powdery. An average-sized person's ashes be would equivalent to a five-pound bag of flour.

If you elect to have your loved one's body cremated, be prepared for this question, "Do you want the bone fragments pulverized?" Cremation doesn't do a total job, and there will be bone pieces. These bone pieces can be reduced to powder if you prefer before they are handed over to you or your funeral director, as you have directed. The ashes will be in a small cardboard box about the size of a shoebox, or you can purchase an urn from the funeral home to place them in. The funeral director can keep them for you, perhaps up to a year, or you can elect to have them interred at a cemetery in a special area for urn burials or in what is called a columbarium. A columbarium is a wall with recesses into which ashes can be deposited and on which identifying plaques are placed.

There are other options for you to consider. You could decide to keep the urn on the mantel or in another special place in the house. You could elect to take the ashes and scatter them in a special place, such as the mountains, the seashore, or a church yard. Or they could be divided and scattered, reserving some to be buried in a more traditional manner. However, you should have the funeral director advise you regarding any laws that may apply. Some states do not allow ashes to be scattered by airplane.

3.6 Memorial Services

Memorial services are similar to funerals but without the body present. A memorial service usually occurs some weeks or months after the death, allowing time for out-of-town friends and relatives to make travel plans. If you are planning a memorial service, you can plan to have it at a time that is most convenient for those who will attend. A memorial service is also appropriate when circumstances prevent recovery of the body.

Your plans for a memorial service can be very similar to a funeral with special songs, music, poetry, and speakers. (See section 3.2 on making the funeral meaningful.) You may want to display a photograph of the deceased in a prominent place to take the place of the body, which would be present during a funeral. Again, you might want to videotape the service for later use, as this could be very meaningful to you and others. I have found that in either a funeral or memorial service it is nice to invite people to share memories of the person who has died. I remember being asked to officiate at the secular funeral of a young woman who had died after a long illness. The most meaningful part came when I invited people to speak and to share memories of their loved one. Through their memories I came to know a person who was very different from the ill, angry, sad woman I knew. I found out about a fun-loving person who would go to elaborate extremes to make a birthday party spectacular. This sharing was so meaningful to those present that they began hugging each other and continued to share memories even after I left.

3.7 Cenotaphs

A cenotaph is a monument erected to honor a dead person whose remains are unavailable for burial. For example, a cenotaph was dedicated some years ago to a prominent person who is believed to have died in a plane crash in impenetrable, snow-covered mountains. You could erect such a monument in the event your loved one died in circumstances where the body could not be recovered. It could be placed in a cemetery, a rock garden in your backyard, your church yard, or elsewhere to provide some closure to a life left otherwise somehow incomplete.

• • •

3.8 Disposing of Personal Belongings

Disposing of the personal belongings of a loved one is a painful process, but one that can help you with your grief. I would avoid having friends and relatives take it upon themselves to do this for you, although they may offer out of wanting to be helpful. This is especially true at the time of the funeral, when hasty decisions can lead to unfortunate mistakes. Only you, helped by close relatives and friends, will know which items should be kept and which can be disposed of. I find this time of sorting out a loved one's possessions a good time to share memories, laughter, and tears. There isn't any set time for this and no rush. Use your best judgment and your own internal time clock. I believe you will know when that day comes. It might be several months after your loved one's death.

As you begin to sort out these things, remember it doesn't all have to be done in one day. Perhaps on the first day you will do the dresser or the closet, saving the rest until later. Keep the things you are sure you want, give away all the things you are sure you don't want, and box up the rest. You can go through those boxes later when you have a clearer idea of what you want to keep.

You might consider having your family and close friends put together a wish list of keepsakes they would like, or you could go by ages of those involved, allowing the oldest to choose one item, then the next oldest, until all items had been distributed.

As you start to give away certain belongings to friends, be aware of two things: first, how will you feel when you see a certain person wearing that green sweater or that watch, and second, how that person may feel about accepting it when he or she is still mourning, too.

There are charitable organizations that welcome used clothing and other personal articles. You might check to see what is available in your community. Your gifts will be appreciated. Whenever possible, get a receipt for tax deductions.

Chapter 4

MOURNING
YOUR LOSS

Discovering Feelings You Never Knew

You Had

If you are caught up in the emotions of grief, I don't have to
tell you what they are like. They are all-consuming. No matter
how much you may have read about the experiences of others,
you can't ever be prepared for the intense feelings that will en-

gulf you when you have suffered a great personal loss. One stricken mother, mourning the death of her son, told me she could not understand why the birds continued to sing or the sun continued to rise in the morning. Intense emotions hit you when you least expect them. I know a widow who had a "grief attack" in front of a box of Special K cereal in the supermarket. Grief is unpredictable and largely uncontrollable, showing us a side of ourselves we didn't know was there. It can be terrifying and unnerving.

If only you could say, "I am going to take a month off and spend that time working on my grief!" Unfortunately, it's not that easy. Grief comes in waves. You can have a good day and then several bad ones. You can be going along, having a good time, and then hear a favorite song of your loved one, dropping you back into the depths of grief. People often see these lows as setbacks in their grief, but they're not; this is how grief is. You will experience peaks and valleys for a long time—peaks of feeling good, valleys of despair. As you start to heal from your grief, you will find the valleys more shallow and the peaks wider until one day you find your life is established firmly on a new course.

However, grief is different for everyone. There are no recipes for grief. Fifty people could be experiencing the cancer death of a seventy-five-year-old mother, and each would have a different experience and cope differently from the others. You may not experience all the feelings I will be talking about in this chapter, but that doesn't mean that they are lurking around the corner waiting to jump out at you. I often hear comments like this: "I was told that if I don't get angry at [him or her] for dying, I would never be able to work this through." This is not true; anger may not be part of your grief. On the other hand you may experience all the emotions of grief daily. Just remember: We are all different, unique individuals coping with life as best we can. (See section 1.3 on the length of grief.)

• • •

4.1 Grief Is Unlike Other Life Experiences

You may be feeling that you are losing your mind; it's a common feeling. You may be wondering if you will ever return to "normal." Since I have gone through this experience myself and worked with thousands of others who have struggled with their grief, I can assure you that you will return to normal if you allow yourself to face up to your loss, to accept the reality of your situation, and to mourn the death of your loved one. However, it may be a different "normal" from what you knew in the past, in part because life does not stand still; what is normal in one period of our lives ceases to be normal in another.

When you are grieving you may find that you are having a hard time remembering things. You may walk into the kitchen to get a pair of scissors and not remember what it was you went there to get. Or you may start to make some point to a friend and then forget what it was. You may miss dates and appointments. If this is happening to you, I suggest that you obtain a small notebook that you can carry with you to record things you don't want to forget. As long as your grief retains its grip on you, don't rely on your memory, because being forgetful will only make you feel inadequate and embarrassed. Your memory will return in time to its usual level of functioning.

You may find it hard to concentrate during your grief. Watching your favorite TV program may be difficult, and reading a book out of the question.

You also may find it difficult to perform as well at work as you have in the past. The loss of your loved one may be all you can really think about. Have patience with yourself and know that it may be some weeks before you will be working at your old speed again. I know of many bereaved people who feel that their employers are not sufficiently understanding of the impact of grief and expect too much too soon. If you have any concern in this regard, you might have a private talk with your employer and try to explain to him or her what you are going through. (You might even let your boss borrow this book for a couple of days.) As the saying goes, things that people aren't up on, they're usually down on. Once you have helped your employer to understand what is happening with you, he or she might even lessen your task load for a while.

Another concern: Be careful in driving your car. When you are stricken with grief it is hard to concentrate, and driving requires concentration. If you have to drive long distances, make sure you break your trip up into manageable segments. Grieving people can be lethal on the highway. This is a time when your mind wanders, when your thoughts may turn to your loved one, and when you may even begin to cry, blurring your vision. I know of many minor (and some major) accidents that have occurred when people were in the midst of grief. You certainly don't need the extra trauma and worry of an accident to contend with on top of your grief.

With your mind so preoccupied, it may seem impossible to focus on anything for any length of time. A woman once told me she had been so preoccupied that, intending to drive to the library, much to her amazement she found herself at the grocery store with no recollection of how she got there.

You may be very disorganized, starting one task only to leave it to start another, completing nothing. Your housework may suffer, causing you embarrassment. You might find a part of you wanting to get on top of things and another part of you thinking, "Who cares?" Yet there is a good feeling that comes from having a clean house. It helps to have this part of your life organized when everything else seems so disorganized. My suggestion is to give it a try for the boost it will give your morale. Here are several things you can consider:

- Have some family members or friends help you.
- Hire a cleaning service to help you catch up.

• Roll up your sleeves and start on one room at a time. One room a week is enough, and before you know it your home will be in proper shape again.

Also you may not be getting enough sleep. You may find that going to sleep is either impossible or that you can get only brief periods of sleep followed by wakefulness. If this is true for you, observe what is happening and see if there is a pattern to your sleep problems. Sometimes, simply changing your sleep routines will help, such as going to bed later or earlier, reading a light novel in bed, taking a warm bath and drinking a glass of warm milk before bed, listening to your favorite music, or, if your physician agrees, taking a mild sleeping pill when all else fails. It is important to have your rest so you can be fully prepared to work with your grief.

It is also important to look at your other physical needs, such as exercise and nutrition. If you are not already doing so, set up a manageable exercise program for yourself. This may involve only a short walk each day, either by yourself or with a friend. If you need more structure to reinforce your commitment, you might consider joining a health club or gym. Once you put out money for the membership, you will be more apt to stick to a routine. Joining a club is also a way to expand your acquaintances and make new friends.

Finally, you need to eat as well as you can. Meals that you used to look forward to may now lack appeal. Cooking, perhaps something you used to enjoy, may have turned into drudgery. If you own a microwave oven, it can be a godsend now, since it will shorten the preparation and cooking time you may have put into your meals in the past. Also, if you find that you can't eat three regular meals each day, try five small ones. But avoid nibbling on junk food such as potato chips, candy, or cookies, as these could lead to excess weight, which will only complicate your situation. Try instead to replace empty calories with fruit, nuts, or vegetables. (See sections 7.23 and 9.1 on helping yourself through grief.)

4.2 Disbelief and Shock

If your grief is still very fresh, you are likely to be experiencing shock and disbelief as you try to comprehend what has happened and what kind of future you can have without the person you loved. This could continue for two weeks or longer, depending on how sudden or how violent the death was, and on whether you experienced some mourning before the death occurred. There are circumstances, however, in which this period could last much longer. The families of soldiers missing in action in Vietnam have been subjected to decades of not knowing the fate of their loved ones.

During this initial period of grief you will feel a numbness and a disassociation with the world around you. People who are going through this often tell me that they feel as if they are watching a play in which they are but spectators. Others feel that what has happened is only a bad dream from which they will wake up to find everything back to normal. I know of a number of people who, after the death of a loved one, have gone back to the hospital under the pretense of taking "cookies or flowers for the nurses." This is a nice thing to do, of course, but I also believe that these people had a need to check out the rooms where their loved ones had been to make sure they were really gone. There is nothing wrong with this; I have done it myself a couple of times. And doing so will help make the death more real. I know a father who could not believe that his son was dead until he saw the car in which he was killed. I know the mother of a young man killed in a plane crash who could not believe that her son was dead until she had gone to the airport and sat in the cockpit of a similar plane, reconstructing in her mind what must have happened. It is during this time of shock and disbelief that you may find yourself waiting for your loved one to come home, or expecting the telephone to ring for your usual noontime conversation, or even picking up the phone and dialing the office in the unrealistic hope that your loved one will answer.

During this time you may also want to believe that someone

77

has played a bad joke on you and that none of what you have been told is true. You may even search for the person who has died, chasing down cars that have passed you because the driver looked like your loved one, or feeling a rush of anxiety when you see a person in the crowd who has a similar way of walking. If you are having such experiences, don't be alarmed; they're a part of this first phase of your grief.

Some Ideas on How to Help Yourself

During this period of grief you may go over and over the details of the death. Reviewing the experience is important because each time you go over the details, the more real the death will become to you. Of course, it must become real before you can move on with your grief process.

If you are worried that your friends may be tiring of hearing your story, all you need to do is to let them know how important it is for you to review the death and that you need people around you who can just sit quietly and listen. Also invite your friends to tell you when they need a break to talk about other things that are going on in their lives. If there is a greater need to talk than your friends can endure, perhaps you need to find a grief therapist or religious adviser who will listen and know how to respond.

During this period you may be devoid of feelings, going through your day like a robot, not remembering or paying much attention to where you have been or to what you are do-ing. A whole day may go by before it occurs to you to eat. I know of one woman who was gently reminded by friends on the third day after her son's death that she was putting the same dress on for the third day in a row. She was amazed; she had no idea that she had done this.

This is probably the state you were or will be in at the time of the funeral and burial. You may overhear friends saying, "Look at how well [she or he] is doing." Little do they know that you are in a state of shock and haven't begun to deal with your grief.

Don't be surprised if there are parts of the funeral and burial that you don't even remember. Someone may come up to you to talk about the funeral, and you won't even recall that person being there. This is normal. If you are really concerned about certain parts of the funeral and you want to remember them, you can have family and friends fill in the gaps for you. If there are any cassette or video recordings of the funeral, you may want to listen to or watch them when you feel ready. In time, as you recover, some of these blank spots will be filled in.

4.3 Denial

As the shock and numbness begin to wear off, lightning bolts of reality will hit—flashes of reality that your loved one is dead and will never be part of your life again. With this return to reality you can expect a new flood of emotions, even physical pain, and feelings of despair. Take heart: This too will pass.

For some people this pain is so great that they look for ways to deny the truth that their loved one is dead. It is natural for us to try to stop the pain when we cut a finger; why not do the same when we feel pain like this? If bandages won't work, then denying we were hurt may be seen as the next best thing. However, allowing yourself to slip into denial can slow down your grieving process, which must continue if you are to get well.

Don't try to fool yourself into thinking that you can avoid the process of grief. I know of a woman who spent six or seven years denying that her daughter had died; only when she finally accepted the reality of her daughter's death did she start to get better. "Time will heal" is a phrase we often hear, often from those who have never experienced grief. It is based on the false idea that you can bypass the pain of grief. Time does heal, but only if you use it to mourn your loss.

Even so, I must say that some denial is probably acceptable, as it can cushion you while you gradually accept the reality of the death. For example, if your loved one died in some horrible

79

way, it may not hurt to pretend for a while that it wasn't so bad. It may not even be necessary to grasp every grisly detail of your loved one's death. Denial becomes a problem when you deliberately look for ways to avoid the pain of grief and the reality of the death.

Some Questions to Ask Yourself

It isn't always easy to determine if your denial is beginning to work against you. Each person and each set of circumstances is different. Each must be examined individually. You may hear comments from well-meaning friends and relatives that may add to your confusion. If you are wondering about your own possible lapse into denial, ask yourself the following questions:

- Is this keeping me from getting on with my life?
- Is this causing conflict within my family or within my circle of friends?
- Has more than a reasonable amount of time passed without resolution or without my making necessary decisions?

If your answers tend to be yes, it is time to change course. If you need help doing this, seek the advice of a professional who can objectively look at what you are doing and help you decide if changes must be made.

Ways That People Avoid Reality

There are a number of ways that people use denial to avoid reality. As temporary coping mechanisms they may serve a purpose, but if they go on for any length of time or start interfering with your life, you need to ask yourself why you are using such devices. Here are some of them:

- Insisting on speaking of the deceased in the present tense. You will tend to do this at first out of habit, but you will catch yourself in midsentence. If you continue to speak of the deceased in the present tense, you may be doing so in an effort to avoid dealing with the death.

- Refusing to believe that the person has died. One day a woman came to my office and announced, "There is nothing you can say that will convince me that my daughter is dead." Needless to say, I could not be of any help to her at that time.

- Pretending that the deceased is on a trip. This is easy to do when separation has occurred frequently, as in military service. I remember talking with a friend whose husband had died and her telling me, "I'm just going to pretend he is on a hunting trip." Later when I talked to her, she said, "You know that hunting trip thing? It's not working anymore. He should have been home by now."

- Leaving clothes and other personal articles just as they were and becoming upset if anyone moves or touches them months after the death.

- Doing just the opposite: disposing of everything that reminds you of the deceased. I know of one case where every personal belonging of a little girl had been removed before her funeral and where plans had been made to knock out the wall of her room to remove every vestige of her ever having lived. I also know of families who, after the death of a child, made plans to move immediately. In early grief memories of your loved one may be painful but, believe me, that changes, and the same memories become as endearing and comforting as being wrapped up in Grandma's old quilt. Memories cannot be erased. If you have moved or disposed of all the clothing and pictures of your loved one, you are very likely to regret it later. If things of this sort are too painful to look at now, box them up and put them away until a later time. (See section 7.1 on other changes in one's life.)

81

- Not talking about the deceased to avoid the pain of hearing or speaking your loved one's name. You may even find it necessary to leave the room when the name of your beloved is mentioned.
- Playing down the importance of your relationship with the deceased in an effort to protect yourself from the pain of grief. I have heard things like, "He wasn't a good father; I am glad he is gone," or, "Who needs her with all her complaining; it's a relief not to have to bother with her anymore."
- "Searching" for the deceased. You may see her drive by in a car, hear his footsteps on the walk outside, see someone with the same walk, hear his voice calling out to you, or smell her perfume. These are all efforts to recreate that person's presence. If you find this happening to you, don't be alarmed. This is normal. It is when you have to work at recreating these images that you may have a problem that will interfere with your recovery.
- Going to a spiritualist of some sort in an effort to communicate with your loved one. This can be a form of denial, especially if it is something out of character for you to be doing. I remember a man going to a medium when his brother died because he felt his brother might have inside information for him on which horse to bet on. It didn't work! Another woman visited a medium in an effort to communicate with her husband and was left very uneasy and anxious after being told about supposed future tragedies.
- Keeping constantly occupied with work or travel; in effect, running away from your grief. Months or years later, when your life has slowed down, you will still have to deal with the reality of the death. This could be even more difficult than it is now if your support system has evaporated in the meantime. I frequently see people who are struggling with their grief two or three years after a death because of this.

- Resorting to drugs and alcohol to block out what has happened. My advice to you: Don't ever take even one drink or one pill to ease your grief. Drinks for other reasons are matters of your personal judgment, and pills are matters for your physician to weigh. But be wary of chemical solutions to your grief; they won't work. They will only delay your recovery.

These are only a few of the ways that you might try to avoid dealing with painful truth. No doubt there are many more. But take heart: This overwhelming grief that you feel at the time of your loss will lessen soon. You will even have happy days sprinkled in with the bad. The more you can work with your grief and mourn your loss, the quicker you will be able to get on with your life.

How to Help Yourself Deal with Denial

Here are some things you can do to overcome the temptation to deny the reality of your loss:

- Talking it out—reviewing with friends and relatives just what has happened. Going over the details of the death, painful as they are, time and again. The more you talk about the death, the more real it will become for you. And it must become "real" before you can begin to mourn your loss. If friends get tired of listening to you, find others you can talk to, such as your pastor or rabbi, a therapist, or your physician.
- As hard as it may be, viewing the body of your loved one, or at least the casket in which it has been placed, will help you accept the reality of your loved one's death. It will help anchor you against the temptation to wait for that phone call or for the front door to open, thus impossibly proving that your loved one is actually alive. (If the body is not presentable, see section 7.12.)

- Planning and participating in the funeral will help you acknowledge the reality of the death. (See section 3.2 on planning a funeral.)
- Gathering as much information as you can about the death by talking to the doctor, police officers, military authorities, or others who may have information to substantiate what occurred. This can be difficult, however, particularly in the first days after a death, and it would help to have a close friend, relative, or therapist with you as you review these painful details.
- Identifying your feelings for what they are. Using your own inner resources, your own sound judgment to recognize that what you are doing is, at least in part, denying the reality of your loved one's death.

When to Consult with a Professional

Denial can become ritualistic, and there are times that you need permission to change your behavior. A widower I know left his bedroom intact after his wife died, waiting for her return. He neither moved nor touched anything except to hang a huge portrait of her over the bed. He didn't use the bedroom at all but slept on a couch in the den. After a time he developed back pain and went to see his physician about it. The physician referred him to me. After hearing his story I suggested that it was time for him to move back into his bedroom and to get on with his life. He readily agreed. His back pains went away. What this story says is that sometimes people need permission to move on with their lives. If you start observing some ritual out of respect for your loved one, and if this ritual is blocking your recovery from grief, you probably need someone who can say, "Okay, you have done this long enough; it's time to let go."

It is appropriate to consult with a professional at any time that you feel uncomfortable with yourself or whenever you are beginning to wonder if your responses are normal. There is a fine line between denial that is normal and denial that is used to somehow pretend that your loved one is still alive. If you are unsure and need guidance, find a professional to help you. (See the Resources section for suggestions.)

4.4 Rage and Anger

Rage and anger are very strong emotions, at times as frightening to you as they are to your family and friends. The anger or rage felt at the time of death is often misdirected at family, friends, or colleagues.

Anger is an isolating emotion, as family and friends often don't know what to do with you or how to help you. They are likely to feel helpless and uncomfortable under your withering attacks and withdraw from you, only feeding your anger all the more. It's not a lot of fun being around someone who is angry, especially when you may be the target of the next outburst.

Anger and even rage are common reactions to the loss of a loved one. You may be terribly angry right now as you think about what you have lost and how your life has been changed overnight. But don't assume that these powerful emotions are lurking around the corner; they may not be part of your grief pattern at all. I know of many people who have said, "I was told that unless I get angry at [the deceased] for dying, I will never complete my grief." Anger is not part of every grief reaction; just as every person in this world is unique, everyone's grief is unique, too.

Anger Is a Powerful Emotion

Anger creates a rush of energy that can get out of hand and cause you to do or say things that you will be sorry for later. It is important to recognize when this is happening and to have ways to discharge this destructive energy in appropriate ways. If you are worried about your own outbursts and your inability to control them, let me assure you that there are ways to discharge this energy without hurting others.

When a loved one dies, leaving you lonely and afraid of what your future will bring, you have every reason to be angry. You don't have to apologize about that; it's okay to be angry. What's not okay is taking your anger out unfairly on yourself or others. One mother told me that she was angry at her husband for dying and leaving her with so many responsibilities. She took out her anger on her oldest son, who then passed it on to his nearest sibling, who in turn passed it on to the next sibling. At the end of the line was the poor dog, an innocent creature without the slightest idea of what was going on.

Does One Have to Express Anger?

Anger won't just go away. It likes to sit there and fester, growing larger and larger until it erupts. Anger that is not discharged can create both emotional and physical stress leading to anxiety and depression. Anger that is not acknowledged and that is misdirected can create all sorts of problems in your life. It is healthier, both physically and emotionally, to learn to identify your feelings and to express them appropriately.

Know Your Anger History

The more you can understand yourself and how you handle anger, the more you can take charge of and control yourself and make the changes that will set you on a better course.

Think back to when you were a child. What lessons did you learn about anger? How did the adults around you express their anger or rage? Were you taught that anger was bad and that you were punished for being angry? Were you hit or slapped and thus learned that anger requires inflicting pain? Did you learn to keep your anger bottled up inside you until you exploded and broke something, thus learning that anger requires destroying things? Or were you taught that it is okay to be angry and given appropriate ways to express your anger? I remember as a little girl, my parents were rather stoic, not showing much emotion of any kind. As a child I learned that anger was something you were punished for. If I was angry, I was sent to my room until I wasn't angry anymore. That didn't help discharge the anger; it just sat there until, at the slightest provocation, I would explode, breaking a favorite toy, hitting a sibling, or saying something hurtful. I came away thinking that anger is bad and destructive.

If you are mourning the death of a loved one, you may be angry about a number of things:

- You may be angry with the hospital staff or the medical professionals for not responding as quickly as you think they should have to an emergency situation or for not providing the appropriate treatment programs.
- You may be angry with friends or relatives who, in their lack of understanding, or because they are caught up in their own grief, make comments that are not helpful—comments like, "He's better off now," or "Look at what you have to be thankful for," or "You're young, you'll get married again," or "It's all part of God's plan." It may help you to know that trite comments of this kind, even though inappropriate, are well meant and stem from the same discomfort and disorientation that you are probably experiencing yourself.
- You may be angry at the person who died and has left you behind facing a lot of legal work and loneliness. Or you may be angry at the situation you are in because of the death.
- Depending on your religious views, you may be angry at God. You may have prayed hard for a cure or for the safety of your loved one, and you may feel that you have been let down, that your prayers have not been an-

swered. A wise lady once told me, "It's okay to be angry with God; He can take it." You may even wonder if you have done something in your life that you are being punished for. If that is the way you feel, contact your pastor or rabbi for reassurance on this score.

- You may be angry at yourself for what you may have said or not said, or for not responding calmly or quickly enough, or for being healthy and alive.
- You may be angry because of the change in life-style that has been inflicted upon you. Your financial picture may have changed, and you may have to make painful adjustments, like moving into a smaller house, having a tighter budget, giving up your travel plans, or taking a job. You may be angry at the things you may have to give up, such as your well-laid retirement plans.
- You may be angry at the role changes that have to be made within your family. You may have to take on jobs that the deceased formerly handled, or you may have to assume added responsibilities—preparing the income taxes, cooking, changing diapers, or mowing the lawn.
- You may be angry at what you perceive as the loss of control in your life. Your loved one's death was one brutal lesson; others may follow.
- You may be angry at the isolation that occurs when family and friends go back to their normal pursuits and you are left alone with your thoughts and your new responsibilities.
- You may be angry that the rest of the world continues on just as though nothing had happened. The neighbors mow their lawns, children play, people tell jokes, the car needs fixing, bills have to be paid, night follows day, just as if your world hadn't stopped.

These are only a few of the many things happening to you that can make you angry. If you are mourning the death of a loved one, no doubt you can add many more.

When Do You Know You Are Getting Angry?

If you can spot the early signs of anger, you may be able to discharge it before it gets you into trouble. The question is, what are those early signs? How do you know you are getting angry?

Think about past occasions when you have become angry. Can you recall what happened first? When I begin to get angry, I usually start to cry, which can be embarrassing at times, but it helps to know that I am not feeling sad but instead I am mad! Where do you feel it first? Is it a tightness in your neck? Do you start perspiring? Does your head hurt? Are your fists clenched? Do you grind your teeth? Do you become irritated at ordinary things, like the squeaking of the floor or the sound of the telephone? Try to become familiar with your anger. The more you know about it and understand it the more control you will have over it, and the more able you will be to express it appropriately.

Now think about how you have expressed your anger in the past. What kinds of things have you done that have not worked? Snapping at people? Turning sullen? Slamming doors and kicking the furniture? Insulting your friends? Making unjust accusations? Driving carelessly? Drinking excessively? Taking drugs? Allowing yourself to become depressed?

Also pay attention to the good ways that you have expressed anger and continue using those techniques. But don't count suppressing your anger as good; that won't work. Anger creates energy that must be released.

In keeping with that thought, think about physical things you can do that will help you expend some energy when you begin to feel angry. These might include brisk walking; any sport such as tennis, basketball, or bowling; chopping wood; hitting a punching bag; kneading bread dough; cleaning your house; or engaging in crafts such as leather tooling, pottery, or cross stitching. (I find there is something satisfying about that needle going in and out of the fabric.) Even taking time out and counting to ten will help. Or letting your arms relax, taking several deep breaths, and saying to yourself, "I am calm. I am calm. I am calm." Simple measures like this will let that first rush pass over and give you time to discharge the energy without inflicting harm on yourself or others.

Sometimes you can turn your anger into humor and laugh at it. Once when I was very upset, burdened with what seemed to me impossible demands, I caught myself yelling out loud while driving alone in my car—and then noticed another motorist staring at me. Visualizing how funny I must look, I smiled at the other motorist and began to laugh at myself.

One woman I know, greatly disturbed by the death of a close relative, decided to vent her anger by breaking a wine jug. What significance that had I don't know, but she waited until all her neighbors were in bed and then took the jug outside to smash it against the side of the house. It wouldn't break! She tried again. It still wouldn't break. She threw it several more times, without success, until she finally broke into laughter. The unbroken jug had done its work. She laughed again when she told me this story.

Tape recorders will give you an outlet for your anger. You can say whatever you want to, play it back and hear yourself being mad, and then erase it. It's safe. Letter writing can serve the same purpose, but I don't suggest that you mail the letter, at least not while you're still angry. Keeping a journal is another option.

If you have a need to destroy something when you're angry, have things around that can be destroyed, such as old telephone books that you can tear up or concrete blocks you can smash with a hammer (wearing safety goggles to protect your eyes). I know of a woman who went to a garage sale and bought cheap dishes just for throwing. She also lived near a construction site and designated that area as the place she could go to throw her dishes whenever she was angry.

Sometimes just talking to a friend who understands you, is sympathetic, and really hears you will also help.

Think about what would work for you, giving you what you need to calm down and take charge of your anger. You may even want to post some of these ideas on your refrigerator or make a list in your journal to refer to when you need them.

Prioritizing the Things That Make You Angry

When your energy level is down and you are in control, take out a piece of paper and pencil and start jotting down all of the things (and people) that make you mad. Look at your list and determine what makes you most mad, prioritize that list, and then look at your list again to see if there are things you can do to reduce its length. For example, if your son plays his music too loud, you could buy him some headphones. If your mother keeps calling you too early in the morning, you could ask her to wait until a certain hour, unplug the telephone, or let an answering machine take the message. There may be things on your list that you can't do anything about—let's say a loved one has cancer—but you will feel better and lighter having gone through such an exercise. Our intellect needs to work with our emotions as we help ourselves through grief.

There are now many books available about anger. Perhaps you might want to get one or two to see if they can be of help. (See the Bibliography for a book on anger.)

When to Seek Professional Help

Anger can take over your life, making you miserable and the people around you miserable. You may be very short on patience and very critical of coworkers, family and friends. You may complain about everything, perhaps even writing "hate" letters to certain people. This will naturally create a lot of stress and tension. You may even take your anger out on yourself by hitting yourself, or risking your life and the lives of others on the highway.

Whenever you feel your anger reaches this level and it's out of control, I suggest that you seek professional help to gain a better understanding of what is causing your anger and how to discharge it.

4.5 Guilt or Regrets

Guilt can be a very powerful emotion. It too can be an isolating emotion, causing family and friends to withdraw for fear of saying the wrong thing. The feeling that accompanies guilt is not a pleasant one. If you are feeling guilty for something, even if there is no basis for your guilt, you may despise yourself and wonder how others could like you when you are such a contemptible person. Because of this, you may be inclined to keep it to yourself, never verbalizing what you are thinking, keeping it a dark secret.

It may help for you to recognize the distinction between guilt and regret. Regrets often get lumped in with guilt, making them more difficult to deal with. Regrets are the things that you wish you had done or said. Examples are: "I wish I had told him I loved him one more time," or "I wish I had gotten her to the doctor sooner," or "I wish we had taken that trip," or "I wish I had gone to the hospital before she died."

Guilt, on the other hand, is what you feel when you believe you have done something wrong. You may feel guilty for having had a fight with your son just before he was struck by a car and killed. You may feel guilty for telling a loved one to "go ahead and kill yourself if that's what you want," whereupon she did just that. One woman felt guilty for being the driver of the car in which her husband was killed. Of course, there are many reasons for people to feel guilty, some well founded, some not. You may feel guilty for being alive when your loved one is dead, as one mother told me she felt after the death of her child. Or you may feel guilty for being angry with God, a very common reaction in religious people.

The possibilities for feeling guilty or regretful are infinite.

What you will want to do is to clarify in your own mind which it is you are dealing with: guilt or regret. Regrets are a lot easier to handle.

How to Help Yourself

There are a number of things you can do to get relief from your feelings of guilt and regrets:

- Identify what is causing you to feel guilty or regretful. Take out a pencil and paper and write down everything that is causing you to feel this way. Then look at your list and put a *G* by the items that you see as the basis for guilt and an *R* by your regrets. This simple exercise alone will give you some relief. If you want, find someone to share this with, someone you trust and who can be objective, not inflicting his or her judgments on you. Then look at your list and see if there is something you can do about some of them. This might be as simple as writing a letter or telephoning someone to say, "I'm sorry." However there will be things on your list that may need more thought and effort to achieve some relief.

- Be careful with hindsight. Now, after the fact, you may be feeling more rested, emotionally and physically, and it can be very easy to become judgmental of yourself. Remember back to past events and how tired or exhausted you were feeling, and how much stress you were under, and remember that you were doing the best you could under such difficult circumstances. Don't assign greater strength to yourself now than those circumstances would have allowed.

- Try to be objective about what happened. There are times when it may seem impossible that you could ever get any relief from your guilt. If you drove recklessly

93

and killed someone, or if you left a loaded gun where your child could reach it, the guilt you feel is real; you may need professional help to find a way to somehow expiate it. On the other hand, your guilt may be more in interpretation than fact. In this case, it may help you to review what occurred with another person in an effort to achieve some objectivity about what happened. The woman I mentioned earlier, who drove the car in which her husband was killed, spent several sessions with me going over and over the fact that she had been driving only as a favor to her tired husband, that she tried to drive carefully, and that she most certainly did not want to kill her husband. Repeatedly we reviewed the reason why she was the driver: She had agreed to drive so her husband could sleep on the way home and be prepared to go to work early the next morning. She was performing a loving gesture for him. Through this approach she eventually worked the guilt out of her system and moved on in her grief. At times it helps to intellectualize the incident repeatedly until you can accept it emotionally. Another woman felt guilty about a quarrel she had with her husband one morning. After that quarrel he went to work, had a heart attack, and died. This woman felt that she had caused his death, that the extra stress of their fight was the one thing responsible for his death. She was also distressed that their last words to each other were unpleasant. We spent time discussing heart problems and the fact that one incident does not create a heart attack. Then we focused on the quarrel. I found out that this was just one of many quarrels the couple had through the years of their marriage and that, in spite of these quarrels, their relationship had been a fairly happy one. It was helpful to her when we talked about how this quarrel would have been resolved if the death had not interfered. In essence she played out the quarrel and then put a finish on it, acknowledging that this fight, too, would have been resolved, and thereby obtained some relief from her guilt.

- Be prepared to forgive yourself. If you refuse to forgive someone who has asked you for forgiveness, your stubbornness not only will hurt that other person; it will hurt you, too, for the matter in question will continue to boil within you. How much worse it would be if you refused to forgive yourself, for in this case you would be both the person refusing forgiveness and the one in need of its blessings. If you have faith in God and ask for forgiveness, you have been taught that you will be forgiven. You must then ask yourself: Why can't I forgive myself?

- Look for ways to work off your guilt. I remember a woman who was feeling guilt for three specific things. She experienced some relief sharing them with me but found the feelings returning in a day or two. We began to think about what task she could do to expiate her guilt and how much time it would take for her to let these feelings go. She decided she was going to scrub her kitchen floor twelve times over a period of one month and then let go of her guilt. Each time she scrubbed her floor she kept in touch with the reason why she was doing it. At the end of her twelve scrubbings, she not only had an immaculate kitchen floor; she felt better. You might think about tasks you could take on that would help you do the same thing: doing community work, visiting a nursing home, building a shed, landscaping your yard, doing some difficult job you long have put off, doing a big favor for a friend or neighbor. However, it is important to put a specific limit on your tasks so they don't become rituals.

- Look for lessons to be gained from your guilt or regret: things you can do that will make you a better person and the lives of those around you better. If you regret you did not say "I love you" often enough, try now to do just that when you feel it and do not assume people know you love them because you do the cooking, earn the living, or provide the allowances.

- Most importantly, don't forget the good things you did do in your relationship with the deceased. So often when you are feeling guilty, that feeling is so powerful that it overwhelms you. Spend time thinking about some of the positive things that went on. Do this task now while you are in the frame of mind to seek help. Write these things down on a piece of paper and put this list somewhere that you can find it easily. Don't forget those good things you did or said; hang on to them.

When to Seek Professional Help

If you have guilt feelings that you can't seem to get relief from, even after trying the suggestions above, you might ask a trusted friend or relative to help you talk them out. On the other hand, if you have guilt feelings or regrets that you cannot share in this way because you feel so horrible about them, find a therapist or religious adviser who can help you deal with them.

I want you to know that you can get relief from this powerful feeling and that you can even discover emotional growth from it. Always reach out for help whenever you have a feeling that you fear is bigger than what you can handle. There is help out there waiting for you, but you need to take that first step and make the phone call.

4.6 Depression

The depression one may experience over the death of a loved one can last for an hour, a day, a week, or longer. It is normal to feel depressed after any major loss in your life. The severity or longevity will vary from person to person. Basic symptoms of depression may include some or all of the following: not caring about your personal appearance, never changing your clothes, withdrawing from friends and activities, low self-esteem, lack of confidence, negative attitudes about everything, feeling empty inside, lacking energy, shedding tears at the slightest provocation, lacking interest in anything (including sex), weight gain or weight loss, insomnia or excessive sleep, and feeling overwhelmed by ordinary daily tasks.

Know Your Own Symptoms of Depression

The list above is a guide to common symptoms of depression. You may experience some or all of them, or you may experience some I haven't listed. Think back to times you have felt down or were having a "bad day." Think about how you felt then. What was the first clue that you were depressed? Was it when you started canceling luncheon engagements? Or was it when you started raiding the refrigerator looking for something to eat— something that would make you feel better? Get acquainted with your own first signs of depression so you can do something about it now before it becomes a problem. I find that when I am heading for a "downer" I withdraw from people, wanting to be by myself. So what I try to do is to have some "people contact," even if that contact happens to be with strangers in the elevator. I find that short, casual conversations help me. Simple approaches like this can be helpful to you as well.

Remembering your loved one could eventually help you with any depression you may be experiencing. However, there are times in early grief when remembering will be painful, putting you in touch with how much you have lost. Just be assured that it will not always be this way; the time will come when you will cherish these memories, when you will feel pride in your loved one's accomplishments, relish your good times together, and laugh at the funny things that happened. Some other suggestions:

- Reminiscing about your loved one's life or your lives together is important. Find people who will be willing to listen and willing to share their memories with you of the deceased.
- Looking at old photographs is a safe way to involve many of your family members and friends in talking about the deceased. Laughter and perhaps tears will ensue as you all go over different memories.
- A nice project to do by yourself or with others is to find a pile of old magazines, some cardboard, scissors, and glue, and cut out pictures and words from the magazines that remind you of the person who has died or of places you may have visited together. Then create a collage, pasting these items on a piece of poster board or cardboard. Share your handiwork with others in your family or circle of friends.
- Put together a scrapbook on the life of your loved one, using pictures, newspaper clippings, bits of ribbon, pressed flowers or whatever you have at hand.
- If you are feeling overwhelmed by your depression and find it difficult to function, try putting yourself on a schedule for daily routines. Do not expect yourself to be functioning at 100 percent, as you were before the death. Set manageable goals for yourself. If you are having problems in getting that stack of thank-you notes done, set a goal for yourself to do four per day. You will be surprised at how fast that stack will dwindle.
- Be careful with the use of drugs and alcohol during this time; they often act as depressants and will only make things more difficult for you.
- Find a support group of people in similar situations.

When to Seek Professional Help

Seek outside help if you find your depression is lasting longer than two weeks without any breaks, or if you find none of the suggestions above giving you any relief from this "down" feeling. Seek help if you find you are exhausted from lack of sleep or if your weight changes are not leveling off after a month or so. You may benefit from some prescribed medication or some intense therapy.

Seek help immediately if you are feeling a strong desire to kill yourself or even if you are feeling more preoccupied with death than is normal for you. It is normal to wish at times that you could die, too. The pain may be so great that you may wonder if you can ever be happy again. Most often, I hear comments like, "I just wish I could go to bed and not wake up," or "I wish God would just take me too," or "I wouldn't really mind if I had a heart attack as well." These are passive death wishes—someone or something doing "it" to you. I think it's good to acknowledge them, but you don't have to worry too much about them. I remember flying back from my first husband's funeral thinking, "I wouldn't care if this plane crashed." At that precise moment the seat-belt light came on and the pilot's voice came over the intercom saying, "Buckle up, we're in for turbulent weather." My immediate response was, "Wait a minute, God, I've changed my mind!"

The opposite of this passive death wish is a more active death wish. It becomes quickly more serious if you become preoccupied with dying or if you start thinking about when and how you might kill yourself. You may start giving away your belongings and finding ways to say good-bye to your family and friends. You may be writing notes to people who are important to you, in effect telling them good-bye. You may even be writing about death or composing poetry about joining your loved one in the hereafter. Or you may have a history of contemplating suicide when other difficult events occurred. This can be very frightening and very serious. If anything like this is happening, I urge you to find someone whom you trust to talk to, and I urge you to tell that person honestly what you have been thinking about. Suicide hotlines are available at all hours of the day, and mental health centers have emergency programs set up to help you. Suicidal feelings are often of short duration, and tomorrow can be a brighter day. If you are harboring such thoughts, reach out and call someone now. Help, understanding, and caring are there for the asking.

4.7 Fears

When a loved one has died, your life will be altered, perhaps even shattered. Normal routines are no longer normal, and new routines have to be developed. Roles within your family may have to be redefined. You may be on shaky ground, feeling very unsure of yourself and unsure of your future. It is during this period that you may become fearful of things you used to be comfortable with. You may jump at loud noises; you may be afraid to go out alone, fearful of new situations, afraid that someone else will die, afraid of driving down busy highways, afraid of the dark, or perhaps afraid of the particular room in your home in which your loved one died.

How to Help Yourself

Help here can be simple. Try to identify each individual fear and take them on one at a time; dealing with all of them at once would be overwhelming. As you get to the particulars, you will have a clearer idea of what you must do to overcome each of them. For example, one woman who was afraid of being in her bedroom alone at night experimented with several things. She tried leaving a night light on with music playing so that when she awakened she would not feel so alone. She also experimented with locking her bedroom door. She installed a telephone with speed-dial buttons on which she could program the telephone numbers of friends and neighbors; if she were to become frightened, she could press a button and summon help. Some people elect to have alarm systems installed in their homes to deal with such fears. Getting a dog might give you the same sense of security. At very little cost, I have a control next to my bed that can turn on lights throughout the house with the push of one button. I never need to walk out into a darkened hallway.

Sometimes your fear may be more serious than this. I know a mother whose daughter killed herself in her bedroom. This mother had great difficulty being alone in her house. She would always call before she returned home to make sure that another member of the family would be there. There were times when she would have to wait an hour or two at a mall before she could return home. Finally, after several months, she was able to overcome this fear and reclaim her house as her home.

The first thing she did was to drive into her driveway and sit there for a few minutes, then leave. When she was comfortable with that, she began driving up, getting out of the car, walking around the yard for a minute or two, and then leaving. The next step was to actually open up the front door and go inside. When she was comfortable with that, she would go inside and do a quick errand, such as starting a load of clothes in the washer. She continued in this manner until, taking one step at a time, she could go home whenever she wanted and feel reasonably comfortable being there.

When to Be Concerned

You should be concerned if you feel that your fears are interfering with your recovery. Perhaps you are afraid now of leaving your house because you fear "something" will happen. This fear could get so out of hand that you would be totally isolated from family and friends, agoraphobic, unable even to get food and other supplies that you need just to live.

Whenever you feel overwhelmed by a fear of this kind and it is controlling your life, or whenever you have tried some of the suggestions above and they aren't helping, I urge you to seek out professional help.

• • •

4.8 Panic

With the death of your loved one, the rug has been pulled out from under your feet. You are probably finding out that you don't really have as much control of your life as you thought you had. With major changes going on around you, you may feel the panic of grief.

The feeling of panic is very close to the feeling of fear. It is a time of high anxiety as you worry about all these changes, perhaps getting legal things done, having enough money to live on, wondering whether you can "make it" on your own, worrying about your own health. With your mind racing, it is hard to focus on one thought or task. You may not be able to remember parts of the funeral service or even how your loved one looked or sounded. You may be forgetful and disorganized and have feelings of losing your mind.

Once again, this can be a normal part of your grief, and there are things you can do to help yourself through this phase.

How to Help Yourself

As one who has experienced such feelings, I can assure you that you are *not* losing your mind; you are grieving. You will return to your normal level of functioning. Give yourself permission to operate at 50 percent for a while. Grief takes time; have patience with yourself. Many books have been written by people who have had similar experiences, and reading their accounts may help you to understand that your reactions are normal. (See the Bibliography.)

If your mind is racing or if you are running from task to task, *slow down*. I remember a man I used to talk to on the telephone who was mourning the death of his wife. He was in such a state of panic that he could not give me a complete thought. He was talking in phrases, jumping from idea to idea. I helped him regain control by telling him that I wanted to hear what he had to say but that I could not keep up with his thinking. In order for us to communicate, I said, we will have to set up this procedure: you can say one thing, and then you must stop and I will say one thing. This slowed him down enough so he could collect his thoughts and we could then communicate.

There may be times when you will feel panic by just knowing that there is so much to do after your loved one's death. Keep this in mind: Not everything must be done today. Make a list of what jobs you have facing you. Prioritize the list, putting a number 1 by the task that needs to be done first. Then put a 2 by the next task, and so on.

Mourning is not a time to be making big decisions about your life. You are not able to think clearly. Whatever decisions you can put off, do so. This is not the time to sell your house or to change jobs. Give yourself time just to get used to this new and different life. However, if there are decisions that demand immediate attention, I would suggest you get help with these from a trusted friend or legal counsel.

Then, too, you may be in a state of panic because you think you are forgetting your loved one. If you find you can't remember how your loved one looked, believe me you will never forget that person who was so dear to you. Just get out some photographs to reestablish his or her face in your mind. There are times when thinking about the deceased can be so painful that our minds blot out sights and sounds. If you are lucky enough to have a videotape or a recording of your loved one's voice (perhaps on an answering machine tape), play it, and the sound of your loved one's voice will come back to you. If you have blank spots concerning the funeral and those events that occurred at the time of death, ask another family member or friend to fill in the blank spots. Find out if anyone took pictures or even a video of the funeral that could help you now. I have found that many of these "blank spots" will fill themselves in naturally over just a few months.

• • •

103

4.9 Physical Illness and Symptoms

The death of a loved one is a highly stressful event. If you have ever taken a stress test, you may have noticed that the death of a spouse rates 100 points. The reason for this is that a spouse death will change your life totally, altering your daily schedule, your responsibilities, your social life, your finances, and many other aspects of your life. However, deaths of other family members also rank very high on the scale. And we do know what stress can do to your physical well-being. It can trigger ulcers, colitis, hiatal hernia attacks, rheumatoid arthritis, and asthma, as well as other psychosomatic illnesses. Stress also weakens our immune systems. You may have a lingering cold that you just can't shake or recurring flu. Other common complaints I hear of include nausea, dizziness, fatigue, and tightness in the throat. I also hear complaints of breaking out in rashes, weight gain or loss, back pain, and insomnia. Some people tell me that they have certain knowledge that they will catch the same illness or have the same fatal accident as the deceased. I do know it is common to take on the symptoms of whatever disease your loved one may have had. I know of a number of people who experienced chest pains after the heart attack death of a loved one. I, myself, had a CAT scan to make sure I didn't have a brain tumor as my first husband did, since I was experiencing some of the same symptoms. I believe we can get so preoccupied with what happened to our loved ones that we will internalize those symptoms and experience them ourselves. I liken it to fathers who have told me that they experienced childbirth pain.

Lastly, you may be sighing a lot. It's not a very serious symptom, but it's another physical reaction to your grief.

How to Help Yourself

I always think it is a good idea to let your doctor know what has happened in your life so he or she can monitor your blood pressure, weight changes, and other indicators of your physical well-being. Once things have settled down a bit, you might even want to get a complete physical.

I can't say enough for eating balanced meals and getting good rest and exercise to help you with your grief. If you find it difficult to eat, that the food sticks in your throat, try eating five small meals a day instead of three big ones. If the joy of cooking is no longer there, a microwave can be a great help; you can heat up things in a hurry and bake a potato in six or seven minutes. (See section 4.1 on how grief differs from other life experiences and 9.1 on helping yourself through grief.)

When to Be Concerned

You should be concerned anytime your grief is showing up in physical symptoms that are painful or uncomfortable to you. Don't wait too long before you see a doctor.

Chapter 5

CONTINUING REMINDERS OF YOUR LOSS

How to Prepare Yourself for Those

Occasions When Painful Memories

Come Rushing Back

There will be predictable milestones in your life when you can expect your grief to well up and to be painful, and then there will be times when you will bump into an unexpected reminder and be caught off guard, left to deal with your grief the best you

can. If this is already happening to you, I want to reassure you
that these rushes of emotion are normal and not to be viewed as
setbacks.

Holidays, normally occasions for happy family gatherings,
may turn into painful reminders of your loss in the first year or
so after the death of your loved one. Let's look at some of the
predictable times for a "grief attack" and at some of the things
you might do to help yourself.

5.1 Public Holidays

Public holidays are impossible to ignore in the hope that they
will go away. Some of them are so commercialized that there is
no escaping them; they are everywhere that you turn—in the
store windows, in the newspapers, on the greeting card shelf,
on TV and radio and in the greetings from your friends. You
may hope that you can just slip through these holidays and that
they will silently pass; it won't work. It is much better to meet
them head on and make plans for them.

Christmas

This is the biggest holiday of the year and certainly the one
that is most advertised, as this is when stores make their biggest
sales for the year. No matter what your religion may be,
Christmas is all around you, coming at you from all sides. It is
the holiday that requires the most preparation for most people.
If it was an occasion for gift giving or special events in your
family, it will certainly remind you of your loss. Here are some
things for you to consider that may help make this holiday
more bearable.

- First of all, think about how much of this holiday you
  can handle. Writing out greeting cards, for example,
  may be too much. In that case, pass them up this year

or at least trim your list down. If decorations are more than you can handle, put up what you can or ask for help from family members.

- There may be times when, shopping in a store, you catch yourself off guard spotting a "perfect gift" for your loved one and then realizing you will never buy a gift for that person again. If going into the stores is unbearable, order from a catalog or give gifts of cash.

- Once you have thought the holiday through, have a conference with your family and find out how the others feel about it and let them know what you are thinking. You should do the same with your extended family and friends so they can adjust their plans accordingly. You may have to compromise a bit to reach a plan that everyone can accept. Young children, of course, have great expectations at Christmas, and they need to know that life continues, even after the death of a loved one. I know of one family in which a child had died and the grieving parents had made a deliberate decision to spend Christmas in bed. After discussing this with their surviving children, they modified their plan so they could open presents with the children on Christmas morning, then have a favorite aunt come over to be with the children when the parents went to bed for the rest of the day. Since everyone knew the plan in advance, this worked for them. The following year, this family returned to their old traditions.

- You may decide to set up a photograph of your deceased loved one with some greens or bright-colored balls around it. It will be as if your loved one was sharing this holiday with you. However, since this can be painful to others in your family who do not find it as comforting as you do, check this idea out on the others. You may have to find a place for remembrance in a less obvious spot in your home.

- Some people elect to do something very different on the first Christmas without their loved one—something so different that the absence of the loved one won't be so obvious. I know of one family that went to a tropical island over the Christmas holidays, and it worked out quite nicely. A widow I know took her children on a trip to her parents' farm to experience a Christmas like the ones she had as a child. However, I find that after that first difficult Christmas, people usually return to their old rituals and traditions.
- You may decide to work on Christmas if you have this option, giving a coworker a chance to spend the holiday with his or her family.
- Oftentimes the anticipation of a holiday is worse than the actual event. But here is an idea to consider if you have children and you want to overcome some of the anxiety associated with this event. Have a basket set in a special place and have it filled with small, inexpensive gifts such as you might find at a grocery store, drug store or such places. They could be combs, bags of candy, costume jewelry, perfume, or miniature toys. Then each day starting December 1 open one gift, providing you and the children with something to look forward to instead of dread as this holiday approaches.
- Look for a lecture that may be held somewhere in your community on how to get through the holidays. Newspapers often have listings of this sort, or you can call a local community mental health center, church, or hospital for information.
- The religious services of Christmas and other holidays can be reassuring, or they can be upsetting. You will want to think about their effect on you and then decide how much or how little you make of them during your period of grief.

•   •   •

Other Religious Holidays

I listed Christmas separately because of the commercial value placed on that holiday. However, depending on your religious orientation, there are many other holidays that you may find difficult—holidays that are a part of your culture and that have special meaning for you. Among them are Easter, Passover, Rosh Hashanah, Yom Kippur, Hanukkah, and Ramadan. You know which ones are important to you and which ones may be most difficult when they are observed. Look back to the ideas listed for the Christmas holiday, and see if any of them can be of help to you.

Secular Holidays

Thanksgiving, Valentine's Day, Halloween, Mother's Day and Father's Day, the Fourth of July, Memorial Day, Labor Day, Columbus Day—these are all traditional American holidays that may have special meaning to you. If you feel that one or more of them may be difficult for you, make plans for them. It is always better to be prepared than to have some wrenching memory sneak up on you. All of them are somewhat commercialized, and they won't pass without your notice.

One thing you can do is start some new tradition that is so different from old celebrations that it has no painful memories for you. For example, a recently widowed nurse worked out a plan with her children that made Thanksgiving an entirely new event in their lives. She posted a sign at the hospital where she worked that said: "We have a turkey. If you're alone and would like to join us, bring a favorite dish and we'll see you at four P.M." She often worked on that day, and this gave her older children something to do that they enjoyed: putting the turkey on and preparing the house for guests. As many as twenty to twenty-five people showed up for dinner. Some brought guitars, and this led to singing and story telling. A new family tradition was founded.

Halloween is usually the easiest holiday to deal with, but it, too, may have special meaning to you. If this is the case, plan ahead for it.

Valentine's Day can be difficult because it is a day that may be filled with sentimental memories. Cards, flowers, candy, and small gifts are often exchanged. During your grief it may be hard to buy a card for family and friends when a loved one is missing from your list. You might consider making some home-made cards or candy instead, saving yourself from having to walk into the card store and face all of those rows of sentimental cards.

Mother's Day and Father's Day can be painful if the person who died was your parent. You might consider honoring a special aunt or uncle to fill the gap of your deceased mother or father—an honor that would be greatly cherished by the recipient. Here too, you might do something different, such as cooking a special meal for that aunt or uncle instead of going to a restaurant where you might see mothers wearing corsages or fathers being honored.

5.2 Special Family Occasions

These are occasions when families get together to celebrate happy times, such as christenings, graduations, bar mitzvahs and bat mitzvahs, weddings, reunions, and sad times, such as funerals and wakes. Once again the rule of thumb is to think this event through and decide what you can handle. If it is too soon and will be too painful, send your regrets, explaining why you can't come. People will understand, but it is better to have been invited than to be left out.

I know of a widow who was invited to a wedding which she knew could prove to be painful. She accepted the invitation but informed the couple that she would be sitting in the back of the church and would leave if she found it necessary. Accompanied by a close friend, she was able to slip out quietly when she found the memories evoked by the ceremony were too much to endure.

If you are invited to a wedding, you may fear that your tears could take away from the happiness of the occasion. Such an escape plan can take away that fear, but be sure to have a friend accompany you to provide you support.

Weddings can be hard, too, if your child has died and now a niece, nephew, or friend is getting married. Your pain will stem from the realization that your child will never have such a ceremony. This same stab of pain can come when attending the christening of a baby or a high school or college graduation.

At gatherings of this kind, friends and relatives may not know what they can say in your presence about your recent loss. If you walk into a group of people and the conversation suddenly comes to a halt, it may be because they were talking about you or your loved one. You may have to take the lead and advise them what you are comfortable with. Give them some guidelines. Say, "It's okay to talk about [the deceased]." Or, if you're not up to that, say, "Today, I just want to be with you and enjoy your company and hear about what's happening in your lives."

Funerals may be especially hard, as they will remind you of the funeral of your loved one. If the death you have experienced is recent, you may want to skip funerals for a while, sending flowers or notes instead. When a favorite uncle of mine died and I could not attend the funeral, I sent a bouquet of flowers that were all golden and yellow—palomino colors in memory of his horse, which was a golden palomino, and a reminder of the days we rode together.

5.3 Anniversaries

I want to discuss four kinds of anniversaries: birthdays, wedding anniversaries, special anniversaries known only to you and your loved one, and the first-year anniversary of the death.

Birthdays

Birthdays never change. Even though your loved one has died, his or her birthday remains the same. You may want to ignore it, or you may want to take your family out to dinner to celebrate it, even though your loved one is gone. I know of people who, on the birthday of a deceased loved one, buy helium-filled balloons, write messages on them, take them to the cemetery, and release them to the heavens. (Because balloons present ecological problems, one would be better than many.) How about buying a present for yourself on this important birthday? I think it is all right to acknowledge this special day unless it interferes with your recovery. On the other hand, if you are making too much of it and family members are objecting, you may want to check with a professional grief counselor to see if there are underlying problems with which you or your family need help.

The other birthday that may now be difficult is your own birthday. This may have been a special occasion with your loved one, and that attention will be sorely missed. A young, unmarried adult whose father died found his own birthdays especially sad after the death because his birthday had been the one time during the year that he could count on having some time alone with his dad. Each year his father, with whom he was extremely close, would come to see him on his birthday. Depending on the memories you have of past birthdays, your birthday might also be an occasion to prepare for. You might make special plans to do something with friends; don't expect them to remember. Or perhaps you may decide to spend the day alone. Whatever it is, make a conscious decision to do it.

Wedding Anniversaries

Wedding anniversaries are particularly difficult when a spouse has died. If the loved one you lost was your husband or wife, this anniversary will be an annual reminder of what you once had. It never changes. What has changed is that you are no longer a couple.

Let your family and friends know how you may want to observe this day, particularly the first year; it probably won't work if you simply try to ignore it. I loved it when my children were living at home and they would buy a flower for me on that day. It was very special to me. Later, after leaving home, they would call me on that date. They might not say much about the anniversary itself, but we would both know why they were calling.

On this special day you may want to write a note and take it to the cemetery to leave on your spouse's grave, or you may want to plan a special religious service in memory of your spouse. You may want attention, or you may want to be alone. You may want to make plans for a short trip, or you may find comfort in staying at home. Maybe you would like to go to work and do no more than quietly know that it is your anniversary. In any case, it's best to plan all this in advance. If you don't, it could turn out to be needlessly painful for you.

Special Anniversaries

A special anniversary known only to you and your loved one might be the day you met or the day you became engaged or the evening you conceived your first child. These are important occasions that are embedded in your memory, and you are going to be very aware of them when these anniversaries occur. You may want to plan something special for such occasions or even share them with a close friend.

The First-Year Anniversary of the Death

This could be a difficult day for you. As the first anniversary of your loved one's death approaches, you may feel that an internal time clock is counting down the days. Your emotions may be welling up without your realizing what is going on. You may be thinking, "One year ago today she was still alive, and we went out to dinner." Or "It was one year ago today that we got the diagnosis." You may once again be preoccupied with your loved one, thinking about him or her as this day approaches and throughout the day itself, dreaming about your loved one at night. This is normal and once again, it is best to prepare for this anniversary.

You can help yourself by letting family and friends know this day is coming up. Don't expect them to remember the exact day; you could be bitterly disappointed. And make plans for what you want to do that day. What will make you feel better? If you have close family members who might also be affected by this anniversary, it would be a good idea to consult with them and make plans together.

Often the anticipation of this anniversary is worse than the actual day. Once it has passed you will have completed a whole year of first-time anniversaries, and the next year these occasions will probably be less painful and more enjoyable for you. At the same time, I would not want you to expect instant relief. I think you will find the pain subsiding, but it will be gradual and not immediate.

5.4 Dreams, Nightmares, and "Visions"

Dreaming about your loved one can be startling at times. You may be trying hard to realize he or she is really dead, and wham, you dream about your loved one, alive and well, the two of you having a good time. Dreaming about the deceased is normal, sometimes pleasant and sometimes unpleasant. You may not have such dreams, though you may want to. I am a big dreamer and dream almost every night, but it was years before I ever had a dream about my first husband after his death.

Many of the dreams people tell me about are pleasant. Parents often dream of their children at a younger age: a safer time in their lives. Some dream of a loved one appearing to them to let them know that he or she is all right and in a better place. But sometimes dreams are anything but pleasant. Especially after a violent death, the dreamer may be trying vainly to get somewhere or do something to save the loved one. These dreams are very unsettling, making it hard to get back to sleep.

Some of these disturbing dreams will recur each night. If you are experiencing such a recurring dream, you may be able to get some relief by figuring out a realistic and acceptable ending for it. I remember a young rescue worker who lived in fear of coming upon an accident and finding someone he knew had died. And it happened! Responding to an accident call one day, he ran to a body on the ground, only to find to his horror that it was his wife. This event then became part of his dream life as he relived that episode. As he and I talked, we began to try to find a realistic, more acceptable ending for his dream. It would have been nice if we could have fantasized that his wife was only injured, but that would not have been realistic. So instead, this young man decided that an acceptable ending to his nightmare would be that a colleague would find his wife dead. Thereafter, when he went to bed at night, this young man would focus his attention on the ending he had provided for his dream, and he did, indeed, get relief from the nightmare. If you are having such a recurring dream, a therapist might be able to help you find a suitable ending for it.

In addition to dreams and nightmares, it is not uncommon for grieving people to have visions, imagining that they are in the presence of departed loved ones. These experiences could be the product of our subconscious minds, making what we so fervently wish for seem to be happening. Occasionally, some of these experiences have a funny twist. A widow told me that one evening she was sitting on the edge of the bed when a wispy figure wafted into the room. She said she was not sleeping, and she knew that this was her husband. She said the figure headed for the dresser, turned and said to her, "Oh, I'm sorry, honey, I didn't mean to disturb you. I came back for some change." Who said you can't take it with you?

If during the period of your intense grief, you imagine that you have had a visit from the spirit of your loved one, perhaps hearing his or her voice, don't be alarmed. You are not losing your mind. However, I would be concerned if these "visions" don't begin to fade or disappear in a month or so. If they persist, it's time to get some help.

5.5 Visiting the Cemetery

I am frequently asked: Should I visit the cemetery? How often? I suggest that you visit the grave at least once to see if this helps you with your grief. That is the reason for going; your loved one will not know if you go or don't go. If you find that it feels good to sit at the gravesite and you go daily for a while, I think that's fine. I was called by some concerned friends who were worried about the daily visits their friend made to the grave of his wife. I was less concerned when I learned that the cemetery was a block away from his home, that his visits were short, and that this was not interfering with his work because he was retired. His visits gradually decreased as the months went by and the weather became cold.

In deciding what you want to do about cemetery visits, your recovery is what is important. Setting up a ritual out of some sense of duty to your loved one is not appropriate. If you have to drive sixty miles, causing you to miss work, and the weather is bad, you might want to rethink the whole thing. Because you do not go every day or even once a month does not mean that you have forgotten your loved one. You will never forget that person. (See section 3.4 on visiting the grave and on the frequency of visits.)

It can be pleasant to visit the grave and have some quiet moments just reflecting on the life of your loved one, but this is not always easily arranged. The cemetery may be many miles from where you live, even in another state, and it may be either extremely inconvenient or impossible to get there often. If you found this helpful in dealing with your grief, you might create a spot nearby that could be a symbolic gravesite. This could be a corner in your garden where you might plant a tree or flowers. You could place a rock there with your loved one's name on it, or you could write a letter to your loved one and bury it there. This special place might then bring you some comfort and give you a special place for you to imagine being in the presence of your loved one or to meditate or pray.

When to Be Concerned

If you get caught up in a routine of cemetery visits that is not helping you recover, such as one that has become ritualistic, you may want to seek out the assistance of your pastor, rabbi, or therapist to find a better way to deal with your grief.

5.6 Revisiting Favorite Places

You may be afraid to return to places you used to frequent with your loved one because you are afraid of the emotions they may evoke. This could be a playground, a favorite restaurant, a grocery store, the beach, a certain resort, an amusement park, or even your church. At the same time, you may feel sad because you miss going to these places. I would be lying if I said that it won't be painful to revisit these scenes of past joys. It could very well be. But I can say that the second time you go there will probably be better, and the third time could actually be enjoyable.

In order to return to one of these places, prepare yourself first. You might arrange for a good friend or relative to go with you. Or, if you decide to go alone, make it a short visit, or arrange to have someone nearby that you can turn to for reassurance if needed. Such was the case of a young widower who wanted to return to the beach by himself. The beach had special meaning for him and his wife; it was where they became engaged. He wanted to return so he could walk along the ocean and just get in touch with what had happened to him. As we were talking one day, I mentioned that my husband and I would be at the beach the same weekend that he was planning to go there. We would even be near each other. We arranged that, since I was at the beach, he could contact me if he needed someone, and this plan made his family and friends feel more at ease.

5.7 Unexpected Reminders

There will be times when you turn a corner and suddenly you are confronted by a reminder of your deceased loved one. Emotions will flood over you, you may feel weak in the knees, and tears may flow without control. Songs on the radio are the biggest offenders here. You have no way of knowing what piece of music will come on as you flip across the dial. I remember a man whose oldest son had died. The son was adept at the guitar, and he and his brother had a certain duet they sang together. After the son's death, the second son taught the song to a friend, and, wanting to please his father, had his friend join him in a rendition of that beautiful duet. This was a very loving gesture, and the father experienced that love as well as the unexpected pain that accompanied this vivid reminder of the singing of his dead son. He told me years later how much he loved it but also how painful it was to hear.

You may get a phone call from a friend who hasn't heard of the death and proceeds to ask for your loved one, reminding you afresh that, but for the death, he or she would be alive today. You then have to relive the shock by hearing the caller's response when you relay the terrible news.

Mail addressed to the deceased often arrives long after the

death. I know of a widower who, following his wife's death, received a notice of approval from an adoption agency that the couple could adopt the child they had been wanting. There may be a time, months after the death, when you are looking for something in your desk and run across the handwriting of your loved one on a note to you. You may find a valentine addressed to you just waiting to be mailed. Or a gift hidden in the back of a closet awaiting your next birthday. All of these can be jolting and are to be expected; they happen to almost everyone in your situation. When they happen, sit down for a while, take a deep breath, shed some tears, and acknowledge your grief. It's all part of mourning.

Chapter 6

DIFFERENCES THAT MATTER

The Variables That Will Govern

Your Grief

There was never another person *exactly* like you in the history of the world, and it is unlikely that any other two people had *exactly* the relationship you shared with the deceased. Recognizing these truths, you may be able to understand why it is that your grief is, in important respects, unique. Neither the intensity nor duration of your grief can be predicted with precision. Of course, the same variables apply to everyone else who is mourning the same death; you are *all* unique.

There are two variables that will play a big part in determining how intense your grief is and how long it will last. These are (1) the cause of death and (2) the relationship you had with the deceased.

Since you turned to this book for help, I doubt that you are feeling insufficient grief over someone's death; on the contrary, you are probably feeling intense pain. However, it may help you to understand the intensity or length of your grief by examining the broad range of situations in which grief can arise. (See section 1.3 on the length of grief.)

6.1 Old Age

To get a grasp of these variables, let's suppose that the death that has occurred is that of a grandparent and that you are wondering why you aren't feeling more grief over this loss. You may not feel the emotional impact that you see in your parents or in the friends of your grandparent. You may wonder why this is so and question whether you really loved this grandparent.

The point here is that grief varies with relationships and causes of death. If a grandparent dies, your emotional response may be affected by the fact that this grandparent is a generation removed, that this is an old person who has lived a long and presumably satisfying life, and that now it is time for him or her to die. This is what life is all about; you are born, grow up, live your life, grow old, and then die. Your grandparent will have fulfilled what you understand is the natural cycle of life. (See section 1.3 on the age of the deceased.)

Then too you may have had little direct contact with your grandparent over the years. Perhaps you lived far away from each other. In such circumstances you should not expect to be greatly affected by that person's death. Any sadness you feel may stem from not having had the opportunity to know him or her better.

However, the death of a grandparent is not always this simple. If you are in intense grief over the death of a grandparent, it is probably because he or she played a large role in your life. This may be the grandparent who helped care for you when you were young, who lived nearby, and who engendered your deepest love. In such a case, your loss can be extremely painful, and generational spread will have little meaning. For help in addressing the pain and emptiness you may be feeling, I suggest that you read or review sections 4.2 through 4.9 on the emotional responses to grief.

6.2 Long-Term Illness

In the case of a loved one who has died after a long and gruelling illness you may actually feel relieved that the ordeal is over, and you may be thinking about how you can get on with your life. The intensity and duration of your grief will be different—generally less intense and shorter—than it would have been if death had come suddenly, without warning and without preparation.

If you are caught up in the terminal illness of a loved one, you may be trying to juggle your feelings. On the one hand you may hope for a cure or remission, and on the other hand you may be dealing with the reality in front of you: your loved one becoming weaker each day. You may be experiencing what is called anticipatory grief. (See section 2.3.) You may even have an opportunity to say good-bye. By the time death occurs you may have completed at least part of the grieving process and to have experienced life without your loved one's active contribution. You may have had an opportunity to take care of unfinished business, and to put some closure on your relationship with the deceased, acknowledging that this chapter of your life is over. (For more on visiting the dying see section 2.2.)

Still, the comparison is not all one-sided. In the case of sudden death you are actually freed of some difficulties that you may now be experiencing in a long-term illness, such as having to watch helplessly as your loved one suffers from pain and the humiliation of mental or physical decay. Another difficulty not encountered in a sudden death is the emotional and physical exhaustion you can feel when a loved one is terminally ill and dying, your home disrupted, medical equipment everywhere in evidence, your privacy invaded by visitors, your sleep interrupted by cries from your stricken loved one.

In spite of all of this, I often find families glad they had the opportunity to take care of a loved one during a terminal illness. People whose loved ones die suddenly often envy those who had time before a death to express their love and to say good-bye.

The illness itself also can make a difference. It is much more acceptable to have cancer these days than it is to have AIDS, yet cancer once inspired similar fears. Orville Kelly, the late founder of the cancer support group Make Today Count, wrote that after he was diagnosed with cancer in 1973, people were afraid of "catching" cancer from him. Once, at a party, he noticed that he was being served his drink in a paper cup while others were enjoying their drinks in glasses because they thought his disease was contagious. For a long time, cancer patients experienced job discrimination, and I still see some of that. It wasn't too many years ago that a frantic husband told me that he had eaten off his wife's hospital tray and was afraid he might "catch" her cancer. Another couple was afraid of making love for the same reason.

I know of a young man who was *relieved* that he had cancer and not AIDS. Public phobias have changed, haven't they? Even with all the education available, people still imagine that they can contract this dread disease in the same way they might pick up the common cold or the flu. Beyond this, AIDS also carries the stigma of social disapproval. I know of many families who were ashamed to tell friends or other relatives the true cause of a loved one's illness or death for fear of being ostracized. "Cancer" is often the cover story. Anger may play a role, too, if family members blame the victim for bringing it on himself or herself, or, even worse, for exposing others to the disease.

It is not uncommon for people with AIDS to withhold this information from their families, fearing their reactions and possible rejection. Often the secret is linked with another secret: a homosexual life-style that is both ill-understood and scorned by a society that is mainly heterosexual. I know of instances of parents finding within minutes that a child is not only gay but has AIDS. Big things to deal with for both parties.

Suggestions for Those Dealing with AIDS

If someone close to you has AIDS, the following suggestions may be helpful to you:

- You know your family and friends best, but the more you can share your grief with them, the more support you will receive. This sharing can be most helpful when done before the final days, enabling your family and friends to provide love and support to you throughout your ordeal. Keeping a secret of this magnitude can be very draining; you always wonder if somehow the news has gotten out. Also, when you do share this information, you may be pleasantly surprised by the support you receive from the person you would least expect to provide it.
- Supply your family and friends with the correct information on the AIDS virus. Use the occasion to dispel needless fears. Your doctor or public health department are sources of reliable facts on the subject.
- Think about how you will answer the question that is sure to be asked: "How did [he or she] catch it?" You may respond differently to different people. You can

tell what you know, or you can simply say, "That's no longer important; what's important is that we make the most of the time we have left with [him or her]."

- When death comes, I now believe it is safe to say that you will not have any trouble finding a funeral director, but there was a time when, lacking adequate scientific information, funeral directors were hesitant to handle the body of an AIDS victim. If you should encounter such resistance, your doctor or local hospital should be able to direct you to a funeral director who will attend to your loved one's body. (For more on AIDS, see section 7.4 on multiple deaths.)

6.3 Sudden Death

If someone you loved died suddenly and without warning, you know how devastating this can be. Sudden death of a loved one leaves the bereaved spinning. It provides no time to brace and prepare for the death. Within hours you may have to make funeral arrangements while, at the same time, you are wondering if all this is a bad dream. You have had no chance to say good-bye or to get answers to your questions, yet the world is descending upon you asking its own questions and demanding decisions, decisions, decisions. Under this barrage of fast-moving events you may have no other choice than to put your grief on hold as you deal with these matters. There it will remain, suspended in disbelief and numbness, until you can get to it at last. (See section 7.5 on sudden illness and death.)

Sudden deaths take many forms. By definition, they come without warning. They can result from a heart attack, stroke, aneurysm, automobile accident, fall, gunshot, plane crash, suicide, drowning, or countless other causes. They can be the result of armed conflict or terrorist attacks. They can be caused by natural processes or hostile acts. I find that the more sudden and violent the death, the longer you are likely to struggle with the shock of it and the anger that accompanies an untimely death. (See section 7.6 on violent death.)

If you are mourning the sudden death of a loved one, here are some ideas that others have found helpful in similar circumstances:

- Talk about what happened. Getting the details from the police or witnesses may actually ease your mind. At the very least, it will help convince you that your loved one did indeed die.
- Attend the funeral, and, if your custom or religious practice allows it, view the body, as this will help you later to acknowledge that the death really occurred. (See section 3.2 on making the funeral meaningful.)
- Reminisce about your loved one. Talk about your life together. Share your past joys as well as your present sorrow with those close to you. Don't keep your sorrow bottled up. Begin the process of mourning. (See Chapter 4 on mourning your loss.)

6.4 Suicide

It is terribly hard to understand why a loved one chooses to take his or her own life. As in any sudden death, disbelief is strong and may last for a long time, interfering with your mourning. In perhaps a majority of cases it will leave survivors with feelings of guilt; in fact, in some cases this may have been a not-so-secret intention of the suicide victim. (Suicide notes often spell this out.) And then, of course, one must deal with the stigma that still accompanies suicide. Social attitudes have become more tolerant, perhaps, but people are still quick to form judgments about these events, either blaming the victim for a selfish act or blaming the survivors for driving the victim to this untimely end. If this is the situation you face, there are now suicide survivor support groups you can join that will help you to get a more objective view of the causes of suicide and what may have been going on with your loved one. (See the Bibliography for helpful books on this complicated subject.)

Few events in life are harder to talk about than suicide. In a suicide survivors group that I formed some years ago, I still hear complaints from people about the unwillingness of family and friends to discuss the suicide of a loved one. "They always change the subject," I am told. Even worse, in my estimation, is the attitude of those few church officials who still refuse to officiate at services for suicide victims. The cruelty of this is beyond belief, needlessly adding to the survivors' sense of guilt and encouraging lies about the true cause of death.

Even though a disturbed person may have an ill-formed notion that certain relatives or friends should feel guilty for his or her death, I believe that a person who commits suicide actually has *no* idea of the pain that a self-imposed death will inflict on his or her survivors. More than once I have heard this kind of comment in my support group: "If I ever knew someone who was suicidal, I would like to bring her here to see what she was about to do to her loved ones."

If you are mourning a suicide death, you may deal with it for a very long time as you search for "the answer" to this terrible event, trying to make some sense out of the death while, at the same time, fearing that you somehow contributed to it.

Did you? I can tell you that you did *not* cause the suicide. It takes much more than one person or one event to cause a person to take his or her life. The life of a human being is much more complicated than that. Just as you can never enter the mind of another person, you can never know everything that contributed to someone's suicide.

However, one's reactions to a suicide can be just as irrational as the act of suicide itself. Feelings of guilt are pervasive after a suicide. I remember going to a school in which a student had shot himself. I was asked to talk to his teachers and expected to be meeting with a group of three or four people. Instead I walked into a large room with thirty or forty teachers and staff members in attendance. I brought up the subject of guilt and asked if anyone felt guilty about the student's death. They all did! One woman who worked in the cafeteria even felt guilty for the way she had frowned at the boy earlier in the day. What a relief it was to each of them to know that others shared their feelings of guilt.

If you are a suicide survivor, there may have been times when your loved one, perhaps suffering from depression or other emotional illness, threatened to kill himself or herself. The stress of such threats can weigh heavily on a person, and you may have thought, "Go ahead and do it; I can't stand the suspense any longer." You may even have said it! Or possibly, when the death did occur, you may have felt relieved, thinking, "At least I don't have to worry about that anymore." If these thoughts occurred to you or if you openly stated such things, you may be experiencing some guilt now for thinking or saying them. Let me assure you that you are not alone; thoughts and statements like these are common among those who have witnessed the degenerative process that often leads to suicide. (See section 4.5 on guilt and regrets.)

Along with guilt, you may be assigning blame to someone else for your loved one's death—a family member or friend who, you think, might have done more to prevent it. These thoughts could be a cover for your own guilt. Be careful with blame. Remember that no one can take responsibility for another's reactions to external events, nor can it be said that suicide is ever the only response to perceived adversity or the result of a single event.

In the days ahead there may be a period in which you find yourself enraged with the deceased, asking yourself, "How could you do this to me? Look at what's happening to this family. I'm sick and tired of dealing with this grief; it's interfering with my life. Why didn't you let us know you were feeling suicidal?" Are thoughts like these further occasion to feel guilty? Far from it. Suicide is a violent act that hurts far more people than the immediate victim. You have every reason to be angry, and this anger must be expressed if you are to begin to mourn your loss. Being angry doesn't mean you didn't love that person. (See section 4.4 on anger.)

For the person who discovered the body of a suicide victim there is an extra burden—a mental image that can't be erased. If you had such an experience and it is causing you unusual distress, I suggest you find a suicide survivors group or possibly seek out professional help to assist you with your grief. (See sections 7.6 on suicide and 7.8 on shock of discovery.)

Finally, there is the matter of religious beliefs concerning suicide. One mother once asked me, "Do I have to die the same way in order to ever see my son again?" Don't fall into that trap! If your grief has led to such thoughts, find a priest, minister, or rabbi to discuss it with. There can never be a sound religious reason to take one's own life.

The suicide death of a loved one, no matter what the occasion, is always difficult. Perhaps some of the following will help:

- Be as open and honest as you can about the cause of death.
- Find people you can talk to who will hear what you have to say and offer comfort and support.
- Read a book on the problems faced by suicide survivors to learn as much as you can about the grief felt by the bereaved.
- Make the funeral as meaningful as possible for yourself. Consider writing a letter to the deceased asking all those unanswered questions, expressing your frustration, and also proclaiming your love of the deceased.
- Find a support group or get help to start one of your own. (See the Resources in the back of this book.)
- Have patience with yourself, acknowledging that grief takes a long time to heal, but also allow yourself to have hope. No matter what, you can work through this and actually enjoy life again.

6.5 Murder

The grief felt when a loved one is murdered is probably the most overwhelming of all griefs. I don't want to make you feel worse by saying this, but I do want you to have patience with yourself. If someone you loved has been murdered, it will take a long time to work through it. However, the grief that survivors of murder experience is at long last being recognized, and help is on the way. (See the Bibliography and Resources.)

Hardly anything in life will prepare you for the shock of learning that a loved one has been murdered. Suddenly you will be feeling many different emotions more or less simultaneously. You will feel disbelief that another human being could do this to your loved one. You will experience horror as you try to imagine what your loved one must have experienced. Also, you are likely to feel white rage against the person, known or unknown, who committed this despicable act against your loved one, and indirectly, you, depriving you forever of the company of this person who meant so much to you. Depending on the circumstances, you may also experience fear for your own life, a fear that can paralyze you. Or you may feel helplessness, not knowing who was responsible or where to turn for help. And finally you may have a strong desire for revenge, a desire that, unless checked, can consume you.

If you have come to this book after suffering such a loss, you may be wondering how you can tell your family what has happened, especially if you have young children. (For help on talking to children about murder, see my earlier book, *The Grieving Child*, which is listed in the Bibliography.) In addition, you probably have other decisions to make for which you are ill prepared. These might include viewing or not viewing the body, becoming actively involved in the search for the killer, or attending or not attending the trial if there has been an arrest. You also may have to face the possibility that the murderer will never be caught.

When working with families and friends of people who have

been murdered I find that the operative verb is never *died* but *was killed*. I can understand why. *Killed* expresses the rage that people feel. Being killed is seen as different from dying; it's unnatural, a form of theft, an act of taking something from you and your loved ones. What is taken is a person's life and all of its promise for future joy and happiness, companionship, and accomplishment. It is the most precious commodity one can steal and the greatest loss one can suffer.

I find that deaths by murder lead to more isolation than most other deaths. If you have had a loved one murdered, you may find that your general support system is so overwhelmed that your friends and relatives don't know what to say or do to help you. Often the horror of the death is so great that it can't be talked about. In cases like this people tend to become immobilized, unable to act. Linked with all of this may be a strong awareness that, but for chance, they could be suffering your fate. Secretly they may be relieved that it happened to you and not them. Ashamed of thinking this way, they may find it difficult to face you. As a result they withdraw.

Also, your rage can be so powerful—perhaps misdirected at others—that it can be frightening to your family and friends, causing them to stay away from you.

Perhaps the murder of your loved one isn't the only horror you have to cope with. Sometimes the circumstances surrounding a murder are as hard to bear. I know of a mother who could tell me about the murder of her child but completely broke down and started to weep when she began to tell me that her daughter had been raped before she was killed. (See section 7.6 on deaths by murder.)

Many families put their grief away somewhere and use all of their energies on the search for or trial of the murderer. You may become a self-trained detective looking for clues to the perpetrator of this terrible deed. You may go to the site to look for clues or interview persons who may have helpful information. You may make frequent phone calls to the investigating officers to keep track of their progress. You may feel frustrated at times that this process moves so slowly. If there is an arrest, you may end up attending all of the court procedures. Only you can judge the wisdom of such involvement, but you should understand that it will tend to postpone what you ultimately must address, that is, facing up to your grief.

Once the legal work is over, you may feel overwhelmed with the emotions of grief. Put up on the shelf while you attended to pressing matters, these feelings now need to be expressed. However, you may be dismayed to discover that you are alone in your grief because, with the passage of time, friends and family assume that the crisis has passed and that you are getting on with your life now. They may have no idea that you are just beginning to mourn your loss and that you need them more than ever. A word to the wise: Don't sit back and feel hurt. Let your family and friends know what you need from them and how they can help you. (Reading Chapter 10 could be helpful to them.)

Here are some things to consider that may be helpful to you if you are dealing with a death by murder.

- Let as many people as possible know what has happened. Talking is therapeutic, and it helps in setting up a support system among your family and friends.
- If you have to make a trip to the police station, morgue, or courthouse, take other people with you.
- If you are asked to identify the body, help yourself by getting information on the condition of the body before you see it. It will be less of a shock. Sometimes even seeing a photograph can help prepare you. If it is too much for you to do, perhaps identifying the body can be done verbally, identifying some outstanding feature. Or perhaps another person, outside of the close unit of family and friends, could do this for you. This might be a pastor, rabbi, physician, neighbor, or coworker.
- If the funeral has to be put off for a day or two because of police/detective work, this could give you time to

make your final farewell as meaningful as possible. Perhaps you might want people in attendance to write good-bye notes that could be placed in the casket or cremated with the body. Perhaps you might want to invite people attending the funeral or memorial service to bring articles that were significant to their relationship with the deceased: photographs, letters, articles of clothing, memorabilia of any kind that can be shared during the service. Favorite songs, music, and poetry can add a meaningful touch, especially if there are friends or family members who can participate in presenting them. There is a purpose in considering such measures. It is to say to Fate that this was a real person whose life had value to the world and that, in spite of this horrible tragedy, you are going to celebrate that life. You are not going to allow that ugly event to characterize forever the memories you have of your loved one. Of course, planning this kind of service may be more than you can handle, and it surely is fine to elect for a more standard service, letting the funeral director and your priest, pastor, or rabbi plan it for you. (See sections 3.1, 3.2, and 3.6 for more help on funerals and memorial services.)

- If there has not been an arrest, you may want to assist the investigators in identifying and tracking down the murderer. This is appropriate and may help bring the villain to justice. But do it from the sidelines, giving the authorities whatever information you have and passing on suggestions that occur to you. Do not take the law into your own hands. Even if you think you know the culprit, the tragedy can only become greater if you attempt to invoke revenge by some violent act. Surely, your loved one would not want this. On the other hand, assisting the authorities can be useful to you in channeling your anger toward a constructive end. At the same time, don't be upset with others who do not want to be that involved. They are entitled to cope with their grief in ways that are most comfortable to them.

- If there has been an arrest, you may have to decide whether to attend the court proceedings. Of course, you could also be subpoenaed as a witness, giving you no choice in the matter. In any event, you may have a strong urge to be there, to look the murder suspect in the eye, and to see him or her pronounced guilty. The opposite could also be true: You might not want any part of the legal proceedings. You also have to be prepared for a disappointing or even infuriating outcome if a person you know to be guilty is able to escape with a light sentence or none at all. The National Organization for Victim Assistance (NOVA) can be a big help to you in dealing with all this. (See the Resources.)

- You may want to consider writing a Victim Impact Statement. In some states the families of murder victims are allowed to submit statements to the court on the adverse effects of the crime on their lives; these statements then may be read by the judge in open court before sentencing. Even if your statement is not read in court, putting these thoughts on paper can serve a useful purpose for you in giving expression to your grief.

- Be prepared for surprises during the court hearings. Under court rules the authorities cannot share with you all the information they have for risk of compromising their case against the accused. Some of these surprises can be brutal as evidence and testimony are presented. (See section 7.6 on murder.)

- I began this discussion by referring to the "white rage" that murder engenders. The description of anger you will find in a dictionary does not come close to what you may be feeling now if a loved one has been murdered. For example, I know of a woman whose son was killed by his girlfriend. To express her rage she nailed a picture of the murderer to a tree and then smashed it repeatedly with a hammer until it was completely destroyed. She felt better afterward. You may want to do something similar for temporary relief from your rage. (See section 4.4 on anger and rage.)

- As I mentioned earlier, if you are fortunate enough to see the killer brought to justice, what you can expect after the trial and sentencing is a return to the depth of your grief. With the distraction of the investigation, arrest, and trial over, you will have time to reflect more fully on what has happened. Don't be surprised if you feel a new rush of emotions that challenge your self-control. If this happens, it is not a setback; it is a resumption of the process of grief.

- Read as much as you can on the subject of grief, particularly murder-induced grief. The knowledge you gain from the experiences of others can help you to get on with your own life. (See the Bibliography and Chapter 4 on the emotional responses to grief.)

- Find out if there is a support group for murder survivors in your community. If you can't find one, perhaps your local community mental health center will have some ideas; possibly such a support group could be started. Your police department could tell you if there is a nearby chapter of the National Organization for Victim Assistance, or you could call the national office. (See the Resources at the back of this book.)

- Have patience with yourself and the loved ones around you. Grief differs so much from one person to another that it may be hard to understand why one person is crying all the time while another shows no emotion at all. Try to keep in mind that you are not the only person having to deal with this harsh reality and that, in some important way, each of you had a unique relationship with the murder victim. Whenever you become concerned about yourself or another survivor, never hesitate to seek help from a professional.

6.6 Extended Family

While you may be dealing with intense grief, it is important to know that grief can neither be turned on nor off. When death comes to a relative that you did not know very well, you may find that the death has little impact on your life. The tears you shed may be, not for the deceased, but for those close relatives or friends who were close to the deceased. You may feel their pain, and this, too, is grief, but of a different kind. You may decide to attend the funeral or you may decide to send a note or card instead. If you do attend the funeral, don't be surprised if you start thinking about loved ones who have died and how much you miss them. If you have an impending death in your family or if someone has recently died, the impact of this funeral may be greater than you expected. (See section 5.2 on special family occasions.)

6.7 Grandparent

As discussed in section 6.1, the grief you experience when a grandparent dies may not be as great as that of your grandparent's offspring, such as your father or mother, or of his or her contemporaries. You may be quite objective about it, recognizing that it is natural for a grandparent to die on reaching an advanced age. This will be especially true if your grandparent had endured long suffering and perhaps had been confined to bed for many months or years, perhaps in a nursing home. However, it is likely that there was something special about your relationship with your grandparent and that this is a loss you will have to cope with. If nothing else, your grandparent's death will serve as a reminder of other deaths to come.

A grandparent's death will make you aware that your parents are advancing in age and that their deaths may be the next ones you will experience. You may also become aware that with this death much of your family history will be gone. There will be no one left to answer certain questions about your ancestors. These are things to reflect on as you attend the funeral and say a final good-bye to this person who helped give you life.

6.8 Friend

Don't be surprised if you grieve more for a friend than you did for a recently deceased relative. The old saying, "You pick your friends, relatives are thrust upon you," holds true here. Friends are special people in our lives because we choose them to be. Friends fill time in our lives that will be vacant when they die. Besides, friends are usually close to us in age, and when they die we are reminded of our own mortality. Thus their deaths can have an acute impact on us. They give rise to the thought, "It could have been me."

The death of a friend presents its own problems. Friends seldom are involved in the funeral planning or are consulted on the disposition of keepsakes and mementos. The grief felt by a friend seldom draws the sympathy or concern given to close relatives. At the same time, family members may expect you to attend to various tasks because you were a friend of the deceased, not realizing how much you yourself are grieving the loss of your friend.

I find that many times at a funeral it is a friend who gives the eulogy. That isn't everything, but it's something—a chance to pay homage to your friend and to express the sorrow you feel. If you haven't been asked, you might volunteer to do this. It may fill a need for you and for the family as well.

There are other complications that present themselves when the relationship is that of a friend rather than relative. An older woman I will call Ellen had a devoted friend I will call Louise. They had been friends since childhood, keeping in touch through the years of marriage and child raising. They shared many interests and enjoyed each other's company through advancing years. Then Louise contracted cancer and moved to the seashore to make the most of her remaining time. For a while Ellen was able to make trips to the seashore to see her friend, but as Louise's condition became worse, younger family members began telling Ellen that her visits were unwelcome, that Louise was too ill to see her. When Louise died, Ellen found herself an outsider. Even though Louise was her closest friend, Ellen was left out of all planning for the memorial service. She attended the service as a spectator only. When she asked the relatives if she could have a certain bracelet she had given Louise, she was told it couldn't be found. She was left with nothing.

The point of this story is simply that the grief one feels as a friend is just as legitimate, and just as heavy to deal with, as the grief experienced by close relatives. It may be that you have come to this book with the same kind of grief. If so, know that your grief, bitterness, and anger require the same mourning process that you would be facing if you were a blood relative. And, like any relative, you can discharge that grief and find life worth living again. (See Chapter 4 on the grieving process.)

6.9 Pet

Yes indeed, when a beloved pet dies, the grief felt can be great. Pets can play a very important role in our lives. Just because they are there they become part of the memories we accumulate through the years. Let's say that you acquired a pet as a child and that fifteen years have passed. For fifteen years that little cat, dog, or other pet has been through a lot with you. It has been there in times of happiness and times of sorrow. It has shared in countless family events. How could its death not be a time of great sadness?

Pets have unconditional love that is offered to you freely. You can have had a horrible day, perhaps become impatient with your pet and perhaps push him or her away, yet your pet will still love you regardless of your mood. Pets make us feel needed as they look to us for all the basic necessities of life: to be fed, housed, cleaned, walked, and cared for in time of sickness. Pets are good company for us and frequently become our confidants. You may carry on a conversation with your pet and by the expression on his or her face, imagine that your pet understands. Pets seem to be responsive to our moods, sensing when we are angry, playful, or sad. They become members of the family.

As with human friends and loved ones, the relationship you have with your pet will influence the amount of grief you experience when he or she dies. If the pet is no longer a central part of your life, your grief may be less. On the other hand, if the pet was your sole companion and has occupied much of your time for many years, your grief can be immense. Don't let anyone tell you that "it was only a cat." You have every reason to mourn your loss.

Burial for your pet may be in the backyard under a tree, or you may contact a pet cemetery and carry out a regular funeral for him or her. You can make the burial meaningful by writing a note to your beloved pet, burying favorite toys with him or her, or even delivering a eulogy or reading some poetry at the burial. No matter what others may think, when your pet dies your grief is real and legitimate. The emotions felt will be powerful and painful. I know that it can be embarrassing to tell people that you are grieving for a pet. The fear is that you will be laughed at. However, pet grief is recognized now as real grief, and there are even support groups for people who have had a pet die. (See the Bibliography for a book on mourning the death of a pet.)

If the time comes that your pet is ailing and in pain, and you must face the necessity of asking the veterinarian to "put her to sleep," this is a hard bit of news to relay to your young children. I am happy to pass on these wise words of a teenage girl to her younger sister. "We are taking Whiskers to the animal hospital," she said, "so the doctor can help her die gently."

When your pet has died, you may find family and friends

ready to get you another animal to replace your dead pet. However, since you have experienced how much it hurts to have one die, you may not want another pet. At least, not right away. Or you may want to get another pet as soon as possible. I would suggest you not get the same species of pet because another pet that looks so much like your old pet will not have a chance in your heart. The new pet will never be able to measure up to the old one. Also, it is important that you do not name the new pet by the same name. That won't work either. I remember when my dog Jocky died, I decided to keep one of her pups, a black female that looked much like her mother, and I named her Jocky. It didn't work. Jocky Number 2 was never loved as her mother had been. Avoid "replacing" your pet. If you do get another, do so because you like the idea of having a pet. Know that your first pet can't be replaced but that you can learn to love this one with its own personality and its own unique ways.

6.10 Sibling

No matter how old or young you are, there are special issues you will have to deal with when a brother or sister dies. Your feeling of guilt may be strong if you and your sibling were still caught up in sibling rivalry; there may be a part of you that is not feeling all that bad that you no longer have to compete with this person. You may secretly feel that you now will have more of your parents' attention. Or you may secretly harbor a sense of relief that it was him or her and not you. These thoughts can create a strong feeling of guilt. However, I assure you that these thoughts are perfectly normal and that by themselves they can't cause someone to die. They zip through our heads and are gone; it's what we do with them that makes them right or wrong. (See section 4.5 on guilt.)

If your parents had only two children and the other one dies, you may suddenly realize that you are an "only child." Not only will you feel the loneliness of life as an only child, but if your parents are still living, you may start to wonder what it will be like to be totally responsible for them as they grow older. You may feel responsible now for your parents' grief and in your efforts to help them, your grief may have to go on hold.

Also when a sibling dies, you are likely to become acutely aware of your own mortality, sensing that you could have been the one to die. I think we pass into another phase of our process of life when a sibling dies; death suddenly becomes very real.

The grief felt when a twin dies is likely to be even more acute. The bond between twins is strong and usually continues to be strong as they go about their lives. If you are a surviving twin, you may feel that a part of you has died. You may even experience something called "survivor guilt." This is the feeling of guilt that stems from being alive when someone close to you has died, of feeling unworthy of continued life when this worthy person has died, of wishing you could change places with him or her. All of this is normal and to be expected; just don't act on it!

6.11 Parent

As an Adult

There are many losses to deal with when you have a parent die, even when you are an adult. Often adult children don't receive the consideration they deserve when a parent dies. Relatives and friends may think, "She's been away for so long, what's the big deal?" You may find you are expected to continue on as before with only a short, "I'm sorry your dad died." Little do others know the losses you may have to adjust to. Little has been written on adult child grief; the one book I have discovered appears in the Bibliography. These are some of the common losses associated with the death of a parent.

- The loss of your childhood. Who else cares that you teethed on a certain chair in your home except your mom and dad? Who else knows or cares that you walked at nine months and were speaking in sentences at an early age? Who else loved to look at your early attempts at drawing other than your mom and dad?
- The loss of unconditional love. Parents often provide a kind of love that is not duplicated elsewhere in our lives. If you have lost a parent, or possibly both of your parents, you know what a loss this is. As an adult I loved visiting my parents at our farm, where I was always treated as if I had never left. My favorite foods were prepared and I felt like a girl again. These wonderful experiences sadly end when parents die.
- The loss of a certain sense of security. There is something reassuring in being able to return to the place where one grew up. If not the very same house in the very same city, at least the home of your parents, wherever it is, with furniture, pictures, and mementos from your childhood. I still love to go to the farm where I was raised and tramp around in the pastures which I so loved as a child. If you have to sell the family home when your parents die, it is another loss you have to deal with— saying good-bye to many of your childhood memories.
- The loss of a friend as well as a parent. Oftentimes a parent is not only your mom or dad but your best friend and confidant. It may be that you kept in regular communication with one or both parents. When one of them dies, it can be a painful loss. I know of a young woman whose father, living in another state, would call her on certain mornings each week before she left for work. How she misses those phone calls since he died!
- The loss of financial support. There may have been times when you needed your parents for financial support. It can be frightening to realize that you are totally on your own.

- The realization that you are now the "older generation" can come as a shock. It quickly puts you in touch with your own mortality. Also, when both of your parents die, it may startle you to realize that you are now an orphan.
- Having to break up the household and dispose of all your parents' belongings. This is always a painful task. If possible, you should try to plan it out in advance with other family members. (See section 3.8 on disposing of personal belongings.)

As a Child

I address this subject thoroughly in my book *The Grieving Child* (see Bibliography), but I do want to touch on some points here that I think are important:

- Unless they are given the right information and allowed to mourn their loss, young children who lose a parent through death may experience a strong sense of abandonment and find it difficult to develop relationships as they grow older. An unconscious fear that loved ones will leave them keeps them from giving themselves totally to any relationship. They also have to deal with the thought that the deceased parent elected to leave and could have stayed if he or she had really wanted to.
- You may hear a child expressing a wish to join the deceased parent. Commonly this is not a suicide wish but simply a desire to see the parent again, based on the child's lack of understanding about the finality of death. However, it would be wise to consult with a professional to be sure.
- The world of young children has a certain magical quality about it that leads to feelings of great power. After the death of a parent, a child may imagine that he or she could have done something to prevent it and feel guilty for not having done so. Unless resolved, that guilt can

become a part of that person's adult personality.

- Children need basic, simple, honest information on all aspects of the death and burial rituals.
- If any of this sounds familiar to you, stemming from your own childhood, be sure to read Chapter 8. Childhood grief needs to be resolved, even if you have become an adult in the meantime.

6.12 Love Relationship

If you have lost a lover who was not your spouse, you may be experiencing some of the indifference or rejection that often occurs when a lover dies. You may hear, "After all, you weren't *married*." It's as if the only love that counts is the love that is sanctified by marriage. The death of a boyfriend or girlfriend can happen early in life or late; the pain is the same. For a teenager it could be his or her first introduction to the reality and finality of death. I have found that the death of an ex-boyfriend or ex-girlfriend can be difficult to deal with as well, often giving rise to feelings of guilt. A teenager whose former boyfriend took his own life was left feeling somehow responsible.

Because the grief you feel over the loss of a lover may not be known or accepted by that person's family and friends, your grief may be exacerbated by exclusion or indifference. This will make your task of mourning all the more difficult. If this is your situation, you may have to look at other ways to resolve your grief.

An unmarried woman I will call Elizabeth had fallen in love with a mature widower. Over several months they had an intense and intimate relationship, which both of them expected would culminate in marriage. However, before he could introduce Elizabeth to his grown children, the widower had a heart attack and died. Upon his death she found that two of his three children would have nothing to do with her, and the third extended friendship only so far as to give her a photograph of his father for her to keep. To the family of this man who had become such an important part of her life she was just an outsider. Much as she wanted to retain some tie to his memory and to learn more about him from his survivors, she could do nothing but keep her grief to herself. What she did then was to write her dead lover a letter expressing her love and her sorrow, and together with an understanding sister she performed a ceremonial burial of that letter at a private place of her choosing, a place with deep meaning for her. If you are caught up in a similar circumstance, this might be something for you to consider as well.

There are other possibilities, too. For example, a widowed group in Elizabeth's church invited her to join them, and this has proven very helpful to her. On occasion I have invited the adult whose "live-in" of several years had died to join a widowed seminar I was conducting. However, this will depend on the makeup of the group; there could be resentment from some other participants who are not ready to broaden the term *widow* that far. I now conduct a group for people who have had either a spouse or fiancé die, and I hope more groups like this will get started.

When your love relationship is a gay relationship, a number of issues may have to be dealt with. If your lover is recognized by both families, your support will be more evident. However, if your relationship was unknown or disapproved of by family members, be prepared for some difficult times. I remember a young man whom I will call Tom, whose lover of three years was killed in an auto accident. The family was very disapproving of the relationship and excluded Tom from all planning involving the funeral and burial. To make matters worse, Tom was given incorrect times and dates of the funeral and burial. When he appeared for the rituals, they had already taken place. If yours was a gay relationship, you may find the family of your lover feeling you do not have any rights, whether to property, keepsakes, or a say in funeral planning. I even know of cases where families have contested the right to proceeds from life insurance policies. If you should be in such an unenviable position, your best support may come from friends who knew and accepted your relationship. If you live in a community where there are many gay couples, perhaps you can find a support group to meet your needs. Or perhaps you can find a therapist who deals specifically with grief issues. (See section 7.15 on "unacceptable" relationships.)

6.13 Spouse

If you are grieving the death of a spouse, you are experiencing a grief that ranks at the top of the list in the hierarchy of stress. Little wonder, then, that you may be feeling at the end of your rope, depressed and without hope.

Two major things stand out in my mind when I think about the death of a husband or wife. One is that the longer you have been married, the harder it will be to pick up the pieces and rebuild a life for yourself. When my first husband died, I had been married for fifteen years and, at thirty-five, was in the prime of my life with four young children. I still had time to develop a career and new relationships for myself. It is easier to make major changes in your life if you have youth on your side; it's not so easy if you are older and have spent much of your life with one person.

Secondly, I find grief for the widower more difficult than it is for the widow. There are several reasons for this. In the United States there are over 12 million widowed people; over 10 million of these are women. Statistically, men die first. In many cases the husband is older and prepares to die first by buying life insurance, providing survivor benefits in his retirement plan, and otherwise arranging for his wife when he is gone.

Many women are more flexible and better able to readjust, in part because their lives typically require adjustment from time to time. As the prime caregiver to their children, she may have had to interrupt a career to be a mother and homemaker. Even if she continued with her career, she probably had to make many adjustments to combine career with motherhood. In many marriages, I still see the husband's job as the main source of income, and if he is transferred to another city, the wife will pack up and attempt to reestablish her career elsewhere. These adjustments, while difficult at the time, help prepare a wife for the adjustments imposed on them when her husband dies. For example, one woman told me that her husband, a military man, often would be gone for six months at a time. She said she hated those long absences but found that they helped her to deal with her husband's death.

Here are some of the special issues, unique to your relationship, that you have to address when your spouse dies:

- Confronting the concept of being "widowed." You are now a member of a "club" you never wanted to join. What is a "widow" anyway? You may have thought that a widow was an old woman who wore black clothes. However, this is not who you are nor what you want your life to be. It is a jolt the first time you have to write "widowed" or to check that box on a form that asks for your marital status. I can remember really resenting that word and becoming angry when asked that question.

- Because of your new, unsought status in life, of being widowed, of no longer being part of a couple, and because of all the adjustments that you have to make, you may no longer know who you are. I am an artist, and during the time that I was struggling with my identity, I was painting. Looking back, it's interesting to see that all the paintings I did during that time are simply signed "Helen." I didn't know fully who I was. I didn't feel comfortable with my husband's name nor with my maiden name. I was a different person, a person I had yet to meet. It takes awhile to establish a new identity to get in touch with yourself as a single person in the world of single people. And it takes awhile to give yourself permission to be the most important person in your life. It is you who needs to take care of you, and it is you who now has to depend on you. It is a time in your life for you to do some of those things you have always wanted to do but put off for some reason or another. It is time for you to travel, to take classes, to redecorate your house the way you want to. It is time for you. As for how you want to be addressed, as Jane Miller, or Mrs. Don Miller, or by your maiden name, the choice is yours. Whatever feels right for you is the choice you should make.

- I am often asked, "What about my rings?" What about them? There aren't any rules that I know of that tell you what to do and when to do it. Do whatever you are comfortable with. Some people have made a vow when they were married to never remove them and have been wearing them for many years. If this is the case, you will probably continue to wear them. I know of one widower who, immediately after the burial of his wife, went to his bedroom, removed his ring, and flung it across the room in a rage that he no longer had a wife. My loving, wise friends bought a ring for me to wear on the third finger of my left hand. When I removed my husband's rings, I had a replacement. Removing your wedding rings can be very difficult as you get in touch with the reality of the death. Because your finger feels naked and unnatural, having a replacement was helpful to me. I did find that my wedding bands went on and off several times before I could comfortably put them away. There were times when I went out as a single person that I would leave my wedding rings at home. However, if the plumber was coming over, the wedding rings went back on. I didn't want strange people who came into my home to know that I was single. Eventually, I had my diamond made into a pendant, and now I wear it as a piece of jewelry. If you are a widow, you might consider, perhaps on your next wedding anniversary, having your rings made into some piece of jewelry such as a dinner ring. As for my husband's wedding band, I gave it to my son as a memento of his father to wear someday, if he wishes.

- Loneliness and isolation are big hurdles for the widowed to overcome. You look around you, and you see a world that is "two by two." You see couples grocery shopping together, or holding hands in the park, or sharing special glances. Suddenly you are acutely aware that the world is made up of couples. You feel out of sync, like a fifth wheel on a grocery cart. You may feel terribly lonely and isolated. Your friends may not be inviting you to be part of their lives as they once did, perhaps because they are uncomfortable with your new single status or because it would make them have to deal with their grief again. The painful truth is that singles are sometimes seen as a threat to this coupled world. A neighbor told one widow friend of mine, "I've noticed it doesn't take John very long to get over to your house when you need something fixed!" The statement came as a shock to her. From then on she was much more careful in the way she asked for help. I have an idea that this sort of problem arises most commonly in those marriages where tensions or problems already exist. However, it is this isolation that can cause you to feel your loss even more as you struggle for a new identity, wanting to cling to the old and familiar but being reminded that it is no longer there for you.

The Loneliness of Widowhood

When a spouse dies, one of the greatest challenges you will face is loneliness. This is quite different from just being alone. "Alone time" is a special time, planned for and anticipated, that you choose to spend by yourself. Being lonely is something else.

It is having the minutes crawl by, every minute seemingly taking an hour. It is feeling restless, walking about, picking up a book but not reading it, dialing a friend but hanging up before the call is completed and missing your spouse terribly.

A loneliness attack can happen anytime. Perhaps it is when you notice another couple holding hands. Perhaps it is when you wake up in the morning and are reminded again that you are alone in that bed. Perhaps it is in the evening as you are about to end your day. Or possibly it is at your office when you hear colleagues making plans for the weekend.

To help yourself, try to zero in on the patterns in your life that give rise to these feelings of loneliness. Once you can identify them, you can alter those patterns to make those times less lonely. This won't cure your loneliness, but your lonely times will be more predictable and you can prepare for them. Here are some suggestions that may help:

- If mornings are the worst times, think about how you might change your morning routines. Waking up in the morning and starting a new day is hard enough as it is. As soon as you open your eyes, you realize, "Something's wrong," and then you remember. No wonder that you want to pull the covers over your head and block out reality or to convince yourself that it's all a bad dream.

  Changing your morning routine can be helpful. Try getting up at another time and doing those morning routines differently, setting the coffee pot the night before so it's ready and waiting, reading the newspaper in a different room, turning on the radio or television for the noise and distraction, rearranging your bedroom so that when you awake you will not be reminded so acutely that your spouse is gone. I found that waking up to a different wall was helpful. There are times when sleeping in another bedroom will help until you can become more adjusted to this life. Perhaps, too, you may have a close relative who can stay with you for a week or two.

- You might want to consider getting a pet. Having something alive in an empty house is comforting. Having something that greets you when you return at night, who welcomes you home with a wagging tail or a jump into your lap can be comforting. Having something that needs you is wonderful. A dog can help with those lonely mornings because it will impose a change on your routine as you take him or her for a walk. Carefully consider getting a pet. Dogs require more active care and do tie you down some, but having a dog in the house can make you feel much more secure. Consider the size of dog. Smaller ones require less exercise and eat less but may not offer the security you want. A large dog needs more walking or a fenced backyard, but the dog's bark will surely ward off unwanted visitors. Cats, on the other hand, are very easy pets to have. They need no walking and even clean themselves. They can be left in the house without your having to worry about them, even overnight. You can leave food for a cat, and it will only eat what it needs when it needs it. A dog, on the other hand, would not only need to be walked but would eat the entire amount of food you left at one sitting. Birds often make good pets and can be tamed enough to sit on your finger and allow you to stroke them. Birds, like other pets, are good listeners, cocking their heads as if they are understanding what you are saying. A pet is a good antidote to help with loneliness, but if you decide to get a pet, spend some time considering what kind of pet will fit best into your life-style.
- If coming home to an empty house is difficult, you can obtain a timer that will turn the lights or the radio on before you arrive so there will be light and noise to greet you as you open the door. You might even try coming in a different door—anything to break up the

old routine, which may have included kissing your spouse as you came in the kitchen door.

- Evenings are likely to be particularly lonely times for you. The end of the day is so often shared with one's spouse. Perhaps you were in the habit of having a glass of wine together, sharing your day's experiences, cooking a meal together, watching TV, reading in bed, making love, or cuddling before drifting off to sleep. These times will be sorely missed. Think about what is hardest for you and do something to change the missed routine.

- Going to bed is particularly hard. Ending the day with the person you love has always had special meaning. There is an intimacy shared here that is unlike any other. The memory of it can make your loneliness seem unbearable. Rearranging your bedroom can be helpful at these times as well as upon awakening. I also found that sleeping on my husband's side of the bed was helpful. I could better deal with my pillow being empty.

- Microwaves are wonderful inventions for the widowed. Not only are you likely to hate cooking for one, but perhaps you find that dishes that you once enjoyed have lost their taste. Since it is important that you eat as well as you can, you might turn to the microwave for quick, uncomplicated meals. A baked potato can be ready in just a few minutes, and frozen, prepared dinners are more nutritious than they once were. Just keep in mind that, as lonely as you are, it's important that you maintain a healthful diet. Many simple meals can be prepared quickly. Also, eating at a different time or in a different location may make dinner more bearable. If looking at your spouse's empty chair is hard, sit in it yourself. It's much easier to deal with your chair being empty. I found this idea to be helpful in the den where I used to watch TV with my husband. I would sit in his easy chair. It was easier than looking at it, and I imagined that it still had some of the aroma of his presence, making it feel good.

- Weekends can be hard. Once they were planned for and anticipated with pleasure; if your spouse has died, all that has changed. Conversations at work on Friday may still deal with plans for the weekend and on Monday how the weekend was spent, but all of this may be very painful to you. However, planning for weekends is still important to help you get through them. You might consider saving until the weekend all of your grocery shopping, trips to the post office, getting the car washed, picking up your cleaning, or going to the bank. With a little effort you can keep yourself occupied through the weekend and at the same time, gain a sense of accomplishment. You might include in your plans overnight visits to relatives or short trips to the beach or to a bed-and-breakfast. Some people do their volunteer work on weekends, filling slots that are usually hard to fill. It may be just the right thing for you. Other people get a part-time job to fill the weekend. If you are already working, it might be possible to move your weekend to Monday and Tuesday instead of Saturday and Sunday. This may help. I don't think it would be good for you to extend your present job to seven days a week, however, as that would be overdoing it.

- When the time comes for you to make important decisions such as those involving your children, living arrangements, or legal actions, you will be reminded that you are on your own. You will miss the advice and shared responsibility of a spouse. You now must make those decisions alone or find someone to advise you. There will be times when family members or friends can help, but there will be other times when their advice would not be helpful. Unacquainted with the nuances of a situation, they may be inclined to recommend actions that would be totally inappropriate. In cases like this don't hesitate to look for professional, unbiased advice. This might be an accountant to help with taxes, or a financial planner to help with investments, or a therapist to help with family problems.

- Holidays and family gatherings, once occasions for joy and happiness, are likely to remind you anew that you are alone. (See sections 5.1 through 5.3.)

- And then there is the still taboo subject of sexuality. So often it is assumed that your sexuality dies with your spouse. Particularly if you are older, it will be assumed by some that this part of your life is over. Of course, it isn't. How you may long for a caress, a kiss, or the touch of your spouse's hand. Now imagine how you would feel if you thought that all such acknowledgments of your sexuality would cease forever. How unbearably lonely you would feel. Take a moment to think about the word sexuality. So often people think sexuality means a preoccupation with sex. Indeed, that is one of the definitions of the word. But I like this dictionary definition: "the quality of possessing a sexual character or potency." In other words, it's being masculine or feminine. It's how you feel about yourself as a woman or as a man. A spouse normally plays a huge part in this, influencing how you think about yourself, what you wear, and even how you live your life. Comments like "You look terrific" or "Your hair looks great" play a big role in how you are likely to feel about yourself. When a spouse dies, your self-image can be one of the first casualties. When a spouse dies, it's not just what happens in bed that you miss. You miss the little things, too. The walks around the neighborhood holding hands, the shoulder to lean on, the arm around your waist, the tender kiss on your forehead, the fingers running through your hair, or the back rub while watching TV. And, of course, you do miss the lovemaking and the glow that follows. The closeness here is unmatched in any other part of one's relationship. The needing and being needed and the sharing are very much missed. I might add that sexuality knows no age and that, whether you are twenty-five or seventy-five, you may be missing this part of your relationship. It may be hard to find a family member or friend to share these feelings with. In fact, you may be uncomfortable bringing up the subject for fear of what others might think of you. For that reason, you may want to find a widowed seminar or widowed group that would provide you with an opportunity to talk about these matters with people who are likely to be having some of the same feelings. But a word of advice: Be careful not to get into an intimate relationship too soon, thinking that it will be a cure for your loneliness. I know of many widows and widowers who have done this, and regretted it later. You need time to mourn the loss of your spouse before you enter into some new romantic relationship. (See section 9.3 on relationships.)

6.14 Child

The death of a child seems to defy the laws of nature. It puts things out of order for a child to die before his or her parents. Many of us have hopes and dreams for our children that may include going to college, starting careers, getting married, having children of their own, taking care of us in our old age, and arranging our funerals when we die. All of these expectations are destroyed when a child dies.

If you have had a child die, you are likely to be feeling both helpless and guilty. As a parent you had a responsibility to love and care for your child. When your child was sick, it was to you that he or she turned to make the pain go away. To your child you were a godlike figure, the embodiment of strength and power. Exaggerated as these conceptions might be, you undoubtedly tried to live up to them to the best of your ability. And yet, when the time of your child's greatest need came, you could do nothing to prevent his or her untimely death. (See section 4.5 on guilt and regret.)

No matter the age of your child or the cause of death, you are bound to have these feelings. But sometimes the burden is even heavier. If your child was killed in an auto accident, you may have been the driver or the person who gave your child the permission to take that trip. How do you forgive yourself for that? If your child was abducted and murdered, your anger toward the murderer may be matched only by your anger with yourself for allowing your child out of your sight even for a moment. Your sense of guilt can be wrenching. (See section 7.3 on unintentional acts with far-reaching consequences and 7.6 on violent death.)

When a child dies, there are special issues that you as a parent must deal with that are different from other kinds of death. Here are some of them:

- It may be assumed by family and friends that the mother and father of a deceased child will be the best support for each other. This is not always true. The strong emotions surrounding the death of a child can create many tensions within a marriage. Husbands and wives are not always the best source of support for each other. I remember a father telling me once, "There are times when I am feeling okay. After all, I have to be okay in order to function at work. Then I come home and Susan is crying and all upset. I know that if I reach out to her, it will bring me down and interfere with my work. So I just go off by myself somewhere." Can you imagine what this does to Susan? And, for that matter, what it does to him? There are times when a wife will tell me, "I expect George to know how I'm feeling; after all, I am sitting on the floor crying, and dinner hasn't been made. It should be pretty obvious how I'm feeling." If either of these examples sounds like you, be careful with such expectations of your spouse. Even though you are living together and know each other well, no one can read your mind. Going off by yourself without explanation may look like rejection. Expecting your spouse to understand and accept what appears to be childish behavior is asking a lot. It is important to verbalize to your partner how you are feeling and what you need from him or her. Maybe all you need is a hug, a gesture of understanding and shared pain; say so. If you are feeling particularly bad, say so. Don't always wait for the other person to act; reach out and give him or her an opportunity to respond in kind. How about sharing a cup of tea and listening one more time to what your partner is going through? And try to be patient with each other. Just remember: Your spouse is mourning, too. Any license for selfish behavior that you can claim applies as well to your partner in sorrow. The more you can communicate with your spouse, the better it will be for both of you. (See section 2.2 on communication and 10.5 on emotional health.)

- If you are a mother, you may have an added issue to deal with, and that is the intense bonding you had with your child. I am speaking not only of the nine months that you carried your child before birth but of the closeness that may have developed between you during the early years of life. This closeness itself is a loss that must be mourned. I know of only one thing to help you with this grief, and that is your memories. Nothing can take them away.

- An added tragedy is the death of a child when it was an only child. Suddenly your house becomes unbearably quiet. The sound of children's voices is gone. Your house seems empty. Even worse, you come to realize that, except in an historical sense, you are no longer a mother or a father. No wonder, then, that the death of an only child ranks near the top in the hierarchy of stress. I know of several couples whose only child died by suicide, an added burden to carry. Another couple, when their only child died, wondered what to do with his toys and his clothes, and even more, whom to leave their estate to when they died. They even wondered what to do with the family pictures and those personal mementos that would be of little interest to others. This kind of death situation is all too common. If you are suffering such a terrible loss, you may want to get in touch with a support group known as the Compassionate Friends, which has chapters throughout the United States. Some of the chapters now have support groups for "only child" deaths. (See the Resources in the back of this book.)

- When a child of yours dies, you lose part of your future and part of your own immortality. I assume that when your child was born, you had a life plan for him or her. You thought about what your child would do as an adult, the grandchildren you would treasure, the vacations you would take together as a family. Although you knew that your child's life undoubtedly would vary somewhat from your plan, the one thing that you were most unlikely to contemplate was the premature death of your child. When death aborts the plan, not only your child's future but *your* future is affected. This is so because, ordinarily, you achieve a measure of immortality through your children, grandchildren, and great-grandchildren. When a child dies, this is yet another loss you must mourn.

- Mourning a dead child is often punctuated by those special occasions associated with growing up. High school graduations, classmates going off to college, class reunions, classmate weddings, christenings, and other such events will serve to remind you of your loss.

You may be invited to these occasions by friends who want to share these experiences with you, not realizing what heartaches they stir up. As these invitations come up, think them through and assess your feelings. Attend those you want to attend, and don't be embarrassed about turning down those that would be too painful. Send a gift or card with an explanation of how you feel. Most people will understand. However, keep this in mind: it is better to be invited than not invited. I think it would be even more painful for you if people simply left you out of their plans because of your loss. (See section 5.2 on special family occasions.)

- The death of a child can be especially painful if it occurs during troubled times. This might be because of turmoil in the family, acting out on the part of the child, juvenile delinquency, the use of drugs, or other problems. I know of a couple who, many years ago, lost a son during his teen years. It was at a time when the son was depressed, couldn't study, and twice had run away from home. This couple's remaining children all survived that terrible time of family stress and ultimately became productive citizens, wonderful parents themselves, and loving children to their parents. I am sure that the son who died would have been an equally productive adult, perhaps going on to the career he dreamed of as a scientist, but his parents will never know because his life ended so abruptly and at such an unhappy time. (See section 7.17 on conflicted relationships.)

- Every year more than eight thousand infants die from no apparent cause, victims of the mysterious Sudden Infant Death Syndrome (SIDS). (See section 7.8 on the shock of discovery.) Infant death doesn't always get the recognition and empathy from family and friends that it deserves. The thought may be, "But you didn't have him for a very long time." What others may not realize is that those first few weeks, months, or years of a child's life are the time of intense bonding between parent and child. The total attention you must give your child is both a burden and a privilege. A closeness develops that will never be forgotten. All of his or her needs are filled by you as you bathe, feed, clothe, and entertain your child. Even your nights are interrupted with feeding times, administering medicines, and checking on the baby. There should be no mystery about this: the loss of a child is severe and painful at any age. I have had grieving mothers tell me that their arms ached, they had such a need to hold their babies. And don't be surprised if you start looking at babies or toddlers who are about the age of your child, wondering if this is what your baby would be like if he or she had lived.

• What do you do on the birthday of your deceased child? What do you want to do? This is still the day your child was born or was expected. You might want to acknowledge this day with a trip to the cemetery, a special religious service, or simply releasing a balloon with a message on it for her or him. (See section 5.3 on birthdays.) If after a few years, however, you still feel a strong need to celebrate this birthday, you might want to see a professional grief counselor to see if there is a problem in your grief that needs special attention. I know a family whose first-born died seven years ago, yet the entire family is expected to continue to celebrate the birthday with a trip to the cemetery each year. This is creating a problem for the younger children, who are now refusing to participate. They didn't know this sister and are feeling less loved because they can't compete with an idealized memory. They see this unending grief and wonder if they have to die, too, to get this much of love. You don't want to do this to your loved ones.

Beyond these suggestions you will find more help on the death of your child by reading Chapter 4 on the emotions of grief. If you are grieving a very recent death, you might also plan some time away from home with your now fragmented family to try to regroup and support each other. A week's trip to the beach off-season, or some other quiet place might give you time for reflection, time to talk, and time to share with each other your innermost feelings and needs. But avoid noisy, busy, hectic places like amusement parks. You could end up being entertained but forget the purpose of getting away. The purpose should be to try to take a break from your grief, get some rest, and to get acquainted with your redefined family. Just be aware that your grief will be waiting for you on your return.

A question I am often asked is, "What do I say when someone asks me how many children I have?" Do you say, "two," and ignore the fact that there used to be three? Do you say, "Three," including the deceased child but feeling that you are not quite telling the truth? Or do you say, "Three, but one died," and risk the awkward silence that could follow, putting the other person ill at ease? I find that you will have different answers for different situations. It is a good idea to think these situations through and decide in advance how you will respond in each situation. In that way you will not be caught off guard and left feeling uneasy. Just because today you claim only your living children does not mean that you are ignoring your dead child or that you no longer love him or her.

Finally, be careful not to have a "replacement" child. The pain of your loss may be so great that you think it would help to replace your little Joey with another son. It won't work. We can't replace a human being as we would a wrecked bicycle. That child who was once part of your life is special in his own right and will demand his own place in your heart. You could come to dislike this new baby because he was not the same as the one you lost. It would be an unfair burden to put upon a child to expect him or her to live up to the image of this mysterious other person he never knew. (See section 7.20 on the replacement child.)

The other caution I have for you is to overcome the natural fear all surviving parents have that another child could die. Avoid becoming overprotective of your living children. Children will soon resent the fact that they can no longer do things or go places they used to. If you are too protective you could be developing an emotional dependence that will create even more problems later on. It is important to explain to your children why you have this tendency to be so protective and to invite them to let you know when they feel smothered. Open communication with your children, spouse, and close friends is the best way to keep your anxiety in check. After a time you should start feeling more comfortable in letting your children move about in their old, normal ways.

Abortion

Abortions, whether they are spontaneous (miscarriage) or voluntary, carry with them intense grief for both parents and other close family members. In both cases there can be feelings of guilt and deep sadness, but in the case of voluntary abortions there is an additional burden: the attitude of many people that the mother doesn't deserve to grieve. Even those who approve the decision to abort may not realize that the loss of an unborn child is a loss to be grieved. No matter how early in the pregnancy the abortion occurred, the mother will always feel some attachment to that unborn child and wonder what sort of person he or she might have been. Adding to this is the lack of more than minimal counseling at some abortion clinics. I know of one young woman who told me that a counselor at the clinic she visited announced, "If there is anyone here who is not sure they want to go through with this, see me in my office." Perhaps the lack of help can be explained by the heavy burden placed on the staffs of abortion clinics, who often are severely overworked. I do know that abortion counseling done by private physicians is often much better. If you are in need of such counseling, you also might look for a support group in your community which you could join.

The grief around abortion is real. So often family, friends and strangers are judgmental about abortion and do not know the hours of desperation, anguish, and sorrow that preceded the decision to abort. I often find women surprised at how much grief they feel after an abortion. The guilt they feel makes them believe they gave away the right to mourn. I have heard women refer to themselves as murderers, even though they had sound reasons for their abortions. This guilt is mixed up with the feeling of being relieved, which in turn makes them feel guilty. And all of this guilt is reinforced by the raging debate over when human life begins, essentially a religious question. (See section 4.5 on guilt and regret.) I do not know of many resources for this grief. Once in awhile I will see a chapter in a book (see Bibliography) that touches upon it, but I know of no support groups. Your best help might come from a professional grief counselor.

The "forgotten" person in this grief is the father, whether married to the mother or not. I often visit a resident treatment center to help people with grief and loss. What a relief it is to some of the men to have their grief acknowledged. For the man who has helped conceive a fetus the decision to abort is seldom an easy one. The more conscientious he is, the more pain and guilt he will carry. If you are carrying such pain and guilt, let me assure you that you have a right to grieve and to mourn the abandonment of this opportunity for fatherhood.

Grief as Part of Your Life

The loss of a child is hard. For the rest of your life you may feel some tugging at your heart when you think about your lost child. I don't think one ever "gets over" grief; it just becomes part of your life, as all our experiences do. And in time it becomes manageable, much less overwhelming than it was in those first months after the death when you were reshaping your future. You may not think that today, but you will.

Chapter 7

COMPLICATED
GRIEF

When You Wish Events Would Happen

One at a Time

Sometimes life's distractions make it hard to grieve. If you are finding it difficult to concentrate on your grief because of everything else that is happening, you may be saying to yourself, "I can't cope with more than one thing at a time!" Oh, if life could be that simple. The reality is that our lives are complex and varied, and the corollary is that the grieving process is also complex and varied. Life's distractions may be preventing you from getting on with your grief. If some time has passed since the death, and your family and friends are getting impatient with you, this might be a time to look closely at the relationship you had with the deceased and the circumstances of the death. There may have been situations requiring your attention immediately after the death that forced you to put your grief on hold. Much later, when everyone else seems back on track, you may feel that you are falling apart.

There could be other complications as well. You may have had a different relationship with the deceased than anyone else, and this may have presented problems in expressing your grief as others did. Listed below are a just a few examples of complicated grief. The possibilities are limitless. The cases I cite are not meant to frighten you. They are true stories with some changes made to protect the identity of the people who shared them with me. They are not unusual stories; I wish they were. But I am including them here to help you understand that, whatever your situation may be, there are ways of dealing with it. Your grief may be more complicated than the grief experienced by the person sitting next to you at your support group or grief seminar. You may need more time and perhaps outside help to move on with your life. This may require more patience than you expected, but know that, no matter what, you can overcome this burden and carry on with your life. You may even be a better person because of the experience.

7.1 Other Changes in Your Life

This subject has been examined in section 1.3 as well. However, it is important enough to look a little further into changes that may occur when a loved one dies.

Sometimes when a loved one dies the memories of that loved

one are so painful that the bereaved feel surrounded by them. After the death of a child or a spouse I have seen people seemingly unable to stay in the same house, filled as it was with memories of the deceased. This has led to the thought that they should sell the house and separate themselves from those memories. When people do this, they may feel better for a while, but soon those memories change from painful to precious. Having moved away, they are denied the comfort of those familiar, memory-filled surroundings.

There are other reasons for you to go slowly if you are considering such a step. For one thing, selling the house and moving will present you with a tremendous task—cleaning the house, repairing it, possibly painting it, listing it for sale, looking for another house, opening your home to agents and prospective buyers, closing the sale, and then moving your furniture and belongings after deciding what to save and what to discard. Grieving people commonly are forgetful, disorganized, and unable to concentrate. How can you possibly do all of this? And there's more: moving from your home also is likely to mean leaving your church, family, friends, family doctor, your children's school, the local library, familiar parks, and many more threads in the fabric of your life. With each of these losses there will be a grief reaction. No wonder that some people collapse with "grief overload." Family and friends may be advising you to move, saying, "It will be better for you." My advice: If you can, sit tight, and give yourself a chance to adjust to the loss of your loved one without introducing new losses. In a few months you will be in a better state of mind to decide what you really want to do. (See section 4.3 on ways that people avoid reality.)

However, you may not have a choice. For example, if you are in the military and living on post, you will probably be given a date by which you have to vacate the house. Help should be available to you on the base. If it isn't offered, seek it out.

Also, you may have to move for financial reasons. If you were a two-income family, and now there is only one, you may have to sell the house. If this is the case, look for help with all of the work involved. Get some professional guidance from your accountant, a financial planner, or someone else who can give you sound advice. Advice from close family members or friends, though well intentioned, sometimes turns out differently from the way you had hoped and can cause hard feelings later on. You need your family and friends, and you don't want to alienate them.

If you are thinking of changing jobs, try to postpone this for a while. Again, give yourself time to get used to your life now without your loved one. When one is mourning, it is hard to give total attention to any task, much less try to learn new responsibilities. If you are in a situation where you do not have a choice and have to find a different job, look for something that is not too challenging at the outset. You can look for a more challenging job later.

Delayed Grief

You may have found when your loved one died that the family became immobile, seemingly unable to make funeral arrangements, much less care for themselves. Maybe you were always the one that others leaned on, telling you their problems, expecting you to "fix" them. When your loved one died, you may have taken a deep breath, put your grief on hold, and stepped forward to make the arrangements, decide on legal matters, be executor of the will, comfort the bereaved, and generally take charge. You may even have thought that you could bypass grief by doing all of this. Sad to say, that won't work. After the estate is settled, funeral bills are paid, and your family members are getting on with their lives, you may finally come to grips with your grief—and feel that you are falling apart! This can be frightening if you don't understand what is happening. You may feel very isolated because now, when you need your family, they are going about their lives and have no desire to relive the death. You have used the time that is normally used to express grief by keeping busy taking care of everyone else. It is now months or years later and your grief is beginning to show itself.

This is fresh, painful grief you are feeling and even though the death may have occurred a long time ago, try to think of your grief as if the death had occurred yesterday. Have patience with yourself, and allow yourself to express your grief and to mourn your loss.

7.2 Unusual Circumstances

This could be a situation in which you do not have a choice—when more pressing, personal things demand attention first and grief has to wait.

I know of several people, children included, who were involved in a tragic auto accident resulting in a fatality and extensive injuries to others. One twelve-year-old girl was in a coma for two months, and a woman was in intensive care for weeks followed by a long hospital stay before she could be released. If you have had such a horrendous experience, you may not even have known about the death of a loved one until you were well enough physically to cope with it. There may have been a conspiracy of silence when you inquired about the fate of others. When you did find out that a loved one had died, quite possibly the funeral was long past, and the people around you were already getting on with their lives. I don't know any standard way of dealing with these situations, but there are times when a hospitalized loved one can be told almost immediately and thus given an opportunity to say good-bye in some way—a flower, a photo, or a note of farewell to be placed in the casket. On the other hand, if you had no chance to participate in the funeral in any way, you may want to do so, in a sense, after the fact.

Now that you understand what has happened, you can take steps to put closure on the death and perhaps have your own funeral service. Talk to your family about the service that was held and get as good a description as you can of what happened. Was there something there that had special meaning for you? Did anyone take any pictures or tape parts of it? Did someone take a rose off the casket and save it for you? Such things could help you overcome the feeling of having been left out of this important event.

Still, you may want to plan a memorial service of your own to satisfy your need to put closure on this part of your life. If you feel the need, I encourage you to do so; it will help you accept the reality of the death. On the other hand, a trip to the gravesite may be enough. There you can place a few flowers, leave notes, and whisper some last words to your loved one. But be aware that your grief will be as painful now, months later, as it was for others when the death actually occurred. You will be just beginning to feel your grief and to mourn your loss. (See section 3.4 on visiting the grave and 3.6 on memorial services.)

Another example of deferred grief is that of an immigrant family that was targeted by murderers. I don't know all of the circumstances, but one night their house was set on fire after the doors and windows had been locked to prevent escape. Two of the five family members died, but, unknown to the murderers, three family members had gone to visit relatives for the weekend and were not in the house. Fearful of the murderers' return, these three had to go into hiding, preventing them from attending the funeral. They simply had to pack their remaining belongings and flee. Not until they felt safe could they return and begin mourning the death of their loved ones. I cite this as another example of how life's complications can interfere with the grieving process. If you have had such an experience, you may need professional help in reconstructing your life and mourning the losses you have suffered.

7.3 Unintentional Acts and Far-Reaching Consequences

If you were somehow responsible, unintentionally, for the death of someone, you undoubtedly will have guilt feelings to resolve. But if that someone was close to you, someone you loved, your burden will be especially heavy. In addition to the grief you feel for the deceased, you are bound to have strong feelings of regret and guilt for having caused, or helped to cause, the death. But don't let these feelings consume you. Remind yourself that you loved this person and that you would never have done anything intentionally to harm him or her. And let me assure you that you are not alone; I know of many people who have had to carry such regrets and who have gone on to live constructive lives. Here are some examples:

- A teenager was backing the family car down the drive when he accidentally ran over his toddler sister, who was playing behind the car.
- Several teenagers were fooling around, taking turns riding on the hood of an auto, when one of them slipped off and was run over by the same car.
- There seem to be endless gun accidents that occur when young people play with firearms carelessly left around the house. For example, I recently read of a fourteen-year-old boy who accidentally shot his seven-year-old sister.
- Almost every day one reads about car accidents in which people are killed but the driver survives.

If you have somehow played a part in such a death, the guilt you feel is likely to complicate your mourning. Even though no one may be blaming you, it is very difficult to forgive oneself for a moment's forgetfulness when it has caused, or contributed to, this terrible result. How desperately you may want to turn back the clock and have a chance to undo your mistake. "If only . . . ," you will say to yourself. Occasionally, especially in the case of an auto accident involving drugs, alcohol, or negligence, there may be charges or a lawsuit to feed into your guilt. Don't be surprised if your grief is still extremely painful months later. Guilt can eat away at you and create all kinds of physical and emotional problems. If you are carrying such a burden and it's not getting lighter after a few months, I think you should consider getting professional help.

Failure to provide help when needed can also leave you feeling responsible for a death. For example, I know of a nurse whose father was living with her. One night he complained of not feeling well but refused to go to the hospital, agreeing instead to see his doctor the next morning. As fate would have it, he died on the way to the doctor's office. Being a nurse, his daughter then blamed herself for not recognizing the seriousness of his condition and acting more aggressively to get him help.

As a parent you may have failed to protect your loved ones from harm. Like the mother who failed to put a bottle of drain cleaner out of reach of her toddler. Or the father who smelled something odd in the house but put off investigating the source just long enough for his wife and child to be asphyxiated. Or the son who was planning to fix the broken step at his mother's house when she fell to her death. Or the wife who knew that her husband needed to be on a special diet but, tiring of its blandness, had abandoned it for a time, only to learn that he had died of a heart attack at work.

The guilt people feel in these situations is overwhelming, often made worse by the condemnation of other family members. If you have come to this book with such a heavy heart, all I can say is that you should be kind to yourself, reminding yourself that life is capable of presenting us with terrible turns from time to time and that your loved one's death was the last thing in the world that you would have intended to happen. Going over and over the reality in a rational way will help you in time to accept this death as an accident. If you fail to get some relief after a few weeks or months, you might want to seek out your pastor or rabbi, or possibly a professional, to help convince yourself that you are not a murderer. (See section 4.5 on guilt and regret.)

7.4 Multiple Deaths

There are times when life's calamities make your grief almost more than you can bear. I am thinking especially of those occasions when several family members die at once. The grief you feel when such a disaster occurs to your loved ones can be overwhelming, made all the more difficult by trying to sort out who it is you are grieving for at any given time. If you have had such a terrible set of losses, be patient with yourself; it's going to take a while for you to work through your grief. Get all the help you can, but don't assume that life has nothing more to offer you.

If a car accident or plane crash has taken the lives of several members of your family, this situation is so overwhelming that you may not know where to begin in dealing with it. I have heard of school bus crashes in which several children from one family were killed, leaving some parents suddenly childless or with only one child when they previously had three or four children. If you have such a terrible set of losses to resolve, you have a long period of mourning ahead of you as you mourn the death of each of your loved ones. But no matter how heavy is your burden and no matter how long it takes to resolve this grief, I want to assure you that the task is *not* more than you can handle. Your life is still important because it is the only life you will ever have on this earth; in spite of your terrible losses, you *can* go on to live a happy and constructive life once you have accepted the reality of what has happened and expressed your grief fully.

Recently where I live there was a car accident in which a mother, a father, their three children, and one of their children's friends were killed. You can imagine the task that lay ahead for the grandparents and other family members. The legal work alone was staggering, and funeral costs were horrendous. Just the management of five or six funerals is difficult, let alone the management of the estate and disposing of personal items. In circumstances like this it is no wonder that grief is complex and often delayed.

I know of families who refuse to fly together on the same flight for fear that a crash could happen, taking the lives of two or more family members at the same time. If you are somehow blaming yourself because you didn't recommend such precautions, be fair to yourself and look at the statistics on fatalities in various forms of travel; it is hard to say that one form is much safer than another. Life presents us with risks, no matter how careful we are. For example, the entire nation mourned when a championship hockey team died in a plane crash; should team members not fly together? Obviously there are limits to the precautions we can take against such losses.

It may not be an accident that takes the lives of several family members or friends; it may be sickness or disease. Over time different diseases have taken their toll: bubonic plague in fourteenth-century Europe, the influenza epidemic of 1918, the polio epidemic of the 1950s, and many more. Cancer, while not contagious, is so widespread today that it often strikes more than one member of a family. And now we have Acquired Immune Deficiency Syndrome (AIDS). You may be someone who has lost more than one friend to this dread disease, and you may be dealing with your own diagnosis, or the possibility of a future diagnosis. This can be a heavy load for you to carry.

Unlike accidental deaths, these deaths come one at a time, sometimes without an end in sight, making you wonder who will be next. This epidemic is not over. Authorities tell us that the disease will continue its course, not just in the gay population or among intravenous drug users, but in the population at large. There are a number of factors that complicate one's grief when dealing with AIDS. For example, you may feel guilty when you visit a dying friend because you are secretly thankful it is not you lying there. You may feel guilty that you are well and healthy and not spending all your time mourning for your friend. You may find it difficult to visit a friend who is ill because it may be too threatening, a reminder of what could possibly happen to you. If you have had friends or relatives die of AIDS and face the prospect of more such losses, it is important that you look for ways to tell your stricken friends or loved ones how you feel about them, that you say good-bye, and that you put some closure on these relationships before they die. (See section 2.2 on visiting the dying.) Also, you might look for ways to make each funeral individual and meaningful for you. (See section 3.2 on making the funeral meaningful.) You might even consider setting up a support group for family members and friends who were close to a loved one who has died, or for the families and friends of other AIDS victims. Sharing each other's pain in this way can help each of you resolve your own grief and express the love you have for the person or persons who died.

7.5 Sudden Illness and Death

When someone you love dies suddenly of an illness you knew nothing about, you are likely to be caught off guard, having had no time to prepare for the event. When this happens, your emotions are likely to take over, making it difficult for you to address the many decisions that must be dealt with: legal matters, funeral arrangements, business details. The period of shock and disbelief will be stronger for you and last longer than it would if you had been given advance warning. Your heart may be telling you that all of this is a mistake, while your mind may be telling you the truth. Your job in these circumstances is to try as best you can to listen to your mind more than your heart.

Sudden illness and death can rob you of the opportunity to say good-bye or to have any final words with your loved one. This is almost a given in such situations, an added complication to an already painful experience. Not knowing what your loved one wanted done about the roof, or what kind of funeral he wanted, or where his insurance policies are, may seem too much to bear, but there isn't anything you can do about it. It is better to find someone to help you with these matters than continue to worry. And if you had no chance to say good-bye, there are things you can do to satisfy that need, too. (See section 6.3 on sudden death.)

There is another kind of "sudden death" that is often overlooked. You may have had a loved one already afflicted with a terminal illness such as cancer, AIDS, or heart disease, but still find yourself having to deal with a sudden death. You may be expecting your loved one to live many more months, or even years, and you find that your plans have been shattered by what you see as premature death. This could be caused by a complication that you had not expected, such as an unrelated heart attack or an abnormal response to a routine surgical procedure, or even a fall from a ladder. You knew death would come, but not so soon. When death comes suddenly to a loved one already diagnosed as terminal, friends and relatives may fail to appreciate that you are dealing with a sudden death and all that this implies. They may say things like "She was saved from suffering" or "You should be thankful you don't have to nurse her anymore." The empathy and understanding you need may not be forthcoming if your family and friends fail to understand that sudden death is sudden death whenever and however it occurs.

7.6 Violent Death

Violent death is not only sudden; it adds complexity to your grief as you try to visualize what must have happened. You are bound to wonder if your loved one knew what was happening or knew that he or she was about to die. In this regard you may find some comfort in what I have learned from talking with people who have had narrow escapes from death. What they tell me is that, for the most part, when their lives are in danger, people become very task oriented, focusing on "How am I going to get out of this" and disassociating themselves from what is really happening to them. It is almost as if they were stepping back and watching the scene being played, like spectators at a play. One woman told me that, after an encounter with an intruder, she was surprised to discover that she had been stabbed many times. Thus, if a loved one of yours was the victim of violence, there is a good chance that he or she did not suffer as much pain as you have imagined.

Accidental Death

Accidental deaths are hard to understand because they upset what we see as the natural order of things. Death by cancer, yes. Death at advanced age, yes. But accidental deaths, so often striking the young, no. We find such deaths very hard to understand. They challenge our cozy beliefs and comfortable assumptions about life, death, justice, fairness, and order in the universe.

If you have lost a loved one through an accident of some kind, you may have the additional burden of dealing with a severely damaged body. If so, and if it would be the normal practice in your family to have a wake or viewing, you may want to have a friend or relative view the body for you and help you decide what to do. There is no point in inflicting greater suffering on yourself than necessary. (See section 7.12 on viewing the body.)

Finally, watch out for guilt feelings. No matter how your loved one died, you are likely to blame yourself for doing or not doing something that, directly or indirectly, contributed to this terrible loss. (See section 4.5 on guilt and regrets.)

Suicide

Suicide deaths almost always lead to complicated grief, varying in degrees of complexity and intensity. The grief you experience when a loved one takes an overdose of pills, injects herself with a lethal substance, or uses carbon monoxide to accomplish the act is a bit easier to accept than when a loved one resorts to violence to achieve the same end. It is very hard to think about a loved one's hanging or shooting himself or throwing herself in front of a train. The more bloody and broken the body, the more intense your grief will be. I mention these possibilities not to frighten you but to assure you that others have lived through such experiences and survived to enjoy life again. Even though your days may seem bleak now, you will get better and you will be able to enjoy life again.

Sometimes there are special circumstances that make your grief more complex and difficult. An example was the experience of a young woman who was talking on the telephone with her boyfriend when she heard heard the gun go off.

You may wish that your loved one had died from anything rather than by suicide. Or it may seem that it would have been easier for you if only he or she had used pills instead of a gun. Suicide deaths are not always discovered immediately, adding more complications. I know of a family that awaited word on the fate of their daughter for months before her body was discovered; she had shot herself after going to a remote forest area, where she was discovered by hunters. This family not only had to deal with the suicide death of their daughter but also the decomposed condition of her body. In addition to everything else, they now have two death anniversaries to face every year: the first, when she died, and the second, when they were notified. (See section 6.4 on suicide.)

Murder

If your loved one has been murdered, your grief will be more complex. Grief will take a long time as you try to cope with knowing that someone purposely killed your loved one. If there has been an arrest and you intend to be present as the case is tried, you should consider seeking counseling by someone who is knowledgeable about grief and what happens at trials. (See the Resources.) More details may come out than you were prepared to hear. I was told by the siblings of a murdered sister that they were doing all right until a witness reported hearing a "death scream" in the woods on the night she was murdered.

If you have had a loved one murdered, I know that you will be wondering what suffering he or she had to endure before death came. All I can say is that the survivors of murder attempts often report disassociating themselves from what was happening. We can hope that this is what occurred with your loved one.

On the other hand, you may know that your loved one suffered, and this will simply make your grief all the more difficult to resolve. This was the case when a young man called the emergency number, 911, for help as an intruder threatened him with a shotgun. These calls are taped, and there is now a tape of his voice pleading unsuccessfully with the intruder not to kill him.

No matter what form it takes, violence complicates the grieving process. While nothing but mourning your loss will lift this weight from your shoulders, it may help you to be aware of why it is that your grief is lasting so long. It will also help you to read Chapter 4 on mourning, to find a support group for people who are coping with a similar death, and to find a therapist who has had experience helping people cope with violent death. (See section 6.5 on murder.)

7.7 Questionable Deaths

There is one circumstance that may be worse—if that seems possible—than knowing that a loved one has been murdered or has committed suicide. And that is not knowing what happened. For example, a woman whose son was found dead in the garage does not know whether his drug overdose was accidental or intentional. She tries to go to a suicide survivor group but doesn't feel that she fits in there. She's not sure whether it was suicide, and she's not sure she wants to believe it could be suicide. The evidence could lead one in either direction. This mother wishes that there had been a note, or something, to help explain the death.

A young adult came home one evening to find his father hanging in the garage. It looked like suicide to the police until the family shared with them some threatening letters that had been sent to the house, and now it looked like murder. Such ambiguities about the cause of death make grief more complicated. When the survivors felt the need of a support group, which one were they to choose? The murder group or the suicide group? The family couldn't find a place where they fit in. Trying to explain what had happened, they had varying opinions, causing more pain. If they only knew!

The anger and frustration you feel in such circumstances can be great. Who should you be mad at? At times like this, it may be best to see a therapist who can help you work on your grief.

7.8 Shock of Discovery

It is pretty obvious that the shock you feel when discovering someone dead is going to make grief more difficult. Even finding an aged grandparent dead in her nursing-home bed is going to be a shock, forming an image that will pop into your head when you least expect it.

Your grief becomes more complicated when you have not had the cushion of another human being between you and the sight of death. It is so much better to have a loving, caring person with you when you hear the dreaded news. Even getting the news from a total stranger is better than gazing directly on the scene of death.

Grief becomes more complex when this happens. This might be arriving home after a shopping trip and discovering the body of a loved one on the floor, dead from a heart attack or stroke. Several people have told me of awakening in the morning to find that their spouses had died during the night. Their grief is complicated not only by having made these discoveries but by the guilt they feel for not being aware of what was happening right there in their beds. If you have had such an experience, you may find that returning to that bed is very difficult or even impossible. If so, I might suggest that you purchase a different bedroom set, rearrange your bedroom, or move into another bedroom temporarily so you are not acutely reminded of your loss every time you go to bed.

You may be a parent who has had the shocking experience of discovering your baby dead of SIDS (Sudden Infant Death Syndrome). Many children die each year from this mysterious cause. Not only parents but grandparents or other child care providers may be the ones to discover such deaths. I even know of one case where the baby died in the baby-sitter's arms. The person in charge of this young life at the time is left not only with the shock of discovery but the guilt that is bound to ensue, no matter how much care and attention had been given the child. Adding to this guilt is the investigation that the police must make in determining whether criminal charges must be filed.

Parents hurt so much when a baby dies in this way that they tend to look for someone to blame, and at times they blame each other. If you are the parent of a SIDS victim, you may be thinking, "Someone caused this; it just didn't happen by itself." But these deaths can and do occur. (See section 4.5 on guilt and section 6.14 on the death of a child.)

If you are a child care provider, in addition to your own grief you may also worry about the legal implications. Will you be charged with either criminal or civil negligence? What will this do to your day-care center and how will this affect your confidence as a child care worker? The National Foundation on SIDS offers up-to-date information and resources that could be helpful to you. You might also consider getting help from a professional therapist to guide you through your grief. (See the Resources at the back of this book.)

Grief becomes even more complicated if you are the one who discovers the violent death of a loved one. The mental picture of what you saw may stay with you for a long time and come up in flashbacks, perhaps in nightmares. Almost always in these cases it is a good idea to consult with a therapist for guidance and help.

I know of several people who upon arriving home discovered the bodies of loved ones who had taken their own lives through carbon monoxide, hanging, overdose, and gunshot. The shock of walking in on something like this is tremendous. You frantically try first aid and call 911. Soon emergency vehicles descend upon the scene, and police arrive. Total confusion ensues. You may be told to stay out of the way and be prevented from spending even a few precious moments with the body. I know of a woman who discovered her father hanging in the garage. She asked the policemen if she could spend a few minutes alone with the body of her dad. These policemen respected her request and left the garage. However, they kept an eye on her through the windows to make sure she was all right and to help her if needed.

Experiences of this kind happen more often than I care to think about. My purpose here is to recount experiences others have had that may somehow relate to your own experience with death.

I know a young man who arrived home one afternoon to discover the bloodied body of his father on the front steps of their home, where he had been shot by a family friend. I know of a young woman who found the body of her mother in the kitchen and the body of her father in the living room, victims of a neighbor's approach to settling an argument.

More often than I wish, suicide deaths are discovered by family members or friends. A husband finds his wife's body hanging in the basement. A mother, checking on her son following a family argument, finds his body hanging in a closet. Grandchildren, racing downstairs to look for Gramps, find him slumped over in the chair after shooting himself. Even worse is the story of a young man whose girlfriend shot herself in front of him as he watched in horror, unable to stop her.

Much of the anger you have to deal with in such cases lies in thinking that the deceased set you up for enormous shock and guilt. While attending a suicide survivors group, you may wish you could be that lady over there whose loved one went to a motel in another state to commit the act. The special circumstances of your situation will make your grief different from others around you.

People who have survived automobile accidents in which loved ones have died have special problems. If this has been your experience, you may have the memory of seeing your loved one die, or you may have feelings of guilt for somehow contributing to this unhappy event. You may be wishing that you could change places so your loved one could live. This experience, too, will make your grief different from that of others in different circumstances.

The discovery of the body of a loved one is always a shocking experience, but the intensity and longevity of this grief will vary with the circumstances. When death was anticipated, finding the body will be easier than when it was unexpected. In either case you may have ambivalent feelings: regretting that it was you who discovered the body, and feeling grateful that it is not your child or another family member who had to have this experience.

It is obvious that the more violent the death, the more intense and enduring will be the grief you experience. Seeing a dead body is seldom a pretty sight, and it may be difficult for you to find someone who can listen to your description of what you saw. Even professionals sometimes have a hard time listening to the details, but it is important for you to unburden what you had to endure, to share this experience with someone else. I remember a man who, being estranged from his wife, hadn't heard from her for a few days during the heat of the summer. He thought this strange and went to her home to check on her. There he found that she had been dead for several days. What he saw and what he smelled was overwhelming to him. After the body was removed, he could not find a cleaning company willing to come in to clean. He had to do this himself, adding to his grief. His therapist could not stand to listen to his story and referred him to me. He needed to talk about the condition of his wife's body, about the smell, about the grease spots on the floor, and other gruesome details. Until he found someone to listen, this man was held in this part of his grief with no means of letting it go and moving on. If you are carrying such weighty images, you also need to find someone to tell them to.

Then there is the story of a young boy who became alarmed that his parents were still in bed as noon approached. He tried the bedroom door and found it locked. Becoming increasingly alarmed, he went outside to climb in through a bedroom window, only to slip and fall onto the bloodied body of his father, who had been killed by his wife, who then had shot herself.

The body you discovered may not have been the body of someone you knew. Such is the story of a motorist who discovered the body of a young girl who had been missing several days and was the subject of a massive search. No matter what the circumstance, discovering a dead body will have an impact on you and plant an image in your mind that you wish weren't there.

I have told you these stories, not to frighten you, but to let you know that, no matter what you have experienced or what horror you have witnessed, someone else has had to carry a similar burden. You are not alone. The discovery of a dead body can be shattering. The discovery of a loved one's body can make your grief more complicated because of the extra issues you have to deal with, issues not faced by other family members or friends. You may see them begin to put their lives back together sooner than you feel you can and you may feel left behind without the support you need. Talking about what you have experienced is important, and if family members or friends aren't available, arrange to tell your story to a therapist. You will feel better if you can discharge these powerful emotions and get on with your grief.

7.9 Hearing the Death News

The way death news is delivered will play an important part in determining how you get started with your grief. There isn't an easy way to deliver such news or to receive it. Delivering the news has to be one of life's most difficult tasks. I often think about those in official positions, like policemen and military officers, who must bear such news frequently as part of their jobs. They have to steel themselves for the reactions they will witness: everything from disbelief to screaming and yelling. For the person receiving the news the manner in which it is delivered will either ease the shock or make it worse, adding to grief's complexity.

Perhaps you found out about the death of your loved one from a minister or rabbi who came into the family waiting room at the hospital and ever so gently told you that your loved one had died. On the other hand, you may have gotten the news from a strange doctor, still dressed in surgical garb, saying only, "I'm sorry," leaving you to draw your own conclusions or forcing you to ask the dreaded question, "Is she dead?" I received the news over the telephone at four A.M. from a voice identifying himself and then stating he was "looking for a Helen Fitzgerald." There was a lot of mumbling as he searched for words to say. Realizing what he was trying to tell me, I put *him* at ease by saying, "It's okay, I have been expecting it." Recently I learned that some people had learned about the death of an elderly parent through a message left by the nursing home on their answering machine. Not a message that said, "Please contact us," but a message that said, "Mrs. Jones has expired." This is *not* the way to deliver death news.

You may have heard your death news from someone coming to the door—a policeman, perhaps, or a family friend. I know of people who, sensing trouble, refuse to open the door. I know of one woman who held her hands over her ears, saying, "No, no, no," in an effort not to hear the news. I know of another woman who told me she began hitting the policeman because

186

he had told her such awful news.

Even more traumatic is learning of a loved one's death through a news report on television. This happened to a couple I know who, when watching coverage of the Vietnam War on the evening news, saw the body of their son being carried off the battlefield.

No matter how you hear news of a loved one's death, it is going to be a shock. But if you received the news of your loved one's death in a way that added to your grief, you will understand why it is taking longer to recover from your intense pain.

7.10 Witnessing a Death

Witnessing a death is not always traumatic. I recall reading about the death of Senator Philip Hart of Michigan some years ago. His family was at his side as his life faded away. Near the end his wife told him she loved him and then said, "If you can hear me, Phil, squeeze my hand." And he did! Shortly after that he died. Can you imagine a better way to say good-bye to a loved one?

I remember being called to the hospital by a man whom I had never met. Someone had written my name and phone number on a piece of paper that he had in his pocket. As the death of his wife neared, he became frightened and anxious. He called to ask if I could come to the hospital to be with him and his children. As I arrived, I had a only few minutes alone with him before the nurse came in to say, "It's time." I sat with the family as this man and his children touched and stroked the dying woman, quietly expressing their love and saying good-bye.

Being with your loved one in such circumstances can be comforting and healing. However there are times when witnessing a death is anything but comforting, and when the emotional trauma it generates adds to your burden of grief. This could be what is complicating your grief.

It could be that you watched helplessly as your loved one

struggled for breath, perhaps drowning on her own fluids. The raspy breathing one hears can be distressing. Often at the time of death a person will make some movement or moaning sound that could be seen as a sign of distress. These are usually involuntary movements and sounds that just happen when one dies, not necessarily signs of discomfort. If you observed something like this, you should not think that your loved one was in great pain or that there was something you should have done to save her life.

Even more traumatizing is the experience of witnessing a sudden, violent death. I think of the millions of children watching TV in their classrooms who witnessed the midair explosion of the space shuttle *Challenger* that was carrying the first schoolteacher into orbit. Even though they did not see the dead bodies, they were all traumatized to know that every person on board was killed in that explosion.

I met recently with a young man whose father suffered a heart attack and died while the two of them were sitting at the kitchen table. This father's life was snatched away in an instant, and there was nothing his son could do. This young man had to spend many hours talking about this experience before he could get on with his grief.

You may have experienced something worse than that. I remember a woman who was driving her car one day with her husband driving a second car behind her. Through her rearview mirror she watched his car go out of control and crash, killing her husband. If you have had such an experience, I am sorry you have to deal with such a memory. It will complicate your grief, but you can help yourself by talking it out and sharing your feelings about it with others.

Witnessing a death can be even more traumatic, as described to me by a stricken widow. She told me that her husband completely "lost it" one day and threatened to kill her before turning the gun on himself as she watched. She was left with the memory of a close scrape with death and the horror of seeing a loved one shoot himself. If you have had such an experience, you should not hesitate to get professional help.

It's hard to believe that things could get worse, but they can. Perhaps you have had to witness something so horrible and terrifying that you wonder just how much a person is expected to take. I know of people who have had to watch helplessly while a loved one was being threatened and then killed. Many of the sad stories I have to tell involve children. I know of a time that an intruder broke into a house, raped and killed the mother as the children watched. I know of a couple who were abducted from their car and the man held at knife point as his wife was raped and killed. For some unknown reason the husband wasn't killed, but he was left with very complicated grief.

If you are someone who has had to experience such horror, I urge you to seek professional help to put this away where it won't interfere with the rest of your life. There are times like this when your mind will block out what happened, giving you some relief. However, this will interfere with resolution of your grief and resumption of a normal life. At some point in your life you will have to deal with it. A therapist can help you through this terrible tragedy and enable you to deal with it in a healthy manner.

7.11 Notoriety

Notoriety? What does that have to do with complicated grief? If you have had a loved one die in some public way with the story appearing in the press, you know what I'm talking about.

There are two situations I want to address. First, there is the prominent person whose death makes news because of his or her prominence. Second, there is the case of an ordinary person who has died in some sensational way, generating news coverage. Either situation can complicate the grief of those who survive.

With the invention of television it is now possible for the death of a famous person to become a major public event. Entire funerals are telecast as the world watches. We see the bereaved family in intimate close-up shots, especially if they are crying or showing the least amount of distress. President Kennedy's funeral set the pattern. Remember how we all watched for the reactions of the family? It seemed the world stopped for days as we stared at TV screens, not wanting to miss any of the funeral events.

Other celebrities that we have mourned in such media spectaculars are Robert Kennedy, Winston Churchill, and Martin Luther King, Jr. All had televised funerals. Years earlier, Franklin Rooscvelt's funeral was covered by radio in much the same way, with Arthur Godfrey narrating the passage of the funeral cortege. While these events enable the public to join in paying respect to a departed leader, they complicate the grief of the survivors. We have the images of the Kennedy family after those two dreadful assassinations, never shedding a public tear. These were remarkable demonstrations of personal strength in the face of great tragedy, but they tell us nothing about the private mourning that ultimately enabled the stricken family members to recover from their grief and get on with their lives.

It's not likely that you are mourning the death of such a famous person, but you may be mourning a loved one who died in some sensational way. There may have been local newspaper or TV news coverage of the event. Suicide deaths are often reported in this way, as are some traffic accidents. Not too long ago a child ran away from an elementary school and was crossing the train tracks when he was hit and killed by a train. At about the same time, a young woman was a victim of a carjacking in which, after becoming tangled in the seat belt, she was dragged to her death. These stories filled the newspapers and TV news for several weeks. While both were newsworthy events that had to be reported, the drumbeat of news stories certainly added to the burden of grief borne by the survivors.

There are deaths that will catch the interest of the national and even world news media, complicating the grief of the survivors. Such was the case with the family of a military officer who was the victim of a random shooting at the Pentagon parking lot in Washington, D.C. Or the parents of a young child who was brutally murdered by children not much older. Or the survivors of the mass Jim Jones suicide in Guyana.

When death goes public, your family may be harassed by TV crews trying to catch glimpses of your sorrow. You and your family may feel that you have no place to go where you can cry privately. You may become known as the "Pentagon murder" family or the family of the "death car driver." Children in school often tell me their classmates no longer know them for who they are but rather as the "girl or boy whose mother was murdered." If you have gone through such an experience, you may be afraid to answer the telephone for fear it will be more reporters. You may feel you have to isolate yourself by staying in the house with curtains drawn. Notoriety adds a complexity to your grief that you may resent but that you have very little control over. It's a complication that adds to your grief.

7.12 When the Body Is Not Presentable

Your loved one may have died in a fire with the body burned beyond recognition. Or your loved one may have died in a plane crash with the body badly damaged. Or perhaps your loved one took his own life in such a way that it would be unwise to view the body. This may be true also if your loved one was murdered.

Or maybe your loved one was dead for many days and, for health reasons, the body had to be wrapped and sealed immediately, preventing any possibility of a viewing. Or during a time of war or hostage taking the body of your loved one had to be shipped in a sealed casket that cannot be opened, leaving you and your family with only the word of a stranger that this indeed is your beloved son, husband, or friend. This type of situation presents a special problem in that, without being able to view the remains, you must depend on the word of others and circumstantial evidence to convince yourself that it is really your loved one who has died. Lingering doubts will complicate your grief, and it may take the passage of time to enable you to put them to rest.

When there is the possibility of viewing, as in the case of the fire-charred body, you face a tough decision: to view or not to view. This is a decision for you to make; there are no hard and fast rules. My advice is to rely on your visceral reaction at the time. You are a better judge of what is best for you than anyone else. If weeks later you start wondering if you did the right thing, I would say you probably made the right decision.

To illustrate my point, I know the widow of a suicide victim who was persuaded by friends not to view her husband's remains, wanting to protect her from pain. She now regrets having listened to their advice and has to cope with the anger she feels toward these well-meaning friends.

In cases like this it is sometimes possible to satisfy the need of confirmation by viewing something else that will help validate the death and give you that last glimpse of your loved one. This could be a piece of jewelry or clothing that would prove to you conclusively that your loved one is indeed dead. A woman I met recently whose son had been murdered raced to the hospital with her family in the hope that what they had heard was not true. She elected to stay in the car, parked outside of the emergency room, while her husband and daughters went into the hospital to make inquiries. As she was sitting in the car, a stretcher was wheeled by with a sheet-covered body. On many occasions through the years she had stepped into the bedroom at night to gaze on the body of her sleeping son covered with a bed sheet. She knew by heart the outline of her son's slim body. As soon as she saw this stretcher with the sheet-draped body, she knew it was the body of her beloved child. She needed to see no more.

7.13 When There Is No Body

If you have lost a loved one under circumstances where there is no body to view or to bury, you may be left with lingering doubts as to whether that person really died, complicating your grief and possibly delaying your recovery. This is the kind of situation one finds after a shipwreck or when an airplane disappears over the ocean. It's what faced the widows of two congressmen whose plane disappeared over the mountains of Alaska many years ago. I remember a couple whose adult child was on an airplane that crashed into the ocean. No bodies were recovered. For years they desperately sought some validation that their child had died and prayed that some identifying piece of clothing or baggage would wash ashore so they would know for sure she had really died. (See section 7.22 on missing persons.)

Of course, this has been the terrible burden borne by the families of military personnel declared missing in action in Vietnam, a burden they have had to carry for decades.

In your case, if there is no body, you may not want to have a memorial service to publicly mourn the loss. You may not want to give up all hope that your loved one could still be alive. Still, you do need to put some closure on this part of your life, and you have the right to have a memorial service when you are ready. Far from an act of disloyalty to the deceased, such a service can help you celebrate your loved one's life and to put closure on your relationship with him or her. You may find family members and friends agreeable to this, but you may find others not yet ready to give up hope. A family meeting can help by allowing everyone to voice their opinions and can be a way of reaching compromises satisfactory to everyone. Don't be offended if some family members or friends elect not to attend. (See section 3.6 on memorial services.)

You can also include in your memorial service a cenotaph, which is a monument erected to honor the memory of someone whose body is elsewhere. It can be placed in a cemetery, if you wish, or on your own property. (See section 3.7 on cenotaphs.) You could also make up a plaque to identify a special tree you have planted in your loved one's memory in a public garden. I know of a family whose loved one was never found after he was lost in the mountains. They contacted the Park Service and obtained permission to construct a shelter to be used by hikers. The name of their loved one is now on a plaque, visible to all who visit the camp.

Building that shelter was a wonderful opportunity for family members and friends to come together for a common cause, to work side by side, and to express their love for the deceased. If you have a similar loss to mourn, you might consider such a project to honor your loved one's memory.

7.14 Secrets Discovered After Death

Often when a person dies the survivors tend to see him or her as some kind of saint. Gone are the realities of life, the arguments, the things that used to annoy others, the "dark side" that each of us has. I have heard eulogies praising the wonderful attributes of a particular person as a wonderful father, as a wonderful husband, as a strong community-oriented person giving freely of himself, when in fact this person was none of these things. In many cases that is the end of the story. But in other cases there is more to come.

When a person dies, it becomes necessary for the family to go through the personal effects left behind. Closets, drawers, and office desks have to be cleaned out so life can go on. And sometimes there are unpleasant surprises. When this happens, grief can become quite complicated. For example:

- Finding divorce papers in your mother's desk drawer. You may have thought that your parents' marriage was their first. Now you may wonder if you have some half-brothers or sisters somewhere. Or you may wonder if your dad is your real biological dad. And surely you will wonder why they didn't tell you and what other secrets they kept from you.

- Discovering that your brother didn't really die at birth but is living in an institution for handicapped children. What do you do? Do you seek this brother out and go see him? Would it be fair to him to know he has a family? Would he be capable of knowing that he has a family? Do you tell others in your family what you have discovered?

- Discovering sexual paraphernalia, membership in certain sex clubs, and subscriptions to pornographic magazines. This happened to a woman while she was at her husband's office removing personal belongings. Because her adult children were with her, she had no chance to decide what to do with this information.

- Learning that your spouse has died while with another lover.

- Finding letters revealing that your spouse had had an affair, or that a child of yours was homosexual, or other secrets.

- Finding evidence that you may have been sexually abused by the deceased when you were a child. In recent years mental health practitioners have found that this aberration is far more common than they had thought. Adults who had blocked these terrible memories as children are seeking help today to address the emotional trauma inflicted on them. If you think that you may have suppressed such memories of the deceased, by all means get professional help, even if the perpetrator is no longer available to be questioned. I do know that support groups are being formed to help you. You should contact your local community mental health center for resources that may be available. (See section 7.17 on conflicted relationships.)

- Learning after the death of a loved one that he or she had been abused by another family member, leaving you feeling guilty for not knowing and dismayed that you did not prevent it. What to do with this information may be something to discuss with another family member, pastor, rabbi, or therapist.

These are only a few examples of what you may find when going through the personal belongings of a loved one. I don't mean to suggest that you should expect anything of a similar nature; most people don't have secrets of this kind. But if you have made such a discovery, I want you to know that you are not alone. Nor should you feel that your life has suddenly lost its luster. You are who you are, regardless of what you have learned about this other person. If you have lived an upright life, you have no reason to feel ashamed because the deceased betrayed you.

Shattered by such a discovery, you will have to sort out your feelings as you move from love, to confusion, to disappointment, to anger, and possibly even to hatred. You may be angry at yourself for ever having grieved for this person. You may feel like a fool for having cared so much. But the one thing you do not want to do is to keep this bottled up inside you. You need to express your anger. Whether you voice this with your family and friends is for you to decide, but you need to discharge it in some harmless way. Depending on the intensity of your anger, you may want to seek the help of a therapist to walk you through it. Others have confronted such disappointments and resolved them; you can, too. (See section 4.4 on anger and rage.)

7.15 "Unacceptable" Relationships

Grief becomes complicated when you are in a relationship that is unacceptable to society and, in particular, to your family and friends, or the family and friends of the deceased. People may feel that you do not have the *right* to grieve, and thus you may be deliberately excluded from all the planning, the funeral, and the burial. Where do you fit in if you were the mistress of a married man who has just died? I know of several people who were told by relatives that they were not to attend the funeral. If you are caught up in such a predicament, you obviously want to express your own grief at the loss of someone you loved. My suggestion is that you plan and carry out your own memorial service to help you say good-bye to your loved one and to put closure on your relationship. (See section 3.6 on memorial services.)

Where do you fit in if the person who died is your ex-wife? Because you are divorced doesn't mean that you won't mourn her death. The good times you had and the children you shared provide a bond that can't ever be totally severed.

Where do you fit in if you are gay and it is your lover in that casket? And his family doesn't know about you, or if they do, they disapprove of your relationship?

Where do you fit in if the deceased is a person with whom you have lived for some years but without benefit of matrimony?

In some of these cases you may not even learn about the death for some time. I know of a woman whose secret lover went home to another state and failed to return two weeks later, when they had planned to meet. She wondered where he was. Had he decided to terminate their affair? Had something terrible happened to him? What should she do? Call his home? Call his office? Read the obituaries in his hometown newspaper? Were there friends she could talk to? In this instance, the worst had happened. Her lover had died, and she was shattered at not being able to say good-bye or even to be able to talk about it. Are we to say that she had no right to feel that way? Of course not. Grief is grief, no matter how it comes about.

There are other problems that stem from these unacceptable relationships. For example, there are unlikely to be any financial benefits for you if your relationship was never made legally "official." No matter that you had invested years, personal sacrifice, and money in the relationship. What keepsakes do you have? There probably are not many, especially pictures, because

197

of the secrecy of your relationship. There are no support groups I know of to meet your needs except a general grief group, but even there you may have to lie a little, because your story could be disturbing to survivors who are harboring doubts about their own spouses. You are, indeed, alone. (See section 6.12 on love relationships.)

Under these circumstances give yourself permission to grieve and consider planning your own memorial service for your loved one, inviting some close friends or family members. I also suggest that you find a grief therapist with whom you can share your pain and your story. You don't want to bear this alone.

7.16 Dependent Relationships

The relationships you have with parents, children, spouses, lovers, and friends take many forms, and these relationships will help determine how you feel when they die. As I review the possibilities, you may see some part of yourself that will help explain why you are feeling the way you are.

Perhaps you spent a lot of time with this other person and saw that person as your best friend and confidante. Perhaps you did almost everything together—even the weekly shopping. Still, you had your own distinct personalities and there were things that you could enjoy separately. This is the kind of relationship that we all might strive for, and you should have no unusual difficulty in resolving your grief.

There are other close relationships that are not so healthy. Possibly you felt that you were part of this other person in some way and that he or she played a key role in determining your own identity. With that person gone, you may not know who you are; you may feel that you're nobody! This other person may have chosen or influenced the selection of your clothes, cooked your meals, paid your bills, selected your friends, shaped your view of the world. You may have been afraid to voice a dissenting opinion, even on something so innocuous as the latest hairstyles. You may have been so involved in this other person's life that you were unable to make simple decisions on your own. As a result, you may be very uncomfortable being by yourself today. You may feel abandoned, lost and alone. You may feel resentment and anger at your loved one for leaving you, and this may make it harder for you to reconstruct your life.

In your grief you may start to look for another family member or friend who can take the place of your loved one—someone who can "care" for you in a similar way because this is the only way you know how to live. Perhaps family members and friends are resisting this role and withdrawing from you, leaving you more hurt and confused.

There are dependent relationships that arise from conditions beyond one's control. These include physical and mental disabilities that leave one person dependent on another for the essentials of life. When the provider of these essentials dies, the dependent person will be faced with intense grief, not only for the loss of a loved one but for the loss of desperately needed support. But I am not talking about that kind of dependency here. What I am talking about is known as a dependent personality disorder. It is a state of mind that will complicate your grief and possibly lead you into new, overly dependent relationships in the future. If you find that any of this applies to the relationship you had with your loved one, or to the way you are feeling now, I think it would be important for you to seek the aid of a therapist who can support you and help you see that you are somebody in your own right—the only person exactly like you in the history of the world! With some reinforcement of your own identity you can resolve your grief and rebuild a life for yourself.

Spouse

Similar dependencies are found in some marriages. If your husband has died and you are having an especially difficult time resolving your grief, it may be that you were also caught up in an overly dependent relationship. You may think of yourself as having been "pampered," but there may have been more to it. There have been many things that you were afraid to do yourself—simple things, like driving into town or doing the banking—and your spouse was always there to do these things for you. I know several examples of working wives being driven to and from work each day by their husbands; some of them didn't even know how to drive. The husbands apparently liked to play this protective role and did nothing to encourage their wives to be more independent. I recall one widow who, protected in this way, had never written a check or filled the car with gas, much less made any of the decisions that demand immediate attention in daily life. She was at first extremely angry at her husband for dying and then later for not helping her prepare for a time when she might be by herself. She looked for other family members who would take over this dominant role, and their unwillingness to do so only made her feel even more angry and isolated.

Sometimes it is the husband who is totally dependent. Surprisingly, this may be a man in the upper reaches of corporate management who the world sees as strong and decisive. At home, it is a different story. His wife is the one who manages the household expenses, buys his clothes and lays them out each night for the next morning, manages their social life, makes all decisions about the children, and plans the family vacations. If this somehow describes you, you may be totally bereft now, wondering how you can face life without her.

Many times people trapped in such dependency will look for a new partner to fill this dominant role in their lives. Often they will remarry or develop a new relationship within a year, to their later regret: They learn quickly that their new partners are not like the old ones and do not fill the roles assigned them. For their part, the new partners usually have a hard time trying to compete with their dead predecessors. If you are considering such a move yourself, I urge that you wait. Give yourself a chance to grow out of such a dependency. Get to know yourself and your strengths. And allow yourself time to grieve for the loved one you have lost; a year is not enough.

Adult Child

Children, of course, are dependent on their parents as they are growing up; this is normal. But adulthood implies independence. Children who remain dependent on their parents after achieving adulthood are often ill prepared to handle life's problems by themselves.

Sometimes a dependent relationship will deprive a child of a chance to succeed as an adult, and when that parent dies, the child will be stricken with intense grief. This might be a son who couldn't seem to hold any job for long and who continued to be treated like a teenager at home, being served his favorite foods and having his clothes lovingly washed by his mother, but also having his freedom restricted by the old house rules. When a parent playing such a protective role dies, the adult child caught in such a dependency not only has to grieve the death of the parent but has to learn how to function on his own as well.

If you are suffering from any variation of what I have been discussing here, you should consider getting professional help. Rushing into a new dependent relationship is not the answer that will lead to future contentment. This may be hard for you to understand right now, but if you will just give yourself such a nudge and make that first appointment with a therapist, you may experience a great spurt of personal growth and find out what a terrific person you really are!

7.17 Conflicted Relationships

Grief will be more complex whenever your relationship to the deceased was marred by conflict. This could be as simple as a single argument or as complicated as continuing tension between you and your loved one. Conflicts occur in all kinds of relationships: between teenagers and parents, between siblings, between lovers, between friends. It is especially unfortunate when death occurs before conflicts are resolved. Recently, a young girl told me after her father's death that the part troubling her the most was the fact that she and her dad had fought a lot. It helped her to share this with someone she trusted and someone who understood her pain. It was a relief for her to learn that it is normal to have conflicts with your parents during your teen years and that these conflicts are usually resolved in time. Because her father died during this time of upheaval, she did not have a chance to work through this period, but at least she knows now that, had he lived, their relationship would have had less conflict.

The same kind of pain arises when a child dies during troubled times. I know of a couple whose seventeen-year-old son was killed in an auto accident. This son had been depressed, unable to concentrate on his studies, often acting out his feelings in behavior that was creating tension in the family. How unfortunate for this couple to be cheated of the opportunity to see their son resolve his problems, to mature and find his place in this world. For the rest of their lives their son will remain an emotionally disturbed seventeen-year-old.

Sometimes a person's grief will be fraught with anger and resentment stemming from violent behavior or sexual abuse on the part of the deceased. Violence can occur in any relationship, and sexual abuse apparently is far more common than we ever imagined. Such offenses are usually well-guarded secrets, carrying with them the burdens of shame and potential embarrassment if others find out. If you are carrying such secrets about a parent, a spouse, or other person who has died, you may feel that you have no one you can talk to. You may hear glowing tributes to the departed and want to cry out, "It's not true. He was a brute!" You may envy others in the family or in your circle of friends who seemingly had loving relationships with the deceased. You may feel that you yourself were somehow to blame for what happened. You may grieve never being able to work out the relationship with your loved one that "could have been." What do you do? I think the most important thing is that you not keep these secrets bottled up in you. Find someone to share them with, whether this is a family member, a close friend, or a therapist. Just getting all this off your chest will provide you some relief and perhaps enable you to see what happened in a broader perspective. It may even enable you to mourn what you have lost: the good memories, the happy times, and the possibility of a better future relationship with that person. (See section 7.14 on secrets discovered after a death.)

These are just a few examples of relationships you may have had with the deceased that will complicate your grief. The more complex the relationship was with your loved one, the more intense your grief will be. Understanding as much as you can about it and about complicated grief will help you to work through it. It will help you to know that the grief you are experiencing is going to be different from that of other family members or friends. It may be a grief that you find impossible to share with others. It may feel unbearable. In cases like this, it may be hard to sit through the funeral or memorial service because of what you know or how you are feeling. It may be hard to play the role of the mourning widow when part of you is saying, "Free at last." My suggestion is to learn as much as you can about grief, apply it to your particular situation, and seek out a therapist who has had experience working with similar cases. Also, you might look for a support group in your community by calling your local community mental health center or noting the Resources in the back of this book.

7.18 Unfinished Business

Whenever there are problems of any magnitude in a relationship and one of those involved dies, there will be unfinished business: arguments not resolved; situations of mental, physical, or sexual abuse not properly terminated; questions not asked or answered; and love not proclaimed. This unfinished business leaves you with no closure on your relationship. You are left dangling with things unsaid, unfinished. You feel restless, unable to grieve as you might wish. Unfinished business with the deceased can hold up your ability to move along in your grief. It is as if, floating down a stream, you are caught on a snag and cannot break loose. Grief becomes complicated as you see others move on, perhaps misunderstanding what is happening to you and withdrawing their support, leaving you in greater pain.

It is important that you resolve this unfinished business and put closure on your relationship with the deceased, either by yourself or with the help, advice, and support of a therapist. Unfinished business can be scary, and if you feel this is more than you can or want to handle by yourself, by all means seek the help of a professional. Working on unfinished business can be simple, or it can be complex and carry a lot of emotion with it. Having someone to assist you can make it less scary. Let's look at how you might get started on unfinished business you had with the person who died.

- Become aware of what your unfinished business is. Is it as simple as not having had a chance to say "I love you" one more time or to say good-bye? Perhaps you have a strong need to apologize for something you said or for a fight you may have had. Do you have a need to confront the deceased on his or her behavior toward you before the death? Get pencil and paper and list everything that was left unfinished when the death occurred.

- Look at that list and think about each of those things listed and about what you could do to get some relief and put some closure on it. Perhaps you could write a letter, make an audio tape, write a song, or paint a picture—whatever you are comfortable with—addressing your unfinished business and stating how you would have wanted it finished. Writing is an excellent tool; you can say everything you want. You can express your frustrations, your fantasies, your hopes. I like letter writing because letters have beginnings and endings. The end is very important when you are trying to put an end to that part of your relationship. Your letter can be placed in the casket with the deceased, providing you with some sense of satisfaction. Often, however, unfinished business is not, or cannot be, dealt with at the time of burial, but instead becomes a problem months or even years after the death. In this case the letter you have written can be buried at the grave site, or, if disposal of the body was by cremation, it can be burned and the ashes scattered or buried. I suggest that you make a copy of the letter in case it could be useful later—perhaps to share with a therapist if you ever decide to go into therapy, or to share with others in the family who may have similar unfinished business. However, it is your original letter that should be buried or burned. You can expect a great deal of emotion as well as relief from letter writing. For some unfinished business, letter writing may follow many sessions of therapy, giving you a chance to work through all the issues you need to and putting the closure on it with the letter. Or you may use your letter to begin your work in resolving your special issues. There are times when writing a letter is all you have to do, and there are other times when writing a letter is only one step in the process.

- If you feel you need to have a "conversation" with the deceased, try putting a picture of him or her in a chair in front of you and talk, yell, scream, or apologize to the picture. When you do this, you may feel that a big burden has been lifted from your shoulders.

7.19 Substance Abuse

If there was a problem of alcohol or drug abuse in the life of the deceased, you may have added issues to deal with. Substance abuse often creates discord within a family that will negatively affect relationships. Given time, your loved one might have gained control over his or her addiction and resolved the problems created by it. Deprived of that time, this person may have died with the problems unresolved, leaving you with conflicting feelings of anger, perhaps, and sorrow, not really knowing how you should feel.

The nature of the substance abuse and the type of problems it creates will vary with each person. Your loved one may have been inclined to drink too much, but it may have been done in such a way that it did not interfere with your life. On the other hand, substance abuse is usually not this benign. Often a family member who has been involved with alcohol or drugs becomes verbally, sexually or physically abusive when under the influence. Paychecks or savings may have been spent on the alcohol or drugs, creating serious problems for the family. In cases like this grief is certain to be complex.

If you are mourning the death of a loved one under such circumstances, think for a moment of the extra issues you have to deal with in addition to the death. Write your issues down so you can look at them, one at a time. Getting them down on paper will help you become more objective about them, and it also will make those issues less powerful and more manageable for you. If you have enlisted the help of a therapist, he or she can be more helpful when you have these particulars clearly in your mind.

It may occur to you or your therapist to bring other family members into the discussion. However, you should not feel hurt if they are not as ready as you are to look at these issues. Everyone has to deal with such issues at his or her own pace. If and when they are ready, they will know that they can come to you to say whatever they have to say on the subject. For additional support contact your local mental health center or substance abuse center to learn if there is an appropriate support group you could attend, such as a support group for the adult children of alcoholic parents.

7.20 Replacement Child

Is it possible to have a grief reaction for someone you never knew? If you are a "replacement" child, someone conceived after the death of a sibling, you may know what I'm talking about. You may be torn by the fact that your parents, never having resolved their grief, keep that loss alive by constantly comparing you to the deceased. They may have expectations of you that would be similar to those placed on the deceased. Throughout your life you may have had reminders that you were alive because your brother or sister died. If you happened to be of the same gender as your dead sibling, your problems may have been greater. His or her clothes may have been saved for you to wear when you grew into them. You may even have been named with some variation of the name of your deceased sibling.

If any of this applies to you, you must have mixed emotions about this mystery sibling, on one hand feeling sorry that he or she died, but on the other hand wishing that he or she had never existed. Ordinarily, you should have little, if any, grief for someone you never met. However, loving your parents and wanting to please them, you may have come to share some of their grief while, at the same time, feeling resentment toward this "perfect" person they talk about endlessly. If you are reading this as an adult and you have been left with doubts about your own worth, I think it would be well for you to get professional help to put your mind at ease. With the advice of a therapist you might yet give your parents an opportunity to show that they love you for yourself.

My point in all this goes beyond what advice I can give a "replacement" child, and that is to discourage grieving parents from rushing to "replace" a child who has died. People can't be replaced. If you have more children, they should be treasured for themselves and not seen as replacements of somebody. The child who died will never walk the earth again, and you do yourself a disfavor by pretending that he or she will. You can't bypass grief in this way; you will merely prolong it.

7.21 Unusual Developments

In addressing this topic of complicated grief, I want to show you how differing circumstances can make your grief more difficult and probably prolong its resolution. If you accept this, you may be more patient with yourself when your grief is slow to lift. Because it's taking longer doesn't mean that it can't be resolved; it means that you have more things to address than someone else in different circumstances. This rule applies to any situation that might arise—even extremely unusual ones.

Some time ago there was a terrible car accident in which two young men were involved. One young man was killed, his body damaged beyond recognition. The other young man was taken to the hospital in critical condition, bandaged from head to toe. One set of parents was notified that their son had died, and a closed casket service was held. The other parents, thankful that their son had survived, were visiting him some days later in the intensive care unit when a remarkable thing happened. Much to their horror, they noticed a mark on the unbandaged foot of their son and suddenly realized that this was not their son but, most probably, the other young man. A dreadful mistake had been made. Imagine the emotional upheaval when the grieving parents realized that they buried their son's friend and that their son was really alive. And imagine the shock of the other parents, who now realized that their son not only was dead but already buried. One doesn't expect to recover quickly from such a devastating experience. Recovery could take months or even years. Needless to say, if your story is anything like this, I urge that you seek out a therapist for help.

Some years ago my husband and I arrived at an island resort and were told in whispers that an American woman sitting in the corner was waiting for some word about her boyfriend, who had disappeared some days earlier while sailing beyond the reef. The rumor was that he had been attacked by sharks and that no body was ever recovered. This woman, without family support, could not leave the island until the police finished their investigation of the matter. Alone in a strange country, she not only had to deal with the uncertainty about her boyfriend's fate and the grief for his possible death, but the rigors of an investigation.

There is no end to the tragic events that can complicate what is already one of life's trials: mourning the death of a loved one. Yet even in the worst of circumstances people somehow have survived such disasters and resolved their grief. I'm sure you can, too.

7.22 Missing Persons

A family I know became worried one evening when their daughter failed to arrive home as scheduled from the university. As hours passed their worry increased, and by the next day they were in a state of panic. Eventually the police issued a missing persons report, but only after the family convinced them that this was not the case of a runaway. Days passed. Then months. No word. No trace of their daughter anywhere.

What do you do in such circumstances? Cling to the hope she is alive? Give up hope and decide she is dead? As agonizing months passed the members of this family saw their hopes wane, yet they couldn't grieve because they couldn't be sure she was dead. They couldn't put any closure on their relationship with her. All their lives were "on hold," in limbo, in a kind of purgatory. One person in the family became active in the investigations. Another went into denial, convincing herself that the missing woman would be found alive. Another refused to talk about it. Conflicts erupted, preventing them from supporting one another. After months of this the support of friends began to diminish. The mother, concluding that her daughter must be dead, began praying that the body would be found so the survivors could move on with their lives. She began following all news stories about the discovery of women's bodies throughout the state and nation. To her even the fact that some unknown assailant was still free began to lose importance compared to her need to know what had happened to her beloved child. What a relief it was when more than a year later the body was discovered in a lake by some fishermen, and the dental records proved that this was her daughter. She and her family could begin to mourn their loss.

In another story, the ending is still in doubt, and the purgatory of not knowing continues after several years! A single mother's young daughter disappeared while the two of them were attending a community Christmas party. Years have passed, and the mystery remains unsolved. Although, for obvious reasons, the mother would like to escape the oppressive confines of this tragic setting, she is afraid to move from her apartment out of concern that her daughter might call or be dropped off one day. This is so even though she probably is convinced that her daughter is dead. Her grief is on hold; her life, in a state of suspended animation.

We see this same suspension of grief in the families of hostages, whose lives hang in the balance at the mercy of terrorists and other desperate people. We see it in the families of servicemen who are missing in action. In some cases these situations stretch out for months or years; the families of servicemen missing in action in Vietnam have had their lives put on hold for as long as two decades because they could not learn the fate of their loved ones. There are few ordeals in human experience worse than this. (See section 7.13 on the absence of a body.)

During such a time of suspended grief there are actually many different losses that have to be put on hold. One is the role that your loved one played in the family. You may have to fill that role yourself. But temporarily or permanently? Unfortunately, life goes on, and decisions have to be made, even though the person who used to make them is not there. Adding to your difficulties, you may find that some or all of your income is cut off and that, lacking knowledge of your loved one's fate, you aren't eligible for death benefits, either. How are you supposed to feel about all this?

If you are in such a state of suspended grief, my heart goes out to you. The only real hope I can provide lies in the knowledge that others have endured such prolonged agonies and survived to live full and rewarding lives. While never forgetting their loved ones, they have been able, finally, to resolve their grief and get on with life.

7.23 How to Help Yourself

Healing takes longer when grief becomes complicated. If you are suffering from a particularly painful loss that will take time to resolve, I urge that you have patience with yourself and not burden yourself with big expectations. Be careful not to overload your workday; take on tasks that seem manageable to you. Information throughout this book will also be helpful as you read the chapters and topics that pertain to your special grief, and especially Chapter 4 on the emotional response to grief.

If you can, inform your friends, family, and coworkers about what has happened. Sometimes your own denial and/or the circumstances of the death may cause you to be uncomfortable with sharing the details. I know that people often find it hard to share details of a death that was caused by AIDS or suicide because of the stigma they carry. Try to let your friends and family know what they can do for you that will help. Encourage them to read this book—especially Chapter 10, "A Friend in Need"—to give them a better understanding of grief. Ask them to tell you how they see you. Do they have any concerns about the way you are acting or not acting? Hear what they have to say, and give it some thought. Are they right? Or do their observations not apply to you?

Talk about the experience if you can. Talk to anyone you are comfortable with. Sometimes it is easier to share personal things with a stranger than a close family member. Talking will give you an outlet for your feelings and save you from the consequences of keeping them bottled up. Talking will also help make your situation more real for you.

Try to relax even if it is for only a short period of time each day. Relaxation tapes will guide you through some simple exercises until you are able to do them on your own; they can be purchased in bookstores or borrowed from a local library. Find a tape that has a soothing voice on it. Women usually enjoy listening to a male voice, and vice versa. There are also environmental CDs and tapes available that play the sounds of birds, wind in the trees, rain falling on the roof, or the ocean surf. You can also relax by doing something each day that you really enjoy, such as reading, sewing, cooking, writing, painting, playing a musical instrument, listening to music, or working crossword puzzles.

As is always true when grieving, it is important to eat as well as you can. Pay careful attention to your diet and try to stay away from the tempting junk foods.

Exercise is another important part of healing. Try to plan a manageable exercise program for yourself—one that you can stick to. If you are planning an exercise program that is strenuous, be sure to consult with your physician before you get started. Find a form of exercise that you enjoy. If you hate it, you will not continue with it. Then think about whether you want to do this exercise with someone else or by yourself. Would joining a health club be the right thing for you? You might ask a friend for advice. There are a number of factors to consider when looking for the right program that will fit into your routine and budget. (See section 9.1 on helping yourself through grief.)

Finally, try to stay involved. Try to continue whatever activities you were pursuing before this crisis began, but not to the extent of being overwhelmed. If there are groups or clubs you belong to, try to continue with them. The structure will be helpful to you and also provide outside contacts and support.

When to Be Concerned

The march of life's events doesn't always provide us with a time to grieve, nor does it always allow us to experience uncomplicated grief. At times these events, circumstances, and surprises pile up, becoming overwhelming burdens. The circumstances of death can be brutal, unlike the romantic deaths we sometimes read about in novels or see in the movies. The shock that accompanies unexpected, violent death can be so strong that our bodies want to collapse from its weight.

You may find that many months after the death of your loved one your grief is more intense than ever. You may be experiencing some of the following symptoms:

- recurring recollections of the death that are disrupting your work, home life, and leisure time
- recurring nightmares of the event
- flashbacks and hallucinations
- intense anxiety whenever you hear of a similar event
- avoidance of any feelings or thoughts concerning the death
- avoidance of any activities or situations that would remind you of the death
- preoccupation with the death many months after it occurred
- overidealization of the deceased and of your relationship that continues for too long a time and too intensely
- lack of recall; blank spots in your memory
- a significant decrease in your interest in normal activities either at home or at work

- depression combined with increased feelings of sadness, loneliness, and hopelessness
- detachment and withdrawal from other people in your life
- feelings of "survivor guilt" and wishes that you could have died, too; perhaps self-destructive or self-defeating behavior
- inability to experience emotions, to feel happy, or to love someone
- avoidance of all intimate relationships out of fear that you will be left alone again
- being overwhelmed with emotions—tense, angry, scared, and out of control
- feeling that you have no future, unable to marry or have children, unable to carry on a career
- problems with alcohol or drug abuse
- new problems, not previously experienced, in falling or staying asleep, or, conversely, sleeping too much.
- irritability or outbursts of anger directed at your children, spouse, or coworkers
- difficulty in concentrating on things you usually enjoy such as reading, music, or simple daily tasks
- difficulty in concentrating on your work, interfering with your performance
- inability to relax, constantly expecting something bad to happen, rushing home to see if everything is all right
- being easily startled, jumping at any unusual or loud noise
- physical symptoms such as cold sweat, rapid heartbeat, or shortness of breath whenever you are reminded of the death

Many of these symptoms are normal, and you may not need to be concerned about them; they will probably disappear in a few days or few weeks. However, these symptoms can be problematic and may need to be monitored. If you are experiencing such symptoms and you feel that they are going on too long, I suggest that you seek some professional counseling to check yourself out. This is particularly the case if you have been dwelling at all on the possibility of harming yourself. (See section 4.6 on depression.)

Also, if you are experiencing several of these symptoms and they have been evident for a month or so, and if it has been six or more months since the death, it's time that you saw a professional therapist to evaluate you. The trauma you experienced could have been so devastating that you could be suffering from something called posttraumatic stress disorder. Often referred to as PTSD, this disorder can develop when a person has experienced an event that is outside his or her range of coping. It is a normal emotional and psychological response to a painful, shocking experience. It can be caused not only by a death but by other events as well, such as war experiences, violent personal attacks, rapes, threats to one's life or the life of a loved one, natural disasters, or witnessing scenes of horror.

Professional therapists are becoming more aware of the effects of complicated grief and can help you evaluate whether or not you need special help. Find someone who is trained in PTSD; your local mental health center can help you find the right therapist. Just knowing more about posttraumatic stress can help you understand why you may be having some of these problems and, in turn, make you more patient with yourself. If you need further help, the therapist can guide you through your recovery, offering you caring and support every step of the way. Your recovery will be much quicker, and you will gain growth and a deeper understanding of yourself. (See the Bibliography for a book on complicated mourning.)

Chapter 8

UNRESOLVED CHILDHOOD GRIEF AND TRAUMA

Looking for the Causes of Those

Obsessions and Fears That Often

Shape Our Lives

I didn't kill my father!" George announced as he burst into my office. "I didn't kill my father!" I could almost feel his sense of relief. He plopped himself into a chair and began to talk. The dam had burst, and tears began to flow.

For more than thirty years George had been carrying a burden of undefined guilt. He believed that, as a child of four, he had done some vague thing that had resulted in his father's death. He never knew what it was that he supposedly had done; all he knew was that he had this terrible sense of guilt that weighed on him constantly. As I heard George's story in earlier sessions it had become apparent to me that this was not a case of Oedipus in the nursery; his father had died of a heart attack. What was plaguing George was unresolved childhood grief. As a child he had never had an opportunity to express his grief or to get answers to his nagging questions. He finally realized that there was no basis for his guilt feelings. As he sat there I could see that he was putting this obsession behind him and, for the first time, would be able to look at himself in the mirror without seeing a murderer staring back.

Through the years I have worked with many adults who have been plagued by such obsessions stemming from early death experiences. In some cases the cause is unresolved grief; in others it is death-related trauma.

8.1 What Is Unresolved Childhood Grief?

Unresolved childhood grief is the state in which an adult, having suffered the death of a loved one while a child, remains trapped somehow in the mind-set of that child because of failure to resolve his or her grief.

In my experience the principal reason that children grow to adulthood without resolving their grief over the death of loved ones is that parents fail to realize how important it is for their children to mourn these deep, personal losses. They fail to include them in funeral planning, and at the same time they give their children absurd explanations for what has happened. Even if they are very young, children are entitled to be told the truth;

falsehood is not the foundation for mental or emotional health at any age.

As you can see from the stories that follow, unresolved grief in children can lead to problems as adults, sometimes not too serious, and sometimes major, long-term emotional handicaps. If you are more troubled than you think is normal when approaching the subject of death, or if you have problems forming and maintaining relationships, or if you still have strong feelings of guilt and/or anger whenever you think about the death of someone you loved, you may be suffering from unresolved childhood grief.

Ideally children are told what has happened when a death occurs in the family. They are included in family discussions, wakes, funerals, and burials, and they grow up experiencing death as part of life. On the other hand, there are many adults today who as children were left in the dark about such matters, seemingly protected from harsh reality but in fact made victims of it. Having nothing more to go on than snatches of adult conversations and glimpses of strange goings-on, and lacking rational explanations for the personal losses they themselves have suffered, these children often grow to adulthood with suppressed fears and fantasies that shape their adult lives.

There are still many people who believe that young children don't mourn and that they quickly forget unpleasant things. Some parents find death such a difficult subject to talk about that they can't bring themselves to discuss it with their children, putting it on a par with sex. Whenever the name of the deceased comes up, they change the subject. Left out of all such discussions and rituals, children must draw their own conclusions, often far worse than the reality from which they are being shielded: "If it's so awful that Mom and Dad can't talk about it, it must *really* be awful."

• • •

8.2 No Detour Too Long to Avoid a Cemetery

For some twenty years a man whom I will call Ralph went to great lengths to avoid seeing or passing near a cemetery, all because of the way he was kept in the dark about the death of two grandfathers, each of whom had spent his last night in the boy's bedroom and then disappeared from his life, never to be seen again, alive or dead.

"I got to the point," he told me, "that if I saw a funeral procession coming, I would go the other way. Or if there was a cemetery and I had to go fifty miles out of my way to avoid it, I would."

How did this come about? Ralph was nine years old when one of his grandfathers had a stroke and came to live with his parents. The day he arrived, he was given Ralph's room. "I didn't know what was going on. They let us go up there, but we weren't allowed to stay in the room with him," he said.

The next morning Ralph went upstairs and asked to see his grandfather, only to be told that he was gone, that he was dead, and that "he's with God now."

Ralph said he cried for hours. Looking out the back door, he imagined that he saw his grandfather and bolted out the door to greet him. But when he reached the spot where he thought he had seen his grandfather, there was no one there.

The answers given Ralph by his parents and their minister didn't satisfy him. "I was very belligerent and angry," he told me. "My attitude was, 'You're telling me that God is good. But last night my grandfather was here, and today he's not. If God is good, why did He do that?'"

Neither Ralph nor his sisters were allowed to attend the wake or funeral or to see their grandfather's body. He simply had disappeared from their lives. Left to his own fantasies and fearing a similar fate, Ralph refused thereafter to sleep in the bed where his grandfather had died. His parents had to buy him a new bed. Then, two years later, his other grandfather was brought there "not feeling well," was assigned to Ralph's bedroom, and the same thing happened! "We woke up in the morning," Ralph told me, "and Grampy was gone!" He also had died and been taken away during the night. The same explanation was given.

As before, the children never saw their grandfather again. "No wake, no funeral, nothing," he said.

Ralph wondered, "What am I doing to these people?" It gave him a creepy feeling, making him worry about sleeping in his own bedroom. Having been told in Sunday school that God punishes wrongdoing, he wondered what his grandfathers were being punished for and what he needed to do to save himself from such punishment.

When Ralph was sixteen, his fifteen-year-old dog was taken to the veterinarian's office to die by injection. Learning of this, Ralph went to the animal hospital to see his dog, but he was too late. He was given the dog's collar, still warm, but was not allowed to see his dog or to say good-bye to him. He told me that he spent six hours driving aimlessly, crying and screaming about what had happened. For the third time, someone or something he loved had been taken from him without his having a chance to say good-bye.

While another child might have started searching cemeteries for his lost grandfathers, Ralph's reaction to these events was to avoid cemeteries altogether. This may have been a way of denying the reality of his grandfathers' deaths or it may have stemmed from feelings of terror prompted by the mysterious way in which death had struck those he loved.

Now in his late thirties, Ralph is no longer afraid of cemeteries after getting to the source of his fears. He even knows now why it was that his parents "protected" him and his sisters the way they did: Their mother had had a traumatic death experience when she was a girl. As a result of his insights, Ralph took his young children to the hospital some years ago when his last grandparent, a grandmother, was dying—but only after asking them if they wanted to go and after explaining why their great-grandmother would look different from what they remembered.

His mother, learning of this plan, became upset and urged him not to do it. "I told her I was not going to have my kids go through what I did," he told me. The children agreed they wanted to go, and the visit was a memorable one for them. "The kids went up to her and stroked her and asked a lot of questions," he said.

As this last grandparent was dying, Ralph was able to tell her it was okay for her to die. She was ninety-three, and she had had several strokes. She died the next morning.

8.3 Ten Years of Not Talking About It

A legal secretary I will call Betty is still grappling with the shock, sadness, and guilt that engulfed her as a fourteen-year-old when her mother died of a cerebral hemorrhage. All of these years she had no one to talk to about it. Her mother's death occurred while her mother was away visiting her own mother and after leaving her daughter at the airport in a rush, forgetting to say good-bye. To this day there is no family member Betty can talk to about it.

As days passed into weeks following the death, this young girl was forced into a kind of parental role, "protecting" her father and grandmother, who seemed helpless after the mother's death. A decade later, she continues to play that role for them. Beginning in the first crucial days after her mother's death and continuing into her adulthood, there has been a conspiracy of silence on the subject. From the outset, she told me, "I couldn't talk to Daddy. I didn't want to upset him, and I couldn't deal with his being upset. So instead of talking about it, I sort of avoided it."

I asked her if she had ever discussed her mother's death with her maternal grandmother, who had been with her mother at the time of the death. "You don't talk to Grandma about this kind of thing," she said. "I'd never think of talking to her about it."

To Betty it is as though her closest relatives want to pretend that her mother had never existed. Even keepsakes are forbidden subjects. The only ones Betty has—a few pictures and a necklace—are things she had to "steal." Eventually Betty's father got around to disposing of some of his late wife's personal belongings, yet he was still so preoccupied with his own grief that, even after ten years, he was unwilling to give his daughter an opportunity to select a few keepsakes for herself.

When Betty was nineteen, she attended a funeral for a great-aunt and, thinking she heard the minister intone the name of her mother, went into hysterics. "They didn't know what to do with me," she told me, "so they threw me into the car and said I couldn't go to the cemetery."

Today Betty is functioning well as an adult, but for years she carried the enormous weight of unresolved grief. She had great voids in her memory, and much of her childhood is blotted out. Every year on her mother's birthday she had to leave work, once three days early, and this was ten years after the death! With the help of a therapist she eventually was able to resolve her grief, but she endured more than a decade of anguish that could have been avoided.

8.4 The Girl Whose Father Killed Himself

Victoria was thirteen when she and her brother watched from an upstairs window as a rescue squad carried their father away on a stretcher. What had happened they did not know, nor did their mother tell them. Finally a neighbor told them that their dad had shot himself. Not wanting to believe that her father was dead, Victoria remembers waiting for him to come back and wishing for this so hard that she imagined she could actually hear his car drive up to the house. She remembers searching for him in crowds of people, desperately wanting to find him. For ten years she dreamed of his coming back to her.

At the same time she was embarrassed and ashamed as she became known as "the girl whose father killed himself." She told me that she has been depressed much of her life and that she has low self-esteem, problems with personal relationships, and fear of rejection.

Ten years after her father's death she was finally able to acknowledge that he was really gone and to cry for the first time. She realizes now that, in important ways, she has never grown up; she has been caught in a time warp. With the help of a therapist she is beginning to address the grief she carried so long without resolution.

8.5 A Not-So-Funny Joke

Forty years ago, when it was common to have wakes in people's homes, a four-year-old girl named Teresa sat on her father's lap as friends gathered in the family living room to pay their last respects to her grandfather, whose body lay in a casket near the bay window. When she fell asleep in her father's arms, he laid her down gently on the sofa, where she awakened hours later. Finding herself alone with the body of her dead grandfather, she became hysterical. This frightening episode has remained engraved on her memory ever since, made all the more disturbing by the lightness with which her family treated the incident.

The little girl's understandable fright became a family joke, the subject of repeated gibes. Cousins delighted in scaring her, putting on white sheets and jumping out at her from hiding places. The story of her experience was frequently recounted and became the subject of many laughs through the years. It was all very funny—except to Teresa, who was so affected by all this that when her father lay dying years later, she could not bear to remain at his side. She had to get away, to remove herself from the site of death, and now she feels that she abandoned her father. The same problem occurs when she tries to attend funerals. With the help of a therapist she is beginning to resolve this childhood experience, but it will take time.

8.6 Problems in the Making

Recently I received a phone call from a therapist regarding a teenage client of his who, ten years earlier as a young girl, saw her mother drown in a lake as she watched helplessly. She has never been able to work beyond the image she saw that day. After all this time most people would be able to think about a loved one, even after a tragic death, and remember happier times. Not so this young woman, who, because she has not resolved her grief, can only see her mother's frightened face and hear her calls for help. Her memory of that day obscures all other memories she has of her mother. I don't know what opportunities she had as a younger child to mourn her mother's death, but I suspect that more could have been done at the time to help her. Fortunately, she sought out a therapist to deal with seemingly unrelated problems, and he was able to identify this history as a possible contributing factor. Whether or not it contributed to her larger problems, the two of them are continuing to work on her obviously unresolved childhood grief and trauma.

Another child whom I saw recently would be a concern of mine if her parents did not pursue therapy for her. This is a toddler, whom I will call Anne, whose grandmother died. This grandmother was more like a mother to her, as she cared for the child while Anne's mother worked. After the grandmother died, Anne was moved into the grandmother's bedroom. This apparently is very upsetting to her, as she screams inconsolably every night. Anne is also a very angry child, breaking and throwing whatever she can reach. She tells her mother that she, Anne, is to blame for the grandmother's death.

I spent time talking to Anne about why her grandmother died. I told her that her grandmother had been very, very sick and that it was the sickness, not Anne, that made her die. I was also careful to explain that the illness that Grandma had was very different from the colds and flu that Anne may experience.

Later, talking further to Anne's mother, I learned that while Anne was viewing her grandmother's body at the church she had been told that her grandmother was only sleeping and that she would be going away to live with Jesus because Jesus loved her so much. I told her mother that this might explain why Anne didn't want to sleep, either in her grandmother's room or elsewhere, as she might be afraid that she, too, would die and have to leave all those she loves. I said this also might explain why she hits, throws, and breaks things; she may not want Jesus to love her too much!

Anne's nightly screaming spells have caused so much disruption in the family that she has been told there may be dire consequences if she continues: namely, that others in the house could get sick and die as well. This is a serious situation that needs prompt correction. How fortunate it is that Anne's mother realized that something was wrong and sought timely help.

8.7 What Is Death-Related Trauma?

There are other experiences children have that contribute to similar long-term obsessions, even though they are not necessarily linked to grief. These are traumatic events associated with death such as discovering a dead body, seeing someone being killed, witnessing a suicide, or being forced as a small child to kiss the cold face of a dead relative. With thoughtful parental support and prompt therapy all such experiences could be resolved, but the lack of such support has left many grown children plagued with obsessions and fears. If, as a child, you suffered through such an event and received little or no support at the time, you could be living with something very similar to unresolved grief: death-related trauma. This disturbing memory may have faded by now yet left you with some irrational fear or an obsession you can't explain. It could even have affected your outlook on life and your ability to enter into relationships with others.

An extreme case of such trauma is that of Chris Sizemore, the Virginia woman whose life was recounted in the book and movie, *The Three Faces of Eve*[6] and her own book, *I'm Eve*.[7] The first incident that she says may have led to her multiple personalities was observing the body of a dead man being dragged from a river. Coming as it did at a critical point in her childhood, this frightening episode caused her to pretend that it was someone else who had seen this terrible thing. While all experiences of this kind do not lead to such extreme consequences, her story nevertheless illustrates how certain death experiences can lead to long-term trauma.

If you have been carrying such a memory and it continues to prey upon your mind, I urge that you get professional help to find some suitable resolution. On the other hand, if your experience and its effects were less severe, you may gain some help from the suggestions that follow.

8.8 Why Review Such Painful Memories?

You may be wondering why you would want to dredge up such painful memories. What good would this do? Won't it simply

---

[6]Thigpen, Corbett H. *The Three Faces of Eve*. New York: McGraw-Hill, 1957.
[7]Sizemore, Chris. *I'm Eve*. New York: Doubleday, 1977.

make you feel bad or frightened or angry all over again? Yes, it may. But that is what the grieving process is all about: facing up to your grief or your trauma and resolving it. Until you do this you will be left with all the unpleasant consequences that we call unresolved grief or unresolved trauma.

Let us suppose that all your life you have had a fear of abandonment. That's pretty serious. Wouldn't you like to rid yourself of that fear? Wouldn't it be nice to be able to give your love to someone without having to hold back in some way because you are afraid that person will vanish from your life? Wouldn't it be nice to be able to attend a funeral or visit a dying friend in the hospital? Wouldn't it be nice to be free of the undefined guilt you feel about the death of some loved one so long ago? Wouldn't it be nice to purge yourself of the feeling of being defiled by some ghastly memory?

If you had a death experience as a child that has left you with such emotional scars, you *can* get relief, however belated, just as many formerly troubled adults I know have done. However, because this business has remained unfinished for such a long time it may take time and patience to resolve. No matter how long it takes, it will be time well spent.

As you work on your unresolved grief or trauma you will learn to do things differently. Your vocabulary may change; your reactions to certain events may change; your ways of coping may change. How long this takes will vary with the intensity of the experience that cast this long shadow on your life. I know of cases where relief came quickly with the discovery of some unknown fact that cleared up a mystery. In other cases, however, it has taken months or even years to resolve long-suppressed grief or trauma. While I don't know what your situation is, if you think you may be harboring such suppressed emotions, I strongly urge that you begin to address them. You have nothing to gain by waiting any longer to rid yourself of these phantoms.

• • •

8.9 Where Do You Start?

If you feel that you may be struggling with unresolved grief or trauma from your childhood, I would like to help you look into your past. Then, if you conclude that you are carrying such a burden, I have some suggestions on ways to resolve it.

You may feel that you can work on this alone with the help of family and friends, or you may seek out help from a professional who is knowledgeable about the grieving process, especially that of children. The reason this is important is that the death experience you are exploring is one that happened when you were a child. Even though you have grown up and are now an adult, the little boy or little girl feelings stemming from that experience were put away somewhere and did not grow up with the rest of your mind and body. The emotions you may feel as you work on your childhood grief may feel like the emotions of a child. Don't let this frighten you, as it is normal and can play an important part in your recovery. However, the reassurance of a therapist you trust will be helpful to you.

Gathering Information

The death you experienced as a child may be dim in your memory. You may remember only bits and pieces of the event, and some of these memories may be incorrect. It may even be hard to separate what you remember from what you have been told over the years or what you have imagined. The following guide will help you refresh your memory and identify what other information you may need to gather from family and friends. Along the way it may enable you to flag any elements, such as family rituals or customs, that could have played some part in suppressing your grief or prolonging your trauma. You may be able to fill in many of the blanks on this guide, or you may find that you really don't remember much at all. If so, you may need to consult with others to fill in the blank spots of your memory.

8.10 Finding the Source of Your Grief

First, let's take a look at who you are and how you were brought up. The answers to some of these questions may begin to explain why your grief or trauma has been bottled up all these years.

1. When you were young, how did your family talk about the subject of dying and death?
2. Was your social background urban or rural?
3. What is your ethnic background?
4. What were your religious views then? What are they now?
5. As a child, what did you believe happened to people when they died? What do you believe today?
6. As a child, what family rituals were played out at the time of death?
7. What family customs were important at the time a loved one died?
8. What family superstitions pertained to illness and/or to death?

Early Death Experience

In this part you are seeking information on that problematic death experience to gain a better understanding of what happened and how the adults responded to you and your reactions. If your death experience was particularly traumatic or painful, be aware that this questionnaire could bring back scary memories to you. In that case, it may be advisable to have the help of a therapist before you start.

1. How old were you at the time?
2. Who died, and what was your relationship to the person

229

who died? Was this person especially important to you?

3. How much attention did you get from the adults around you? Did they give you a chance to mourn your loss? Did they ignore your concerns? Did they pretend that this death meant nothing to you? Did you feel angry and rejected? Did you feel depressed? How long did this last? Do you still feel that way?

4. How old was the person who died, and what, if any, significance did this have?

5. What was the cause of death? Was it expected? Was it sudden? Was it violent? How much did you know at the time?

6. What fears did this death generate in you? Were they well based or the result of childhood fantasies? What did you think would happen to you? Were they borne out in any way? Did you discuss them with anyone? Were they dismissed or laughed at? How have they affected you through the years?

7. How did you find out about the death? Were you present at the time of death? Did you witness the death? Did you overhear hushed conversations and draw half truths? Were you told abruptly by family members and left on your own to process it? What did you do? Where did you go? What did you think? How did you feel? Who did you talk to? Was there any part of it that you felt you had to keep secret? Are you still carrying that secret? What parts of this discovery of the death remain with you in your adult life?

8. Did this death involve police investigations? How did you feel about that? How do you feel about it today?

9. What were you told about the death? Do you still have unanswered questions? Do you trust the information given to you as true, or was there information kept from you? Can you trust people today?

10. Were you given a choice about attending the viewing, funeral, and burial? Did you want to attend, or were

you taken there against your wishes? How do you feel about attending these rituals today?

11. Were you prepared for what you might experience at the viewing and/or funeral?

12. What memories do you have of the viewing and/or funeral? Was there anything about it that bothered you? What feelings can you remember? How did you behave? How do you feel about the way you behaved? Is there anything about this that makes you feel guilty, ashamed, embarrassed, or angry?

13. What do you remember about the burial at the cemetery? Again, were you prepared? What feelings can you remember and how did you react? How do you feel now about the way you reacted?

14. Try to remember as much detail as possible about the death, funeral, and burial. What stands out in your mind? If there are blank spots, try to find someone who can help you fill in the gaps.

15. How did the adults act? Could they show their emotions? Were they stoic? Did they encourage or discourage you to show emotions? What are some significant things you can remember that they may have said to you during this time?

16. What followed? Were people aware of your continuing problems, or did you have to keep them bottled up inside you? Did your parents or other family members offer to help you, or did they make things worse by complaining about your changed attitude? Did you have anybody to talk to? Did you receive any therapy?

17. What was it like for you to return to school? Were teachers and classmates told? If so, what were they told, and was it helpful to you? Were you treated differently? What changes, if any, occurred in your schoolwork? What changes, if any, occurred in your circle of friends and classmates?

18. If you were quite young, did you return to bed wetting,

thumb sucking, baby talk, or other regressive behavior? If so, how long did this last? Has any variation of this pattern, such as intense sibling rivalry, persisted in your adult life?

19. When you think of this experience, what is the first thing that comes to your mind?

20. What was the worst part about your experience? What are you least likely to discuss with others? What is buried the deepest?

21. Did you have nightmares? For how long? Do you still have them? Are they the same nightmares?

22. Do you feel responsible for the death? Why? Is there any validity to this?

23. What feels unfinished for you?

24. What changes would you make with this death experience if you could do it over?

8.11 Other Things to Look For

Having started this exploration with the questionnaire in the last section, you may want to apply some other tests to see if you really are carrying unresolved grief or trauma from your childhood:

- This may be a difficult question to answer, but it does give you something to start thinking about. What part of your early death experience do you bring with you to your adult life now whenever you experience a loss, death, or even a major change in your life?
- How do you feel when talking about your early death experience now? Are you comfortable with it or do you feel a lot of emotion welling up?
- What carryover fears about death and burial do you still experience now as an adult? For example, do you avoid

visiting a seriously ill person or going to funerals or cemeteries?
- Are you able to visit the grave of the person who died so many years ago?
- Are you able to speak of the deceased, or do you become fearful or tearful even though many years have passed since the death?
- Do you use alcohol and/or drugs to avoid dealing with dying or death?
- Do you fear getting close to people because of a fear of being abandoned?
- Are you overprotective of your children, fearing that one of them may be injured or killed?
- Do you obsess on the topic of death?
- How do you react around young children regarding the topic of death? Would you like to change some of these reactions?
- Do you experience physical reactions like sweating or increased heartbeat whenever the topic of death comes up?
- Are you overly fearful about your own death?
- When you think of the person who died, do you remember happy times or do you think only of a body in a casket?

As you explore these questions, their implications may start to become clear to you. For example, if you are terribly fearful about death, you probably know that this is not normal. Although people don't normally relish the prospect of their own death or the death of loved ones, they don't agonize about it either. They face it when they have to. They don't obsess about it. Also, if you live your life constantly anxious without really knowing what you are anxious about, you may come to realize that this is based on the death experience you have left unresolved since childhood. Similarly, if you have problems in developing close relationships because of the fear of abandonment, you probably know that this is not normal. Ridding yourself of this obsession could make your life much richer. (See section 7.23 on when to be concerned.)

8.12 Restarting the Grief Process

Let's now turn to ways in which you can restart the grief process that was arrested so long ago. It need not be an arduous undertaking unless the grief or trauma is intense, in which case I urge that you get professional help. Here are some simple things you can do right now.

Recording Your Recollections

Using a tape recorder or journal, record the things you remember about this early death experience. This will help you reconstruct what happened and, quite possibly, provide a record to be shared with other family members. It will also be valuable in case you decide to consult a therapist at a later date. If you decide to share your story with other family members, you may be surprised to discover that others remember certain things differently; they might even be able to correct certain details that go to the heart of your grief or trauma.

Books

Read a book on the grieving process in children. (See the Bibliography.) What you want is information that relates to the age you were when this death occurred. You can't assign adult feelings to that special child within you; the feelings you must address are the feelings of that child who never resolved the grief or trauma of that death experience. Reading about childhood grief can help you understand why these feelings, arrested for all these years, need to be released.

Healing Old Wounds

This could be as simple as attending a funeral or burial of a distant relative or friend with the purpose of reliving that earlier death experience and making it come out right. As you attend this funeral, let yourself think back to that important death of long ago and feel those feelings. Bring flowers or whatever you would have done then to make that funeral meaningful. (See sections 3.2 and 3.6 on planning a funeral or memorial service.) Since this could be a very emotional time with sobs and tears, you might want to sit near a door so you can slip out if necessary. Also, you might want to have a friend with you who knows what is going on and who can support you. Afterwards, find time with your friend or a therapist to review how it went. What feelings did you have? What questions remain unanswered? Did it help you to understand what it was like for you as a child when this person died? Are some of the pieces of the puzzle beginning to fall into place? Did it give you some relief? Do you feel better?

Depending on your talents and abilities, you might consider one or more of the following techniques to come to grips with your unresolved grief or trauma.

Writing

Even if you do not feel that you are an accomplished writer, the act of writing down your experience can be very helpful. Writing is a good way to get feelings out. You take them from inside yourself and put them down on the paper in front of you. Also, writing helps you to be more objective about what has happened, making it easier to see where the trouble spots are. You can look at those areas and rework them. I suggest that you write down what happened long ago and then what you wish had happened. In doing so you will be resuming the mourning process that has been awaiting its resolution all this time.

Letter Writing

Many times when there is unresolved grief there is unfinished business with the deceased. In a symbolic way letter writing can be a useful way to finish some of this business. You might try writing to the person who died. Tell her or him all the things you wish you had done or said so long ago but, for one reason or another, you didn't do. Tell this person what you are doing today and why you wish that he or she could be here now. Talk about memories, the good and the not so good. If there is unfinished business between you and the deceased, this is a way to lay it to rest, and it is a way to say good-bye. This will be the hardest part of the letter because good-byes are always hard. Don't be surprised if you find tears welling up. Make a copy of this letter and save it for yourself, but take the original, conduct your own ritual, and then bury it or burn it. The feelings and tears that well up will be the very same feelings and tears that have been suppressed all this time. When you're finished, you should have some closure on that part of your life and new peace of mind. (See section 7.18 on unfinished business.)

Drawing

Like writing, drawing is an excellent tool to help you resolve grief or trauma. You use it in the same way that you use the written word, substituting pictures for words. Your drawing does not have to qualify as art. Even stick figures will work fine. What you draw is what counts, not how well you draw it. Draw the part of that death or funeral that is still giving you problems, and do a second drawing "making it right." I have used this approach with grieving people of all ages. You may be amazed at how helpful it is in starting to put closure on your grief.

• • •

Funeral Home and Cemetery Visits

If that early experience has left you fearful of funeral homes and cemeteries, you might consider going to these places when there hasn't recently been a death, simply to exorcise this spirit from your mind. As you approach the funeral home or cemetery gate, try to get in touch with what you are thinking and feeling. Approach it slowly. Whenever it seems more than you can handle, stop there and wait for another day, when you can proceed further. Have a trusted friend or therapist along to support you and help plan the next visit, if that is necessary. Add this experience to your journal if you are keeping one. It will contribute to your healing.

Symbolic Burial

If something about that original funeral and burial was either flawed or traumatic for you, or if you weren't otherwise able to say a final good-bye to that person, you may want to consider a symbolic burial now. This would provide you an opportunity to recreate that early death experience and make it right, the way you feel it should have been done so many years ago. You could plan this one to make it as meaningful as possible for you. However, symbolic burials can produce very strong feelings and need to be thought out slowly and carefully. Once again, it would be a good idea to discuss this with a professional before you proceed.

There are several ways to approach this symbolic burial:

- You will need something symbolic of your deceased loved one to bury. It could be a picture. It could be something that represented this person's life such as a flower, a book, an article of clothing, or a letter written by you. This might be the one you just wrote to say good-bye and finish whatever business there was between you. If your loved one was cremated, I would suggest that you burn the letter after having made a copy and bury the ashes.

- The container you use for the burial can be anything you feel appropriate, from a highly decorated box to an envelope.

- In planning this event consider if you want to invite others to your symbolic burial. Would they be comfortable, or would they feel that they were indulging you? Perhaps you will want only one or two other special friends or relatives to share this private ritual. One might be your therapist. However, I don't advise your doing this all by yourself as you could find some powerful emotions coming to the surface; you may feel the way you would if the death had been very recent instead of long ago. Having someone there to give you support is important.

- Next you will want to choose where this should take place. It could be at the gravesite, in your backyard, in the mountains, or at a beach. Find some place that feels right to you.

- There are some pastors and rabbis who recognize the importance of such delayed observances and will be willing to help you if you want this to be religious in nature.

- What kind of ceremony do you want? It's fine to have meaningful readings or special music. If others are there, you might invite them to speak. You're in charge. Do you want a record of this service, either taping it on a cassette tape or using a video camera? If it's at the gravesite, you may want to write messages on a helium-filled balloon and loft it toward the heavens. (Because of environmental concerns, use only one balloon.)

- When it's time to bury your symbolic casket or to spread the ashes, don't be alarmed if tears flow freely. That's what is supposed to happen at burials. You will be releasing feelings that have been locked up for a long time. Let them go!

- After the service, as after all funerals, it will be good to spend some time with those who have attended your burial service to talk about the significance of what has happened. This will be a time for you to thank them for attending and to relax a bit after a highly emotional experience. If there were members of your family and other friends present, this will give them an opportunity to offer you their love and support. Sharing a meal or refreshments would be a fine idea. This symbolic burial can be a bonding experience for all of you.

When to Be Concerned

There are certainly different degrees of unresolved childhood grief and trauma. Some experiences can be resolved simply by clearing up misconceptions of what happened when you were a child. Others are very traumatic and emotionally powerful and will be frightening to you as you take yourself back to that unhappy time. It is always appropriate to talk with a therapist who can help you decide how to proceed.

You should be concerned if the emotions you are feeling seem overwhelming to you or if you start to have nightmares or flashbacks. If your experience from years ago has left an obvious mark on your self-image or on the way you relate to others, get help; don't try to work this out all by yourself. If you continue to be plagued by the spectre of something you experienced as a child, this is more than you can handle on your own; get help.

Be concerned, too, if you are becoming depressed and you can't shake it, or if this early death experience is creating problems for you in your relationships at home or at work. If you are overwhelmed, slow down with your research and find the support you need to proceed. (See section 7.23 on how to help yourself.)

As you work on your early death experience you should experience a new freedom. Whether the burden you have carried was light or heavy, you should start to feel better about yourself and about those around you, recognizing, perhaps, that you live in an imperfect world where mistakes are made, where people are forgiven, and where life somehow adjusts itself to the spectacle of death.

Chapter 9

THE ROAD TO
RECOVERY

When Will You Know You're Getting

Better?

If you are suffering the agonies of grief, you may be asking yourself, "When will I recover?" There is no simple answer to your question because, in part, the definition of recovery will vary from person to person. However, I suggest that you reflect on the goals you have set for yourself: what you feel should take place so you can recover. Are your expectations realistic? Do you expect never to feel some sadness for your loved one? Do you expect to return to life exactly as it was before the death? Do you expect never to feel the need to cry again? If your answer to any of these questions is yes, you probably know that you're being unrealistic.

While I can't tell you when you will recover from your grief, I can assure you that people *do* recover. And while some sadness will always be there, the tears and grief will become more manageable as you integrate them into your life and live with them. I do know that the intense pain of early grief goes away after a while, leaving an ache that will also subside. I know countless people who have had to endure shocking, devastating losses and yet have gone on to live happy and productive lives.

I know that, like them, you can develop a life for yourself again, different as it may be from what you knew before. All of life's experiences change us, including those that involve pain and suffering. Out of this loss you can experience personal growth, and you can become more sensitive to the needs of others. Your priorities in life may change with less attention paid to material things and more to relationships and the world around you.

The process of grief takes time. It requires work and patience, not only on your part but on the part of those around you. Healing doesn't happen all at once but in bits and pieces as you reconstruct your life. Because it is slow, healing is often not recognized. I remember when my husband was dying, I kept a journal of my feelings on a tape recorder. Listening to it one day, I was surprised at the tone of my voice. I heard myself in the beginning of the tape, speaking slowly in a depressed, sad voice. As time went on, I noticed my voice changing to a voice with more animation and enthusiasm. I carefully listened to the words in the early part of the tape. The words were words of despair and loneliness. Later the words began to sound more hopeful as new things were happening in my life. This was certainly a good tool to let me know that I was getting better.

In the self-help groups that I lead I often hear participants react when someone says, "I just can't seem to move ahead with my life." Others quickly point out improvements they have observed. For example, someone may say, "You are getting better. I remember the first time I met you; all you did was cry. You cried so much that you couldn't even tell us why you were here." Sometimes it takes an outsider to help you see the subtle improvements you have made. Your family and friends may be able to share similar observations that will let you know that you, too, are moving through the process of your grief.

9.1 Helping Yourself Through Your Grief

Mourning is more than waiting for things to get better. There are many things you can do to help yourself during this difficult time to make your way through your grief. Fortunately they include the basic rules you should follow anyway in pursuing good physical and mental health but that you might forget during this time of disorientation. The three basics are diet, rest, and exercise.

Diet

Eating proper, well-balanced meals is essential. In times of stress it is easy to nibble away on snack foods and difficult to organize yourself enough to plan proper meals, much less sitting down to eat them. Food may have no taste to you; it may be unappealing; it may seem to stick in your throat and make your stomach uncomfortable. If it is impossible to eat a well-balanced meal at one sitting, try spreading meals throughout the day, eating smaller portions but eating more frequently. Microwave ovens can be very useful in these circumstances, since they cook food quickly and can easily reheat food you didn't finish earlier. You can have a meal within minutes.

Exercise

Exercise, always important to good health, is even more important now. During times of stress you may forget about your exercise routine, yet regular exercise can help reduce that stress, discharging anger or frustration. Unless your doctor advises otherwise, you should devote at least twenty minutes three or more times a week to walking, running, bicycling, tennis, or other exercise that works for you. Find the exercise you enjoy doing and work it into your schedule. You will find that exercise not only reduces your stress level but increases your energy level and your sense of well-being. It will also help your appetite and your sleep.

Rest

Shaken by your loss, you may be having a hard time sleeping at night. You may find that as soon as you end a busy day and lie down for a night's sleep, your mind starts churning, thinking about your loved one. Or you may fall asleep quickly, only to awaken a few hours later, wide awake, restless, and unable to resume your rest. Grief is very tiring by itself, and going without sleep merely adds to the problem.

If you are not sleeping well, developing and maintaining good sleep habits is the first step to take in addressing your problem. Here are some suggestions that may help:

- Go to bed at the same time each night, and get up at the same time each morning. Try to follow this pattern even on weekends. If you find you have already fallen into a bad sleeping pattern on a routine basis, try to break it by changing your routine.

- Warm milk can work. It is a natural sedative and relaxes you. Even if you wake in the early morning hours, warm milk will help you go back to sleep.
- If you awaken during the night, it may be best for you to stop fighting it and get out of bed, read for a while, drink a glass of warm milk, watch some television, and then go back to bed. You will have a better chance of going back to sleep.
- Experiment with exercise. Some people find exercising at bedtime relaxing, and it helps them go to sleep. Others find it too stimulating, interfering with sleep.
- Try a hot bath before you retire to see if it relaxes you.
- Soothing music will give your mind something to focus on other than thoughts of your loved one.
- Lying down while watching TV may cause you to fall asleep. The more boring TV program the better.
- Try reading before you retire, but be sure it is something that is not too stimulating.
- Avoid daytime naps unless you need them to catch up on your sleep.
- It's best to sleep in your own bed. But if the bed is a painful reminder that your spouse is dead, try sleeping on his or her side of the bed. It is easier to deal with your own pillow being empty. Or try propping a pillow behind your back to give you the feeling of not being alone.
- If you feel fearful at night, experiment with leaving lights on or turning them off, try having your bedroom door closed and locked or wide open. Look into alarm and light systems. Call your local police department to go through your house and advise you on how to make it more safe. Take whatever steps are necessary to make you more secure, as this can help you sleep better.

- Experiment with the temperature in your home. Usually a warm, humid room will relax muscles and make you more drowsy. However, if it is too hot and dry, you may be unable to sleep. Or perhaps you sleep best when it is cool. Find the temperature that is best for you.
- Meditation helps some people relax and fall asleep. You may want to find a tape on relaxation or meditation to help you get started if you are unfamiliar with this concept. Prayers are a form of meditation that some people use.
- Certain foods and drinks should be avoided at bedtime. Coffee, tea, cocoa, chocolate milk, and many caramel colored soft drinks contain caffeine, which may keep you awake. Drink herbal tea, decaffeinated coffee, or juices. Avoid eating a heavy meal before bedtime, and stay away from chocolate.
- Try an environmental CD or tape to listen to. Some are available with sounds of the surf at a beach with gulls crying out, sounds of birds in the forest, sounds of rain on the roof, or sounds of wind in the trees. It is even possible that you will find the hum of the air conditioner comforting.
- Take time to unwind before you get ready for bed, especially if you have had a harrowing or strenuous day.
- Try not to force sleep. If you have been in bed for half an hour and do not feel that sleep is approaching, get up for a while and then start your bedtime routine all over again.
- Avoid alcohol and cigarettes at bedtime. They might help you go to sleep, but as soon as they are out of your system you will probably awaken.
- If your problem is severe, you may want to ask your physician for a mild sleeping pill. This should be a last resort because you could become dependent on pills or they could actually cause more insomnia.

While attending to these basics, there are other things you can do to help yourself during this period of mourning:

- Decide which relatives or friends are most comfortable with your grief and with whom you are most comfortable discussing it. Develop a support system of people who can help you if you have a "grief attack."
- Support groups for many different grief reactions are springing up in different places. You may find such a group a good support system that fills a need not being met by relatives or friends for one reason or another. If you don't have the energy to find such a group, this is a fairly easy thing to ask someone to do for you. (See the Resources for information on support groups.)
- Read as much as you can about the process of grief. (See the Bibliography.) You will gain a better understanding of yourself, and your grief will be less frightening.
- Find time when you can be alone: time to just sit and think about what has happened and what you need to do to reconstruct your life. Friends and relatives may be uncomfortable with this, but you need the reassurance that will come from formulating at least the beginnings of a plan for your future.
- Occasionally you need to take time off from your grief. This might involve a short trip to visit relatives or a short vacation to a favorite spot. Make the most of these times, but don't expect your grief to go away. When you return, your grief will be waiting for you, and you will have to work on it again. However, you will be better able to deal with it.
- Pamper yourself. Often the person who died was the person who would pamper you, the person who would do those little special things for you: rubbing your back, bringing you flowers, or buying you that special dress or sports jacket that you had been coveting. This may have been the person who really cared about how

you looked or the person who cooked you special meals. You may miss those little things that were done for you. Now it's time for you to pamper yourself a bit. However, do this within reason. If money is tight, it is not the time to carpet your home or go on an expensive vacation. But it is time to do some nice things for yourself, to give yourself rewards or things to look forward to.

- Have patience with yourself; grief takes time. Be gentle with yourself. Take it easy. If you can, avoid any new responsibilities that can wait. You have enough changes to cope with that can't be put off.

- Don't compare your grief to others who may be mourning a similar loss. Every person's grief is unique. No two are alike. (See section 1.3 on the length of grief.)

- Lean into your pain. Try to experience your grief as it comes. As tears well up in your eyes, let them come. Since others may want to stanch your tears, this may mean finding a place where you will feel more comfortable letting this happen. The more you can let your grief out and express it, the quicker you will feel better. It is always okay to seek the help of a professional if you feel it would benefit you.

- Deal with one day at a time, and if that is too overwhelming, break the day into manageable chunks.

- If you have heard that the first year is the worst, which is generally true, be careful not to get caught up with the magic of this idea. Don't assume that once the year is up, everything will be fine. Sometimes grief takes longer than a year. Also don't be surprised that as the first anniversary of the death nears, you are counting down the days while your emotions build. I often hear from people that the anticipation of that anniversary is worse than the actual day. (See section 5.3 on anniversaries and holidays.)

9.2 You Know You Are Getting Better When . . .

There are clues that will help you to see that you are beginning to work through your grief. These ever so slight clues can be missed unless you are aware of their importance. Such clues might be:

- when you are in touch with the finality of death
- when you can review both pleasant and unpleasant memories
- when you can enjoy time alone
- when you can drive somewhere by yourself without crying the whole time
- when you realize that painful comments made by family or friends are made in ignorance
- when you can look forward to holidays
- when you can reach out to help someone else in a similar situation
- when the music your loved one listened to is no longer painful to you
- when you can sit through a religious service without crying
- when some time passes in which you have not thought of your loved one
- when you can enjoy a good joke
- when your eating, sleeping, and exercise patterns return to what they were before the death
- when you no longer feel tired all the time
- when you have developed a routine to your daily life
- when you can concentrate on a book or a favorite television program
- when you no longer have to make daily or weekly trips to the cemetery

- when you can find something to be thankful for
- when you can establish new and healthy relationships
- when you feel confident again
- when you can organize and plan your future
- when you can accept things as they are and not keep trying to return things to what they were
- when you have patience with yourself through "grief attacks"
- when you look forward to getting up in the morning
- when you can stop to smell the flowers along the way and enjoy experiences in life that are meant to be enjoyed
- when the vacated roles that your loved one filled in your life are now being filled by yourself or others
- when you can take the energy and time spent on the deceased and put those energies elsewhere, perhaps on helping others in similar situations or making concrete plans with your own life
- when you can acknowledge your new life and even discover personal growth from your grief

If you observe some of these behaviors in yourself, you can take heart in the knowledge that you have started to put your life together once again and to find new important directions for it. As you work with your grief you can experience new personal growth and a new awareness of the pain and suffering of the people around you. You will find others who are experiencing a loss turning to you for help and comfort, knowing that you are someone who has been or is going through something similar to what they, too, are experiencing. Helping others in like circumstances can help you to further resolve your own grief and to accept that the loss you have suffered is, regretfully, a common human experience.

• • •

9.3 New Relationships

Some time ago a widow told me that her marriage of eighteen years was one that she would like to repeat someday. She said that before his death her husband had encouraged her to marry again, and she felt that this was his parting gift to her. She told me that she knew she was capable of loving another person without diminishing her love for the husband who had died. Still, she wondered just when she should consider starting to date again and how she might go about it.

Not every person who has been widowed or lost a partner may be interested in establishing another romantic relationship, but for those who are, it is hard to know either when or where to begin. When you were young and in high school or college, it was an easy matter to meet other single people; everyone around you was single. But when you are older, it is likely to be a different story. Chances are that most of your friends and associates are married. Where, you might ask, do I meet single people my age? You may also be apprehensive about meeting someone, spending an evening with him or her, wondering what might happen and how you might react. You may find the thought both exciting and terrifying. You may wonder what the norms are for dating.

When Do You Know You Are Ready?

The answer to this question will vary from person to person. You may feel so lonely that you want to rush into courtship and marriage. Don't do it. I have seen many mismatches and disappointments. For one thing, if you are still mourning your loss, if you have yet to resolve your grief, some new person in your life will have great difficulty filling your needs and may become confused and angry in trying to do so. In order to have a healthy, fulfilling relationship with another person you must first become reacquainted with yourself as a separate and distinct, independent human being, not just one half of a couple.

Be firm with yourself on this score. Don't be too quick to decide that you have passed this test. For one thing, you need some time to get comfortable with yourself as a single person. At least a few months should pass before you make any moves toward dating again. And as for remarriage, go slow! Don't rush into anything. Remarriage in less than a year after your partner's death is not a good idea unless you had a long time before the death to anticipate and, in effect, mourn your loss. (See section 2.3 on anticipatory grief.) When my husband died after an illness of many years that included a final seven months in a coma, I felt ready to accept a date just a few months after his death. Many weeks passed before I had another opportunity. Thus, while my reentry into the dating world was earlier than yours might be, it was slow and relaxed. There is something to be said for taking your time.

Now for a word to the wise: If you sense that you are looking for someone who looks like and has many of the same qualities as your deceased spouse or fiancé, be careful. You may be trying to "replace" the person you lost, a clear sign that you haven't completed your mourning. When people do this, they are often terribly disappointed. You can't replace people; each person is unique. Instead, try to look at the qualities each new person is presenting and appreciate them for what they are. Try to see each person as an individual and not as a reincarnation of your deceased mate.

Where to Start

The place to start in finding people to meet is with your friends. Ask them if they know someone. This is always a touchy subject and, generally, friends won't approach it without your leading the way. You might ask friends if they would mind putting together (with your help) a small dinner party, or perhaps just a small gathering for drinks. This would give you a chance to meet someone in an easier way than going out on a blind date with a stranger. If it turns out that you and this person do not have a lot in common, there would be other people around for both of you to enjoy.

However, friends aren't always the best avenue for finding single people to meet. They may not know many single people that they feel would be appropriate for you, or they may be hesitant to get involved in your life on that level. You might also consider joining a widowed or grief group: either a seminar or a support group. Such groups provide a safe way to begin your reentry to the world of meeting people. In addition, since these seminars are often educational, they may enable you to continue to learn about your grief and to see how others have dealt with certain common problems or concerns. Through a group of this kind you can better prepare yourself for dating, and, at the same time, expand your circle of acquaintances. Since being with someone one on one can be frightening, seminars for the widowed are helpful in giving newly single people a chance to practice talking to someone of the opposite sex. They provide a safe atmosphere in which you can come out of your cocoon. I might add that they usually have a ground rule prohibiting dating one another while the seminar is going on, which is a wise policy. However, you are likely to make new friends of the same sex with whom you may find companionship right away.

Churches often have groups geared to the single adult. It usually isn't necessary to be of a particular faith to join these singles groups. If you feel this might be helpful, scout around and find out if there is one to your liking.

Post Cana is an organization for the widowed that was started by the Catholic church years ago and is now open to all widows and widowers, regardless of religious affiliation. It is a national group with local chapters. A phone call to a nearby Catholic church can help you make contact with one of the groups.

There is another organization that you might consider joining in order to expand your acquaintances and possibly meet someone of interest. It is called Parents Without Partners, or

PWP. You need to be a parent to join, but your children can be of any age. This group is open to people who are not only widowed, but divorced and separated as well. Some PWP chapters have special groups devoted to the widowed only. In these subgroups you may not need to be a parent, but only widowed. PWP is a national organization, and, once you join, you can attend activities in any state. There are scheduled events, like wine and cheese parties, hiking or bicycle outings, and discussion groups almost every day of the week. Many of the activities include children. PWP chapters are usually listed in the phone book. (See Resources.)

As you put the word out to your friends and/or join a group of one kind or another, you will be finding out about other local groups that you can explore. Usually if you start with attending a widowed or grief seminar, there will be a session on dating that will include a listing of local resources that are available to you. Also look in your local newspapers for announcements about groups or functions that may be of interest to you: progressive dinners, tours, or special interest groups. If you can't locate a group, perhaps, with the help of someone from your church or mental health center, you could start your own group.

You might also consider signing up for a class. Taking a class of some sort will not only fill up some lonely time but stimulate your mind and help you meet people. Select a class that sounds like fun, one that you will enjoy but also one that will attract both sexes. Even if you don't meet someone to date, you will have had the opportunity to make some friends and expand your horizons.

Personal ads in your newspaper or local magazine can be a source of meeting people if you feel brave enough to venture out on a one-on-one date. The personal ads offer you an opportunity to be in control. You can respond to an ad without giving your address by using a post office box number. If you respond by telephone, you don't have to give out your telephone number. However, now that devices are available to reveal the phone numbers of callers, you might want to play it safe by calling from your office or a pay phone far removed from your home. After one or more conversations, and perhaps after checking on what the person tells you, you may feel sufficiently comfortable to arrange to meet him or her at some public place, like a restaurant, possibly for lunch and possibly in the company of a friend or friends. If you do this, you will have your own transportation to make it easy for you to leave whenever you wish.

On Dating

Right now it may be hard to even think about dating someone. You may still feel married or engaged, and the thought of going out on a date may feel as if you are cheating on your spouse or fiancé or having an affair. It will take you a while to convince yourself that dating is perfectly all right and that you are, indeed, eligible again.

Going out on a first date with someone may feel comfortable for you, or it may feel terrifying. One widower told me that he felt the same way he did when he was a teenager: He had sweaty palms and butterflies in his stomach. He even arrived at the home of his date too early and had to drive around until the proper time came to pick her up. Don't be alarmed if you also find these teenage symptoms returning; they're to be expected when you try to pick up where you left off years before, experiencing many of the same feelings you had when you were seventeen.

You may remember all the rules you had as a young person and wonder if they apply now: rules like, "Nice girls don't call boys" or "The guy always picks up the bill" or "The guy always drives." Times have changed. Today it is perfectly all right for a woman to call a man. I have had a number of widowers tell me that they appreciated calls from women. In big cities going out for an evening can be expensive, and it is fine for the woman to offer to pay the tab or at least her share. However, if you are planning a date with someone, this is a matter that should be discussed in advance and agreed upon, whether you are planning dinner or the theater. One woman who lived on a tight budget had met a man she found interesting and called him one day, inviting him to a performance at a local theater. She had to stammer a bit when he said, "Yes! What are we going to see?" In fact, because of the cost, she had not bought the tickets yet and wanted to make sure he would be willing to go before doing so. Fortunately, she was able to buy the tickets, and they had a very pleasant, get-acquainted evening. It is also fine for a woman to call a gentleman and invite him to dinner at a restaurant, making it clear that he is to be her guest. I did that with my future husband. It was our second date, and it was during that evening that I came to realize that I wanted to continue seeing him. If you make such an offer and the gentleman insists on picking up the tab, perhaps you could invite him to your home for dinner when you feel comfortable doing so.

Asking someone for a date can be frightening to both men and women. You have already had the ultimate rejection when your spouse or fiancé died. Thus it may be helpful to have a backup plan when you ask someone out. If plan A fails, activate plan B. For example, I know of a widow who had decided to ask a certain widower out for dinner. However, in case he turned her down for one reason or another, she had a friend on standby to go to the movies with her. Insecure as you may be about dating, you need to understand that people have many legitimate reasons for turning you down. A "no, thanks" doesn't have to mean a rejection. People do have other plans, and sometimes they are not ready to date, particularly if they, too, are mourning the loss of a spouse or fiancé. There may also be financial problems. Rather than feeling rejected if the answer is negative, you might go on to ask if there would be another night that would work out. This will give the other party a chance to let you know if he or she is interested. One widow who was invited to go out for dessert had to say that she was busy that night but let the caller know she was interested by saying, "I would like a rain check." If you are interested, don't fail to communicate your own interest in similar fashion.

On Children and Dating

I'm talking about *you* dating. If you have children, you may have many different reactions from them when you start to date again. They may say they want you to date and eventually re-marry. But when you begin to do this, they may find themselves equivocal on the subject. They may find it difficult to see another woman setting the table with their mother's china or see another man sitting in their dad's chair. Each person you bring home will be sized up as a prospective stepparent, and, of course, they have all heard horror stories about stepparents. They fear the prospect of having stepbrothers and/or stepsisters and having to share their rooms and you with them.

If you should develop a serious relationship with another parent, you may have visions of creating a happy unit similar to the popular TV show "The Brady Bunch." In my case, I quickly found that this would not work. Each child had to move at her or his own pace. Many times after I had gone to great lengths to plan a picnic, various children announced that they did not want to participate. When this involved children too young to be left home, I found that I had created a problem with my eagerness. I found that each child needed time to get used to the idea of my dating, and each child needed to evaluate such an arrangement for himself or herself.

If you start dating, you will discover that role changes can occur as older children become the parent giving you advice and even setting curfews. You can expect many questions from them the next day as to where you went, why were you so late, and what you think of this person. Sounds familiar, doesn't it? One woman returned from a date late one evening to find a sign strung across the doorway that stated, "Wake me up when you get home." You have to be prepared to accept these intrusions gracefully. After all, your children have had to adjust to the loss of a parent and it is understandable if they resist more changes stemming from the prospect of your remarriage. They may even exhibit obnoxious behavior that is totally embarrassing to you. My advice: Be patient but firm in what you know is right.

On the other hand, there are times when your children may become fond of a particular person you bring home, and then feel disloyal to the parent who has died. If this is the case, you will hear all the reasons why they do not like the person. This is likely to be an effort to remain loyal to their deceased parent. They may also need reassurance that you will always remember and love the parent they have lost.

Younger children do not like being without a father or a mother. If you have young children and decide to bring a date home, your children may make an effort to move your date right into the family to fill the void of the missing mom or dad. Do not be surprised if they try to do all the things with your date that they used to do with their parent: sitting on his or her lap, having the person read them a bedtime story, asking your date for help with homework or work on a model car, or even inviting your date to dance class or a T-ball game. Understanding what is going on and explaining this to your date will help avoid some embarrassing moments.

Just being a teenager is hard enough; adding to that the death of a parent and then a parent's dating can be more than an adolescent child can take. In the mind of a sixteen-year old, dating, kissing, and the like are for the young only, and it is a deep embarrassment to them to have a parent acting like a teenager. Your teenage children may worry about someone's taking advantage of you and may become protective of you. They may simply act disgusted and refuse to acknowledge that you are dating at all. Or you may find one of your children developing a "crush" on the person you are dating. Finally, you may sense some kind of competition between you and your adolescent child if you develop a more active social life than your son or daughter.

Still another concern may be that if you marry again the children may be deprived of some of their inheritance. None of these are reasons for not trying to develop a new relationship, but they are possibilities to be aware of.

How to Help Your Children

If you decide to begin dating, be aware of your children's special needs and the grief they feel for their deceased parent. (See *The Grieving Child* in the Bibliography.) Talk to them and let them know when you are thinking about dating and ask them how they will feel about it. Invite them to talk to you and make an effort to hear them out. It is so easy to let conversations of this nature turn into arguments; try to avoid this by listening carefully and responding thoughtfully. However, don't let your children dictate what you should or should not do; they really don't want, nor should they have, that much control. Remember, if it's not best for you, it won't be best for your children either.

Keep your children informed, but don't feel that you have to go into great detail. Also, don't spring any surprises on them. One widow came home one day to announce that she was going to get married in a week. Almost in passing, she said that she hoped it was okay with her children. Well, it was not okay, and the children were rebellious and hateful to the new stepparent. The situation became intolerable.

Try to give your children some options and some control. For example, you could let them know that you will be having someone in the house for a few minutes before the two of you go out to dinner. Then let them decide whether they want to meet this person. If they have a choice, most likely they will be curious enough to be around when that hour approaches. Later on you could invite them to give you their impressions of your guest. Listen to their comments, but don't let these comments dictate whether you see this person again; that is for *you* to decide.

Also set some firm ground rules. The clearer you can be the better it will be for everyone. A basic rule is that they be polite to any guest you have in your home just as you will be polite to their guests. Homework, bedtime, and clean-up rules continue to apply, even when you have a date visiting.

If you develop a serious relationship that consumes much of your time, you can expect your children to be jealous of that time and show it in their behavior. It is difficult for children to share a parent with someone else. To avoid this I suggest that you set up some regular times to spend with them. I know of two single parents who consistently scheduled one weekend a month for each family to go its separate way, doing the things they enjoyed doing together.

On Sexuality

Sexuality is more than having sex with someone. Sexuality is the way you feel about yourself as a man or as a woman. In a happy relationship your spouse or fiancé provides constant re-inforcement of your self-image with comments like, "Honey, you look terrific," "I love the smell of your perfume," or "I love to watch your hands while you work." When that other person dies, this source of reinforcement will be gone. You may be good-looking and very attractive, but you may suddenly wonder if you have anything to offer that someone would find interesting. It may take a special effort to feel good about yourself again and to be aware of your sexuality. Here are some ideas:

- Take an active interest in what colors or styles of clothing look good on you.
- Have a color analysis done. (Even men can benefit from knowing what colors look best on them.)
- Get a new haircut or hairstyle.
- If you are a woman, review your makeup with a professional.
- Start an exercise program or possibly join a health club to put yourself in the best shape.

As you focus anew on your manhood or womanhood, keep in mind that you are who you are whether or not you are involved in a special relationship with a member of the opposite sex. Nice as it is to have that reinforcement, your sexuality doesn't depend on anyone else. Sexuality is your *capacity to love* and not the actual performance of any act. One definition reads, "The quality of possessing a sexual character or potency." You can have sexuality without ever developing a new intimate relationship.

Of course, intimacy is the ultimate expression of sexuality; it's the closeness one feels being next to someone; it's the excitement of having a shoulder to rest your head on; it's the exhilaration of holding hands while watching the sunset.

And sexuality can show itself in more intimate acts, like that first kiss or that first act of lovemaking. This is the part of sexuality that many people wonder about and find scary. You may wonder if you really want to get that close to someone again, fearing that this person may leave you as your beloved did. Also, your spouse or fiancé may have been the only person you ever made love with, and the prospect of doing so with another person may be frightening.

You may be worrying about how you would respond if someone were to put an arm around you. Would you stiffen up and move away, or would you just melt into his or her arms, perhaps regretting it later? You may have been comfortable giving hugs to friends of the opposite sex before but feel wary about it now. It's all part of rediscovering your sexuality.

You may be worrying too much about all this. When you are in the company of someone, try to relax and enjoy the person for who he or she is. If your relationship leads to making love, it should happen easily and naturally. However, for the widower, don't be alarmed if you experience temporary impotence. The feelings of disloyalty, or of being still married, can contribute to this. The problem usually disappears in a short time. If you are a woman, you can help a great deal by being patient and relaxed about it. However, if the problem persists, it would be well to see a doctor to make sure there isn't any physical basis for it.

You may be worrying, too, about how you will react if some-one puts pressure on you to go to bed before you are ready. In fact, you may worry so much that you resist invitations to go out for social evenings. Since you obviously could be subject to such pressure, it is a good idea to think through in advance just how you will deal with it. First, fully understand how you feel about sex. Are you comfortable with casual sex? Or do you con-sider lovemaking a form of commitment? Are you likely to feel guilty about it the next morning? Once you have a clear idea of your morals and values it will be easier to set your guidelines. Try to stay away from situations where your actions might be interpreted incorrectly, such as accepting a solo dinner invita-tion at someone's home a week after you met. If you can, have a conversation early in your relationship on the subject of sex. Be as clear as possible. The other person can then decide whether she or he wants to continue with the relationship. Good rela-tionships will not suffer from such openness. If you ever feel yourself being pushed in a direction you do not like, let your partner know that you are not comfortable with what is hap-pening. One woman whose new boyfriend kept pressing her for sex in spite of her frequent refusals finally told him, "It's time for you to go home. You are wasting my time, and I am obvi-ously wasting yours." He left.

Openly discussing the ground rules will take the pressure off both of you. For example, if you two decide to go away for a weekend, are you comfortable with the sleeping arrangements? Make your desires known before you agree to go on the trip. Work out as much as you can in advance. This includes not only the sleeping arrangements but the finances as well.

As a newly widowed person you also may encounter the old friend or neighbor who feels that you must be starved for sex and sets out to satisfy that need. I know many stories of people who were approached in this way by neighbors, friends, or cowork-ers. Be forewarned; this could happen and, indeed, may already have happened to you. Be prepared to let these people know clearly that you are not interested. If, in spite of the clarity of your message, someone persists, you may have to threaten to expose the person to his or her spouse, boss, or the neighborhood.

On AIDS

If your relationship is progressing to the point that you are considering making love, AIDS is something to be concerned about. It is of utmost importance to practice the safest sex possible, and the rules are few and simple.

- Know the person as well as you can before you consent to having sex. Is this a promiscuous person or someone who has remained faithful to one person at a time for long relationships?
- Is this a person who has been or is an intravenous drug user?
- Has this person ever been tested for the HIV virus? If so, what were the results?
- Most important, practice safer sex using latex condoms. Always have some with you "just in case." Never falsely assume that "it will probably be okay." Both men *and* women should take the responsibility to have a condom available when needed. Yes, women, too. If the man doesn't have a condom, the woman should make sure that she does. Before long you will have a choice of male or female versions, as the Food and Drug Administration has approved a female condom that should be on the market soon. Not only will this save you from the possibility of disease but it will save you from an unwanted pregnancy. If your relationship has reached this point, discuss safe sex with your partner before you get into a situation where emotions take over and can lead to bad judgment. AIDS does infect heterosexual couples, and the numbers are large enough for people

to be concerned when considering sex with someone new. You *can* contract AIDS. If you need more information, contact your local health department.

When a Relationship Breaks Up

If you decide to break off a relationship, you may find it as painful as it was when you were a teenager. Experiencing this loss may take you back to thinking about the death of your spouse or fiancé, revisiting your earlier grief. You may even feel some anger at your spouse or fiancé for leaving you in this predicament. You may even promise yourself not to date anymore because this part of it hurts too much. Breaking up a relationship generates its own grief—certainly not as strong as when your spouse or fiancé died, but it is grief, nonetheless. Also be aware that if you have children, they may share some of these feelings of loss.

On Remarriage

It *is* possible to have a happy second marriage. It *is* possible to love another person as intensely as you did the first time. However, when you start thinking about getting married again, you and your fiancé need to consider some things that aren't a part of first-time marriages.

- Where will you live? If each of you has a house, which one will be your new residence? Will the other person be comfortable in your house, and vice versa? Look carefully at which house meets your needs and the needs of the children involved. Which house will create less turmoil? Or is it possible to sell both houses and buy a different one without all the memories?
- A huge task is deciding which furniture to keep and which to give away or sell. A suggestion: If you have grown children or special relatives or friends, they may

be very happy to take or buy some of the pieces. If you have children who will soon be on their own, you might consider storing the extra furniture for their use when they set up housekeeping. There are always some things you would like to save. If you don't have a place for them in your new home, they can be stored in an attic, garage, or rental space.

- If both of you are working, who pays what bills? This is often a touchy subject to discuss; try to clear the air on money before the marriage.

- Wills need to be looked into. Is there a sum of money that should go to certain children or relatives and not others? In the event of your death, are you satisfied with what will happen to your estate? If not, be sure you work this out with the aid of a lawyer before you get married.

- What are you going to do with the photographs of the deceased? Are you both comfortable with them around the house, or do you both agree to put them away?

- Make sure you don't expect your new spouse, without advance agreement, to perform the exact same household chores performed by your former spouse. These matters need to be discussed and agreed upon before you remarry.

- If there are children, be sure to discuss discipline. What kinds of discipline do each of you believe in? What works and what doesn't work? Do you have similar ideas on child rearing? Spend a lot of time on this subject as differences here can create a great deal of tension. Reach clear understandings to avoid future trouble that could threaten your marriage. If it seems necessary, seek out some professional help to make this part of your marriage work.

- How does the extended family fit into your marriage? Are holidays going to have conflicts? What will everyone's expectations be about vacations and holidays? Is there an aging relative who may have to live with you eventually? How do you feel about that?

The more you can predict problems and address them in advance, the better your chances will be for a happy second marriage. Be open about your preferences, but be prepared to compromise, too. The willingness to compromise is what makes married life possible.

Even though you have been married before, you need to remind yourself that relationships require constant work on everyone's part. Caught up again in the excitement of a new love affair, you may have forgotten that mutual agreements are necessary to make your relationship work. Try not to take the other person for granted and assume that you know how he or she feels on a certain issue. Talk things out. I have a wonderful second marriage and have always found the rewards for our efforts worthwhile and enriching. If this is what you seek, I wish the same for you.

Chapter 10

A FRIEND IN
NEED

Knowing What to Do and Say When

It's Your Turn to Give Aid and

Comfort

At one time or another everyone will have a close relative or friend who suffers a painful loss—the death of a spouse or child, parent, sister or brother, or best friend. When this occurs, you want to help but may not know what to do. This chapter is about what you can do.

If you yourself have not yet experienced the death of a loved one, you're not going to know what it feels like to suffer such a loss. Even if you have suffered such a personal loss, it still may be hard to relate to your friend's feelings because of the special circumstances of the death. But that doesn't mean that you can't be of help to a friend in need of support during a time of crisis.

There are many practical things you can do to help someone suffering intense grief. And there are many ways in which you can offer strong emotional support. But there are also things to avoid, like meaningless clichés and senseless euphemisms that fail to account for people's feelings when faced with great loss. I want to help you learn the difference.

10.1 Preparing Yourself

If you have the opportunity, you can be of greater assistance to a grieving friend by preparing yourself for the task. You can feel helpless when you see someone in need and don't know what to do. You may actually dread visiting your friend or offering help because of your uncertainty about what is appropriate, and, in turn, your friend may be confused and angry because he or she hasn't heard from you. Following are some suggestions that should help.

- Review your own death experiences, if you have had any. Remember who died, how he or she died, and how you reacted. What did your own friends do for you that was helpful, and what wasn't? You might even take yourself back to when you were a child and review your first death experience, whatever it may have been. This may give you an understanding of how you react to death even now as an adult. (See Chapter 8 on unresolved childhood grief.)

- If you have time, read as much as you can on the process of grief to gain a better understanding of the emotional impact of this death on your friend. (See the Bibliography.) The more you know about the process of grief the better you will be able to identify how your friend is feeling and what to do to help. It will also give you some guidance on whether your friend needs professional help and support.
- Think about the special circumstances surrounding the death of your friend's loved one, and then inform yourself as well as you can on how they may complicate your friend's grief. (See Chapter 7 on complicated grief.)
- Use the correct language and avoid using euphemisms. If a person has died, he is "dead," not "gone to his greater reward" or "lost" or "passed on." Using the correct language is a way of saying that you, at least, understand and accept the reality of what has happened. Because grieving people often fall into patterns of denial your correct use of language can help steer your friend away from such beguiling fantasies.

10.2 When Death Occurs

In most cases the time between the death and the funeral is very short, and there is much to do. You can provide a lot of assistance, some of which is practical, but there are some other things that need planning.

Upon hearing news of the death contact your friend immediately, either by telephone or by visiting the home. There is no more important time to have a friend than this. Your friend will be looking for your support, comfort, and guidance.

At the same time, this first contact can be difficult as you wonder what to say. If the death was sudden and/or violent, there may even be a part of you that wants to deny that this happened. You may wonder where to start. How do you get validation of the death? You could start by saying, "I hope there has been a mistake, but I have just heard John was involved in a car accident. Is this true?" This will then give your friend a chance to say yes and to explain exactly what happened. This will give you a chance to let the reality sink into your own mind. Usually the bereaved have a strong need to go over the details as they struggle with the reality of what has happened. Talking about it helps. After this recitation your simple, "I'm so sorry," will be comforting.

After a death there are many immediate tasks that need attending to. Since you may not be able to handle all of them, your first task may be organizing other friends and neighbors to share in the work. Here are some typical tasks:

- Making phone calls to other friends or relatives of the bereaved if he or she would like help with this. Close relatives and friends need to be called as quickly as possible so they can proceed with travel or work-related arrangements. Find out what your friend wants you to say to each of the people you call. (See section 10.9 on delivering death news.)
- Checking the house of your bereaved friend to see if it is presentable. People may be stopping by to offer their condolences and bring food, and if your friend is Jewish, the family may "sit shiva" for some days. The bereaved person may need help getting the house in order.
- Answering the telephone. There may be many telephone calls coming in, and your friend may appreciate having someone to sort them out. Your friend will want to talk to some callers but may want you or another friend to talk to others. It would be a good idea for the person doing this to keep a record of who calls, their phone numbers, the messages they leave, and the date

and time of each call. This will enable your friend to review them later.

- Keeping track of food that people bring and dishes to be returned. Your friend will appreciate this list when it comes time to write thank-you notes. Someone needs to organize the food, putting some out for immediate nourishment and storing other things for later when it may be needed for family gatherings or receptions.
- Helping with the children. The death of someone close can be very frightening and upsetting to children, yet parents are often so caught up in their own grief that they are unable to give their children the support they need. This might be one of the best things you could do for your friend. (See the Bibliography for reference to *The Grieving Child*.)
- Running errands such as picking up the laundry or the groceries, delivering a visiting child back to his or her parents, or getting the car washed. Find out what needs to be done, make a list, and decide who will do what.
- Picking up people at the airport or train station, and delivering them to their lodgings.
- Finding places for people to stay, such as the homes of friends or relatives, your own home, or hotels and motels.
- Helping your friend select the proper clothes to wear to the funeral. This may even involve a shopping trip.
- Making travel and other arrangements if the death necessitates an out-of-town trip. This could include a ride to the airport, stopping the mail and newspaper, calling your friend's office to inform them what's happening, making arrangements for baby-sitters if this is necessary, or even feeding pets and watering plants.
- Encouraging your friend to take time out and rest.

• • •

10.3 Funeral Arrangements

Few people are prepared to make the decisions thrust upon them at the time of a death. This is another area where you could be of help to your friend if he or she would like it. When my husband died, I greatly appreciated the offer of his employer to go to the funeral home with me. I had never planned a funeral before and was overwhelmed by the thought of it. If your friend would like to have your assistance in making funeral arrangements, here are some suggestions that may help:

- Identify the funeral homes available, find out what they have to offer, check their prices, and then present the options to your friend. Costs for burials vary even within the same area. If cost is not a factor, it might be important to have a funeral home that is conveniently located rather than some distance away.
- If the funeral is to be conducted at a church or synagogue, contact the pastor or rabbi and make arrangements for him or her to meet with your friend to work out details of the service. Funeral services may also be conducted at a funeral home by anyone you choose. (See sections 3.2 and 3.6 on funerals and memorial services.)
- You might help your friend select a burial site. Perhaps the deceased is eligible to be buried in a national cemetery. Perhaps your friend wants the body interred some distance away, possibly in that person's home town. You might help your friend decide on such options as cremation and disposition of the ashes. Once your friend makes some of the decisions the funeral director will probably be able to help you locate a cemetery and arrange all necessary transportation. Selecting a monument can be done at a later date. (See sections 3.3, 3.4, and 3.5 for information on selecting a cemetery, burial, and cremation.)

- After most funerals there will be a reception at the church or at the home of the bereaved. Help is needed to arrange this. It will involve preparing the house or the church room, ordering the food, and organizing people to prepare it, serving the food, and cleaning up later. You could take the lead in making these arrangements.
- No matter what else you do, you can provide a valuable service by helping your friend and his or her family to set aside some time to be alone, to mourn for the deceased, and to share with each other their private grief.

10.4 Funerals

Because funeral customs vary among religions and religious groups you may be unsure whether you should attend a friend's service or, if you do, how to conduct yourself. My advice is to ask your friend and then to pass on this information to others. Lack of familiarity with a given religion should not prevent you from showing support for your friend.

Another thing you can do is talk to the pastor, rabbi, or other person who will officiate at the funeral service. You can be sure that he or she will be happy to set your mind at ease. Also, it is likely that during the service the officiant will let people know when it is time to do something, like stand or sit or sing a hymn. You can also watch the family of the deceased and follow their lead.

Years ago, when Catholics were not allowed to attend services at other churches, two thirteen-year-olds, Mike and Al, had a very good friend who belonged to a Russian Orthodox church. When their friend died from a genetic disorder, the two boys wanted to attend the funeral but, knowing it was a violation of church rules, decided to sit in the rear of the church. However, their plan was thwarted when the family of their deceased friend insisted that the two boys sit with them in the very front of the church. Things went all right until they saw a crucifix being passed down the row, with each person kissing it. Now this was a matter of some concern. Kissing the crucifix of another religion would surely mean that they were worshipping another God and would constitute a serious sin. They didn't know what to do until Al, an innovative fellow to this day, came up with a new plan: They would hold their hands in such a way over the crucifix that they would kiss their own hands instead of the Christ figure! The revised plan worked, and no one was the wiser.

Fortunately times have changed somewhat, and there is more of an ecumenical spirit among religions today. While you may be uncertain about others' religious and funeral customs, it should not be at all difficult to find out what is, or is not, expected of you. Funerals are not tests for theological purity; they are tributes to the departed.

10.5 Emotional Help

There are few times when life demands more of a person than when death strikes a loved one. It is a draining time, a time when your very identity is brought into question, a time when one difficult decision after another tests your strength and your self control. During such times you need understanding friends who will listen to what you have to say, share your sadness, and help you mourn your loss. Performing such a service is one of the greatest acts of friendship that a friend can provide.

If you happen to be that friend, this may sound like a huge task. However, what I'm talking about is not that difficult; you already have the key ingredient: love and concern for your friend. All you need to do is brush up on your basic communication skills. Here are some starters:

- Let your friend know that you are available and willing to be there whenever he or she wants to talk. When you make this offer, be sure that you are prepared for an immediate response because this could open the flood-gates. On the other hand, it may not be the right time to talk but your friend will know you are available and willing to listen.

- As your friend is speaking, ask questions that require more than a simple yes or no response. This will encourage your friend to listen to your questions and to think through his or her answers. It will keep your friend talking.

- Communication enhancers such as, "I see" or "and then what did you do" or "yes-s-s-" will encourage your friend to continue talking and also show that you are interested in what he or she is saying.

- Communication doesn't always have to be in words. Nonverbal communication may involve leaning toward your friend, nodding your head, intermittent but comfortable eye contact, touching the arm or shoulder of your friend, and thoughtful facial reactions all tell your friend that you are listening and hearing what he or she is saying.

- As I repeatedly advise people, it is important to use the correct language and to avoid euphemisms when you are talking to your bereaved friend. While sugarcoating seems to take the edge off a difficult subject, it encourages denial. And yet there are exceptions to this rule. If your bereaved friend is badly shaken and simply can't stand to hear words like *murder* or *suicide* or *killed* right now, think about the relationship you have had with your friend and how you have communicated on other topics. If in your judgment the time is not right to speak so bluntly, you may have to tone down your honesty a bit. Let your past experiences with your friend govern how you handle this.

- If you knew the person who died, sharing your memories with your friend will be welcomed. I know of a mother who was visited by young friends of her dead son and was greatly comforted by the stories they told about him. Bereaved persons are usually anxious to hear stories that bring their loved ones back to life in happier roles. Sharing these stories will also help you cope with some of your own grief.

- You can help your friend solve problems by carefully verbalizing them. Solutions frequently become clear when the problems have been stated correctly and available alternatives laid out for consideration.
- You can help your friend organize his or her day by pointing out what needs to be done first and what can wait until later.
- Allow your friend to mourn. If your friend needs to cry, let him or her cry. This is an essential part of mourning. You don't have to do anything but sit quietly by, offer a hug, or make a pot of tea. If your friend needs to be angry, listening to the anger will help him or her discharge it and, in turn, feel better. (See sections 4.1 through 4.9 on the emotional responses to grief.)
- Be a good listener. People often feel uncomfortable just listening and feel pressured to say something that will "make things okay." Silence really is golden. Sitting quietly next to your friend and letting him or her say anything or everything that comes to mind is one of the best things you can do to help. Your friend will feel better after being able to talk about his or her pain to someone who really listens and doesn't change the subject or offer superficial advice on how to "get over it."
- If something you have said seems to confuse your friend, or if you feel he or she is not really listening, ask for feedback. Make sure that what you said has been understood. It's also all right to ask your friend to repeat to you what you have been saying if you think there may have been a misinterpretation. This is part of communicating correctly. To help your friend you have to be understood.

Taking Care of Yourself

At the same time as you are helping your friend, keep your own health in mind. After such a session you may feel very tired. Listening to someone's emotional pain can be very draining, even though it leaves the other person feeling much better for your efforts. Take care of your own needs, too. Occasionally do something that will enable you to regain your own strength. Because of what is happening in your own life you may not have the energy or strength to take on all of your friend's pain. If this is the case, it is all right to say this to your friend and to offer to find someone else to pick up some of the load.

10.6 Things to Avoid

Our good intentions are sometimes misread, causing tension where good will was intended. In talking with your bereaved friend you want to be sure you are understood. Following are some pitfalls to avoid.

- Vacuous platitudes like:
  "I know how you feel."
  "It's part of God's plan."
  "You're young and you can still get married again."
  "Look at what you have to be thankful for."
  "He's in a better place now."
  "Now you can put this behind you and move on with your life."
  "Call me if you need anything."
  Such superficial comments would only leave your friend angry and frustrated. (See the Bibliography for a humorous but helpful book on the clichés of grief.)
- Doing all the talking. When emotions are high, you may be anxious and inclined to talk too much. If this happens, stop for a second and get control of yourself.

Then invite your friend to talk and concentrate on what he or she is saying rather than on what you can say next.

- Statements that begin with "You should." Such statements are too directive and tend to imply that the other person is incapable of making his or her own decisions. Grieving people receive a lot of gratuitous advice that leaves them confused and overwhelmed. I suggest that you replace the "you should" statements with, "Have you thought about—" or "What do you think about—" or "What do you want to do about—." By doing so, you will leave your friend in control of the decision process. When one's life is out of control, as often occurs following the death of a loved one, some control, any control, is important to have.

- Making decisions for your friend. If you make the decisions and they turn out to have been wrong, your friend will blame you. You can help your friend best by helping him or her look at all the options for each decision that must be made. The final decision must be your friend's—not yours—even though you may disagree.

- Discouraging all emotion or expressions of grief. Do not change the subject when your friend needs to talk. If you are uncomfortable with the emotions your friend is displaying, you can offer to find someone he or she can talk to. This could be another friend, a minister or rabbi, or professional therapist.

- Promoting your own values and beliefs. If your friend does not believe in an afterlife, for example, this is not the time to try to convince him or her of that concept. This is a time to be an objective listener and to accept your friend's beliefs and values.

- Passing yourself off as an authority on grief. Be careful not to predict what the next phase of your friend's grief will be. You may have done your homework and know about the process of grief, but remember that grief is always unique, shaped by the special circumstances of one's life. (See section 1.3 on the length of grief.)

- Encouraging your friend to be dependent on you. He or she needs the opportunity to gain the personal growth that can accompany grief.
- Dominating your friend's time. Be sensitive to the needs of your friend. Are there other friends who want to help as well? Be sensitive to the times your friend may want some time alone or time to be with others. Watch for times when you can take a break and slip out for a while.

10.7 Long-Term Help

Your bereaved friend is going to need your caring and support as the weeks and months go by. He or she may even need you more when family members return to their homes and other friends get back to their families and daily routines. The reality of the death may just be sinking in for your friend, and the need to talk to someone may increase. Here are some pointers.

- Pace yourself. Often following a death people rush forward to do the many things that need doing and soon realize that they can't keep up with the schedule they have set for themselves. They become exhausted and their families become upset with them for being gone so much. They run out of energy. It is at this point that friendships begin to fray. Unable to keep up the pace, they become embarrassed and withdraw. The friend becomes confused and angry, and the friendship starts to fall apart. To avert this you should recognize that your friend has a lot of mourning to do and that it is going to take a long time—months or even years—for the grief to be resolved. Decide how much time you reasonably can give, and pace yourself so you will have the time and energy to help your friend for as long as he or she needs your help and counsel.

- Developing a regular visiting schedule will be helpful to both of you. This may be once a week in the early weeks and then stretched out to every other week as time goes by. Your friend will appreciate knowing that on a certain day you will be there to talk, walk, cry, or simply enjoy each other's company.

- The writing of the thank-you notes is often seen as an overwhelming job. If your friend feels this kind of pressure, perhaps you could write a few under your friend's guidance.

- Has your friend been back to the gravesite since the burial? Does he or she want to go, and would he or she like some company? (See section 3.4 on visiting the grave.)

- You could offer to research community resources that might be helpful to your friend. There may be lectures, support groups, or seminars that would be helpful to your friend. Are there some things that you could attend with him or her? Would you want to do that? Don't go if you would rather not. You might also seek out the availability of professionals who specialize in grief in case your friend would benefit from such counseling. (See the Resources.)

10.8 Writing a Letter of Condolence

Letters expressing sympathy to a bereaved friend are difficult for most people to write, yet they are very necessary, especially if one is unable to contact the friend directly. Because this is such a difficult letter to write, you may have put off the task so long that it has become an embarrassment to you. If so, I suggest that you pick up paper and pen and get started! It is better late than never. Here are some thoughts that may help.

- A condolence note should be written within a day or two of your finding out about the death. If, indeed, the death occurred several weeks or months ago, note that you have just heard the news or explain the difficulty you have had in writing and apologize.
- A condolence note can be short. A few sentences may be enough, or you can write a page or two in which you share not only your sorrow at the death but perhaps some memories of the deceased that would be meaningful to your friend.
- You might think of the words you would use if your bereaved friend were sitting in front of you. These would be the same words you would want to convey now.
- If you feel that you are not one of the most gifted writers of our time, it is better to elicit the help of the greeting card rack than not doing anything at all. Greeting cards are improving, and there are some nice ones now that focus on very specific death situations. They even have cards for pet deaths. There are also some very nice cards on the importance of friendships, which would be a nice lead-in to a short condolence note you could compose without too much difficulty. Never just sign a card, but try to add at least a line expressing your love and support.
- Here are some examples to get you started:
  My thoughts and prayers are with you during this sad time.
  I am so sorry to hear about the death of your Uncle Ralph. I know how important he was to you.
  I regret that I live so far away from you, especially during this sad time. I wish I could talk with you about the death of your sister and give you a hug to comfort you.

I will be calling you before the end of the week.

I have wonderful memories of the three of us. The telephone calls, the shared letters, the vacations, and even the problems we had. I shall miss Mary not being part of our group.

Although I had never met Lucy, I feel I knew her through you. I am so sorry to hear of her death. I also feel a loss.

Even though your mother died several weeks ago, I have only just now heard of her death. I am sorry I wasn't there to be with you at the funeral.

Even though I cannot physically be with you during this sad time, I am with you in spirit.

Words seem so inadequate to express what I want to say to you. I am so sorry you have to be going though this. I am available to talk with you whenever you feel you would like to talk.

10.9 Delivering Death News

One of the most difficult tasks that the police, clergy, physicians, and military officers have to carry out with some regularity is delivering death news to the families of those who have died. But at some time or other you, too, may have to carry out such a heavy assignment, either by telephone or in person.

By Telephone

It may be your task to help notify other relatives and friends of the death of a loved one. Be aware that getting death news by telephone can be extremely traumatic. A woman whose brother had just killed himself was informed of his death by a phone call. She was at her doctor's when she was informed to call home immediately; when she did, she was told that "we no longer have Charley." Her knees gave out on her as she slumped to the floor. She now says that she understands why people often ask if you are sitting down when bad news is delivered. Here are some things to consider:

- The age and health of the person you are calling. If it is a person with a heart condition, news of this sort could trigger a heart attack. In cases like this it would be best to contact another relative, minister, or rabbi who could either be there when you call or actually deliver the death news.
- The relationship to the deceased. If it was a close relationship, you might want to call someone else to be there when you call or else relay the news directly.
- The need for detailed information. If the death was of a traumatic nature, it is best not to go into a lot of detail. For most people details can come later.

If you are making such calls for a bereaved friend, find out if he or she would like to talk to the person later on, after you have done the initial calling. Try to use a soft, calm voice, and speak slowly and clearly. Give people time to absorb the information. If you're not sure that the person has heard or understood, ask him or her to repeat what you have said. Here are some other pointers.

- Avoid a lot of small talk, but take a few seconds to build up to the death news, giving the listener a chance to prepare for what is to come. However, don't spend too long in your buildup; this will only create more anxiety and be equally as devastating. You might begin by saying, "My name is [your name] and I am making some phone calls for [your friend]. I am so sorry to have to tell you that [the person who died] was killed last night in a car accident." Then give the listener time to absorb what you have said and to ask questions. If you don't know the funeral plans yet, you may have to call back later. If you do know the funeral plans, relay that information.

- You may want to ask the people you are calling to help with phone calls, too. They may think of relatives or friends who need to be notified, and they may offer to make those calls.
- If the person you are calling is alone and is someone who might be shattered by the news, try to arrange for a close friend, minister, or rabbi to be with him or her when you call.
- Some phone calls may take longer than others. If the person you call is tearful and there are long lapses without conversation, stay on the line! Let the tears flow. He or she will eventually be able to talk, and then you can assess when it is okay to end the call. In the meantime you could say things like, "This must hurt a lot," "I can hear how painful this is for you," or "I'm still here; are you still there?" You will be performing that person a service by waiting quietly until he or she can respond.
- Invite people to call back if they need further information.

In Person

There may be a time when you have the unenviable task of visiting a friend to inform him or her of the death of a loved one. Or you may be asked to go with the police or clergy to assist them in delivering such news. What a difficult assignment! How one would wish to go through life without ever having to do such a painful thing. Faced with such a task, you might ask yourself: How can I soften the blow I am about to deliver? Is it even possible to soften the blow? The following suggestions may help you to prepare for your task.

- When you first find out about the death, give yourself some time to think it through. Think about the words you will use. Think about what effect this death will have on your friend. Think about what your friend's reaction might be. Think about how your friend reacted in the past when crises occurred. You may see a similar reaction this time.

- Consider taking another person with you. This might be a minister or rabbi, another friend, or a family member. Taking another person along can be helpful for several reasons: (1) moral support, (2) having someone there to share in decisions if your bereaved friend becomes extremely upset. (3) having someone there to stay at the side of your friend while the other person makes phone calls or attends to urgent matters, (4) having another set of eyes and ears to assess what is happening and how your friend is doing, (5) having a backup in case you forget something important, and (6) having someone to debrief with later. Delivering such devastating news is very draining, and it will help to be able to review what happened with someone who was there and shared in that experience.

- Gather as much information about the death as you can. Your friend may have many questions and will be eager for answers. Make notes if you need to. Your friend may want to know the time, location, exact cause of death, and other details. Making notes will help you as well, since it is hard to remember everything when you are under some shock yourself, but refer to them only if necessary.

- Consider the physical and mental health of your friend. If there is a history of physical or mental problems, it would be a good idea, if possible, to contact your friend's physician or therapist before delivering the dreaded news.

- Dress comfortably. This is not the time to wear those

new shoes that are going to be hurting your feet. That discomfort will show up on your face, adding to your friend's anxiety.

- This is not the time to have a shot of liquor or a Valium to bolster your courage. You need to be clearheaded and able to think quickly. If your friend senses that you had to boost your nerve in this way, his or her fantasies may conjure up something even worse than what you are about to say.

- Give some thought to whether you should call in advance or take a chance that your friend is at home. A phone call might trigger anxiety. If you go to the house and your friend is not there, you could wait for his or her return. You know your friend best; use your best judgment.

- The seriousness of the expression of your face is going to let your friend know that something is wrong. That's fine; it will give him or her a few seconds to prepare for what is to come. Your friend might even start asking questions before you have a chance to say anything.

- Don't keep your friend waiting by using small talk. Get to the point as quickly and as gently as possible. Invite your friend to sit down, touch him or her if that is comfortable, and proceed with what you have to say. You might start with, "I had a phone call from your father and it seems that your mother collapsed" or "I wanted to be the one to tell you that your brother's car was struck on the freeway" or "I hate to have to tell you this, but . . ."

- Allow time for this news to sink in. Don't feel that you must keep talking. Your friend will need a few moments to reflect on what you said and then will probably have a lot of questions. If you then observe your friend becoming very busy making lists, calling people, ordering flowers, and otherwise showing remarkably stoic control, he or she may be in a state of shock. Your friend may not yet have embraced the reality of what you said. Don't be fooled by this aura of detachment; the grief is yet to come. (See section 4.2 on disbelief and shock.)

• Be prepared to stay for a while. Delivering such news is not something that can be done in thirty minutes. You might even offer to spend the night unless there will be other friends or family members arriving. A father once told me that when his son died, friends moved into their home for several days to help out with the arrangements that had to be made. This might be helpful to some, but others will want time to themselves, time to think things through.

Looking Out for Yourself

Delivering news of a death to a beloved family member or friend is very draining, and it may be necessary for you to get away for a while to attend to your own feelings and fatigue. Having done this, you will be better able to carry on. Here are some suggestions on things you can do.

• Spend some time alone, reflecting on all that has happened.
• Take a long walk.
• Listen to some of your favorite music.
• Find someone else to talk to outside of the grieving circle.
• Spend some time with your own family.
• Meditate, read, or enjoy a favorite hobby for a little while.
• Visit someplace that you find relaxing and peaceful, such as a church, synagogue, art gallery, or park.
• Write in your journal.
• Eat well and try to get adequate rest.

Even though it can be very draining, sharing a friend's grief is more than a painful duty; it is a privilege, a sharing of the most intimate part of that person's life. You will want to be careful not to be intrusive and not to impose yourself if this is not what your friend wishes; but the experience of shared grief can make your friendship more precious than ever. That is not a reason to help, but it can be a reward for doing so.

Epilogue

As you and I come to the end of this journey of pain and sorrow I wonder how you're feeling. Grief is a powerful emotion. It's so pervasive. It's so demanding. Much as you may try to escape it, it's always there. Has reading this book, or parts of it, helped? Do you have a better understanding now of what you're going through and what you can do about it? Can you see now that there are still things to look forward to in life? Do you recognize the difference now between grieving and mourning, that is, the difference between feeling the pain of grief and expressing it?

This book was meant to start you on the way to recovery, not to give you instant relief. A piano student doesn't become a concert pianist in one lesson, nor will reading one book bring you to the end of your grief. In each case it is what follows that initial step that will decide the outcome. Knowledge by itself can be illuminating, but it is knowledge combined with its application that achieves results.

If you have suffered a great loss, the days ahead will not be without sorrow and tears. You will have bad days. But don't feel guilty if occasionally you have a good one, too. By expressing your grief, releasing your anger, acknowledging your guilt, overcoming your fears, and addressing the changes in your life, you will find after a while that the good days come more frequently and the bad ones start to decline, both in number and in intensity. After all, there is nothing written in the stars that says you can't be a happy person again. Much as you loved that person or those persons who died, you don't have to wear black for the rest of your life!

I have been there. I have known intense grief, and I have heard just about every sad story one could relate. I hope that relating my experience and the experiences of others in this book has been helpful because, although we may never meet in person, I wrote this book for you, my fellow passenger on the confusing, unpredictable, often cruel, but always interesting journey we call life.

—Helen Fitzgerald

Bibliography

General Grief

Grollman, Earl A. *Living When a Loved One Has Died*. Boston: Beacon Press, 1977.
> A book about feelings after the death of a loved one. It is easy to read and to understand during the confusion of bereavement.

Kries, Bernadine and Pattie, Alice. *Up From Grief: Patterns of Recovery*. New York: The Seabury Press, 1969.
> Describes the various stages of grief from the authors' own experiences and those of three hundred persons interviewed. Reassuring and educational.

Kushner, Harold. *When Bad Things Happen to Good People*. New York: Schocken Books, 1981.
> Explores the challenges to religious faith that often follow a tragedy.

Neeld, Elizabeth Harper. *Seven Choices*. New York: Clarkson N. Potter, 1990.
> Informative book on general grief, addressing the choices people can make along the way.

Rando, Therese A. *How to Go On Living When Someone You Love Dies*. New York: Bantam Books, 1988.
> In this compassionate, comprehensive guide, Therese A.

Rando, Ph.D., leads you gently through the painful but necessary process of grieving and helps you find the best way for yourself.

Schiff, Harriet Sarnoff. *Living Through Mourning*. New York: Viking, 1984.

An excellent guide through grief that looks at the different paths people take. Comprehensive.

Schoeneck, Therese S. *Hope for Bereaved*. Hope For Bereaved, 1342 Lancaster Avenue, Syracuse, New York 13210. Mail order only. Cost is about $11.00 plus $2.50 for postage.

A handbook of helpful articles for all kinds of grief situations. A very practical "how to" book.

Widowhood

Armstrong, Alexandra, and Donahue, Mary R. *On Your Own*. Chicago: Dearborn Financial Publishing, 1993.

A book to assist the widowed to emotional and financial well-being.

Elmer, Lou. *Why Her Why Now*. New York: Bantam Books, 1987.

A man's journey through love and death and grief.

Ginsburg, Genevieve Davis, M.S. *When You've Become a Widow*. Los Angeles: Jeremy P. Tarcher, 1987.

A compassionate guide to rebuilding your life.

Lindsay, Rae. *Alone and Surviving*. New York: Walker and Company, 1977.

This book addresses the emotional and practical problems of widows from ages thirty-five to fifty-five.

Loewinshohn, Ruth Jean. *Survival Handbook for Widows*. Chicago: Follett Publishing Company, 1979.

This book explores what is known about a woman's reaction to the death of a husband. It provides hope following one of the most traumatic of human experiences.

Kohn, Jane Burgess and Willard K. Kohn. *The Widower*.

Boston: Beacon Press, 1978.

> A book written especially with the man in mind. It looks at what the widower faces, what he feels, and what he needs.

Nudel, Adele Rice. *Starting Over*. New York: Dodd, Mead & Co., 1986.

> Help for the young widow and widower.

Suicide

Bolton, Iris. *My Son . . . My Son . . .* Atlanta: Bolton Press, 1983.

> Written by a mother after her son's suicide, this book has been helpful with other types of deaths as well.

Giovacchini, Peter, M.D. *The Urge to Die: Why Young People Commit Suicide*. New York: Macmillan Publishing Company, 1981.

> A look into the "whys" that motivate young people to think of and commit suicide.

Hewett, John H. *After Suicide*. Philadelphia: The Westminster Press, 1980.

> Probably the best book on suicide bereavement. Speaks to the emotional reactions that follow this most difficult kind of death.

Sandefer, Kathleen. *Mom, I'm All Right*. Garretson, SD: Kathleen Sandefer, 1990.

> A mother's story about the suicide death of her fourteen-year-old son. Directed at parents who have children on some type of long-term medication.

Smolin, Ann, C.S.W., and Guinan, John, Ph.D. *Healing After the Suicide of a Loved One*. New York: Simon & Schuster, 1993.

> An informative book that will provide suicide survivors with new insights into the emotional responses they may be experiencing following the self-inflicted death of a loved one.

Wrobleski, Adina. *A Guide for Those Left Behind*. Minneapolis: Afterwords Press, 1991.

> Practical advice for dealing with the problems faced by suicide survivors, offering encouragement and hope.

Parent Grief

Berezin, Nancy. *After a Loss in Pregnancy*. New York: Simon & Schuster, 1982.

> Help for families affected by a miscarriage, a stillbirth, or the loss of a newborn.

Borg, Susan, and Lasker, Judith. *When Pregnancy Fails*. Boston: Beacon Press, 1981.

> For families coping with miscarriage, stillbirth, and infant death.

Friedman, Rochelle, M.D., and Gradstein, Bonnie, M.P.H. *Surviving Pregnancy Loss*. Boston: Little, Brown and Company, 1982.

> This book contains descriptions of reactions to pregnancy loss and practical approaches to coping with the associated emotional problems. A comprehensive discussion of the physical and emotional consequences of pregnancy loss.

Rando, Therese A., Ph.D., editor. *Parental Loss of a Child*. Champaign, IL: Research Press Company, 1986.

> A series of articles written by many different authors covering all aspects of this special grief.

Schiff, Harriet Sarnoff. *The Bereaved Parent*. New York: Crown Publishers, 1977.

> A book of counsel for those who suffer the heartbreaking experience of a child's death.

Parent Death for Adult Child

Myers, Edward. *When Parents Die*. New York: Viking, 1986.
    A guide for adult children.

Children

Fassler, Joan. *My Grandpa Died Today*. New York: Human Sciences Press, 1971.
    A book about the love shared by a young boy and his grandfather. When Grandpa dies, David cries along with the adults around him. In spite of his sadness David goes on playing and eventually learns why Grandpa was not afraid to die.

Fitzgerald, Helen. *The Grieving Child: A Parent's Guide*. New York: Simon & Schuster, 1992.
    Organized like a book on infant care with detailed cross-references, this book provides practical advice for surviving parents and others charged with the care of grieving children. The last chapter addresses the unresolved grief that many adults carry from their own childhood and suggests how they may use some of the same techniques described in the book to resolve that grief. For the parents of grieving children as well as adults with unresolved childhood grief.

Grollman, Earl A. *Straight Talk About Death for Teenagers*. Boston: Beacon Press, 1993.
    A book for teenagers who have experienced the death of someone they love. It includes a journal section where the reader can record memories, feelings, and hopes.

Grollman, Earl A. *Talking About Death: A Dialogue Between Parent and Child*. Boston: Beacon Press, 1990.
    A book that the parent can read to a child. It includes a parent guide and recommended resources.

Hughes, Phyllis Rash. *Dying Is Different*. Mahomet, IL: Mech

Mentor Educational, 1978.

> Helps children to see death as part of life. Invites questions and exploration. Focuses on increasing the child's awareness of life and death in its most common forms. A sensitive and honest introduction to a serious subject.

LeShan, Eda. *Learning to Say Good-by When a Parent Dies.* New York: Avon, 1978.

> Written for the whole family, *Learning to Say Good-by* opens the way to genuine communication between youngsters and adults. In simple, direct language, the author discusses the questions, fears, fantasies, and stages of mourning that human beings must go through.

O'Toole, Donna. *Aarvy Aardvark Finds Hope.* Burnsville, NC: Celo Press, 1988.

> Aarvy Aardvark comes to terms with the loss of his mother and brother with the help of his friend, Ralphy Rabbit. This story of loss and grief needs a parent to translate the animal story to human terms, then to the child's particular situation.

Rofes, Eric E., and the unit at Fayerweather Street School. *The Kids' Book About Death and Dying.* Boston: Little, Brown & Co., 1985.

> Fourteen children offer facts and advice to give young readers a better understanding of death.

Slater, Dr. Robert C. *Tell Me, Papa.* Council Bluffs, IA: Centering Corporation, 1978.

> Children have many questions about death. This book takes the great unknown of death and, through the words of Papa, tells it as it is. The feelings that are triggered by death are explained and shared, showing the child that feelings are normal.

Stein, Sara Bonnett. *About Dying.* New York: Walker and Company, 1974.

> A family book for parents to share with very young children. The use of photographs makes death very real. It contains guidelines for parents.

For the Family When a Member Is Seriously Ill

Duda, Deborah. *Coming Home*. New York: John Muir Publications, 1984.

> A guide to home care for the terminally ill.

Fiore, Neil A., Ph.D. *The Road Back to Health*. Berkeley, CA: Celestial Arts, 1990.

> Dr. Fiore uses his personal experience with cancer to guide patients and their families through the psychological and emotional consequences of cancer and its treatment.

Garrison, Judith Garrett, M.Ed., L.S.W., and Sheperd, Scott, Ph.D. *Cancer and Hope*. Minneapolis: Compcare Publishers, 1989.

> Provides the cancer patient and family members with a resource when they feel most isolated. An excellent "how to survive" book.

Kelly, Orville E. *Until Tomorrow Comes*. New York: Everest House, 1979.

> The late Mr. Kelly was the author of *Make Today Count* and the founder of a nationally known organization by the same name. This book is for the cancer patient and his or her family. Many resources included.

Martelli, Leonard J., Messina, William, C.S.W., and Peltz, Fran D., C.R.C. *When Someone You Love Has AIDS*. New York: Crown Publishers, 1987.

> A practical guide for both the professional counselor and the families of AIDS patients.

For Family and Friends

Donnelley, Nina Herrmann. *I Never Know What to Say*. New York: Ballantine Books, 1987.

> Your friend's wife or husband has died. Your neighbor's child has died. Your friend is dying. What can you do? This book offers answers for all such situations.

Geary, David Patrick, Ph.D. *How to Deliver Death News.* San Francisco, CA: Compass Publishing Co., 1982.

> Even though this book carries a heavy title, it is full of information that will be helpful if ever you have the task of informing a friend or neighbor of the death of a loved one.

Grollman, Earl A., editor. *What Helped Me When My Loved One Died.* Boston: Beacon Press, 1981.

> Helpful suggestions from people who have experienced the death of a loved one.

Linn, Erin. *I Know Just How You Feel—Avoiding the Clichés of Grief.* Cary, IL: The Publishers Mark, 1986.

> A humorous book with practical information.

The Death of a Pet

Fischer, Arlene, and Nieburg, Herbert A. *Pet Loss.* New York: Harper & Row, 1982.

> A book that deals openly and honestly with the impact of the death of a beloved dog, cat, or other pet. Thoroughly researched and expertly written.

Dealing with Anger

Hankins, Gary, Ph.D. *Prescription for Anger.* Beaverton, OR: Princess Publishing, 1988.

> A practical daily guide to changing self-defeating behavior and channeling one's anger.

For the Professional

Garfield, Charles A. *Psychosocial Care of the Dying Patient.* New York: McGraw-Hill, 1978.

A collection of articles on working with dying patients and the grief they experience.

Kübler-Ross, Elisabeth, M.D. *On Death and Dying*. New York: Macmillan, 1969.

The most influential book ever published on the subject. Still widely read by professionals as well as laypeople facing a life-threatening illness.

Moos, Rudolf. *Coping With Physical Illness*. New York: Plenum Medical Book Company, 1977.

A book that addresses how people cope with serious illness and injury. Basic adaptive tasks and types of coping skills are identified. Covers a wide range of physical illnesses.

Rando, Therese A. *Grief, Dying, and Death*. Champaign, IL: Research Press Co., 1984.

Clinical interventions for caregivers.

———. *Treatment of Complicated Mourning*. Champaign, IL: Research Press Co., 1993.

An important resource for professionals working in the field of bereavement.

Redmond, Lula Moshoures. *SURVIVING When Someone You Love Was Murdered*. Available only from Psychological Consultation & Education Services, Inc., P.O. Box 6111, Clearwater, FL 34618. Published 1989.

A professional's guide to group grief therapy for families and friends of murder victims.

Worden, J. William. *Grief Counseling and Grief Therapy*. New York: Springer Publishing Co., 1981.

Required reading for anyone working with bereavement. An excellent handbook for the mental health practitioner.

Resources

Finding Professional Help

Most of us live our lives with only a vague awareness of the resources that become very important to us in times of crisis. We may be aware of our police and fire departments, but we may not know where to turn for the kind of professional help discussed in this book. If you have need for such help, you might start by asking a well-informed friend for suggestions. If you are a member of a church or temple, you might ask your pastor or rabbi. You could ask your family physician to recommend someone. Or, if you live in a community with a mental health center, you could call there, state your reason for calling, and ask to be referred to an appropriate therapist. Don't be embarrassed to spell out what it is that concerns you; that's what these caregivers are there for.

At the same time, keep in mind that it is for you to decide whether a given therapist meets your needs. Interview the person. Get a feel for whether this is someone you will like and trust. Find out whether he or she knows about and has experience working on problems like yours. Find out what the charge will be for this service, whether your health insurance will cover it, and whether you can afford it. If the first therapist you interview doesn't quite fill the bill, don't hesitate to look for another. You're in charge.

Support Groups

1. National Self-Help Clearinghouse
   Room 620
   Graduate School and University Center
   City University of New York
   25 West 43rd Street
   New York, NY 10036
   (212) 642-2944

   A source of information on all kinds of support groups.

2. American Self-Help Clearinghouse
   St. Claires-Riverside Medical Center
   25 Pocono Road
   Denville, NJ 07834
   (201) 625-7101

   A source of information on support groups by state.

Death of a Child

1. The Compassionate Friends
   P.O. Box 3696
   Oak Brook, IL 60522-3696
   (708) 990-0010

   A national organization for parents who have had a child die. They can tell you about local chapters and the possible availability of "only child" support groups.

2. National Sudden Infant Death Syndrome Foundation
   10500 Little Patuxent Parkway, Suite 420
   Columbia, MD 21044
   (301) 459-3388 (Maryland residents)
   (800) 221-SIDS (outside of Maryland)

   Support in the form of education and information for parents who have had children die in this way. There are chapters located throughout the country.

3. Parents of Murdered Children
   100 East Eighth Street, Room B41
   Cincinnati, OH 45202
   (513) 721-5683 (emergencies)

   Support and resources for the families of murdered
   children. There are local chapters.

4. Resolve Through Sharing Bereavement Services
   Lutheran Hospital–La Crosse
   1910 South Avenue
   LaCrosse, WI 54601
   (608) 791-4747

   An international support group for parents who have
   had an infant die during pregnancy or shortly after
   birth. They provide educational materials as well as information on local support groups.

5. Center for Sibling Loss
   The Southern School
   1456 W. Montrose
   Chicago, IL 60613

6. Mothers Against Drunk Driving (MADD)
   511 East John Carpenter Freeway, Suite 100
   Irving, Texas 75062
   (800) 438-MADD (Victim Line)

   A national organization supporting families who have
   had someone killed by a drunk driver. Support groups
   are located in many cities.

7. SHARE (Source of Help in Airing and Resolving Experiences)
   St. Elizabeth's Hospital
   211 South Third Street
   Belleville, IL 62222
   (618) 234-2415

A national self-help group devoted to helping parents who have had a miscarriage, stillbirth, ectopic pregnancy, or an early infant death.

Suicide

American Association of Suicidology
2459 South Ash
Denver, CO 80110
(303) 692-0985

A source of information about local support groups.

Death of a Spouse

1. Widowed Persons Service
   AARP
   1909 K Street, N.W.
   Washington, D.C. 20049
   (202) 434-2277

2. Theos Foundation
   1301 Clark Building
   717 Liberty Avenue
   Pittsburgh, PA 15222
   (412) 471-7779
   (800) 408-4367

   Support and education for widowed persons.

3. Parents Without Partners, Inc.
   8807 Colesville Road
   Silver Spring, MD 20910
   (301) 588-9354

   A national organization providing support to single parents. Many local chapters. May be listed in your local phone directory. Many have subgroups that are limited to the widowed.

Death by Murder

National Organization for Victim Assistance (NOVA)
1757 Park Road, N.W.
Washington, D.C. 20010
(202) 232-6682 (counseling line)
(800) 879-6682 (information and referral)

An organization that provides advocacy for victims' rights and has local chapters.

Death of a Pet

Holistic Animal Consulting Centre
29 Lyman Avenue.
Staten Island, NY 10305
(718) 720-5548

An organization that provides education and consultation for those who have had a pet die.

Illness with Cancer

1. Make Today Count
   (Call the Mid-America Cancer Center for information and location of support groups.)
   (800) 432-2273

   A national organization with local support groups for victims of cancer and other life-threatening illnesses.

2. American Cancer Society (ACS)
   1599 Clifton Road
   Atlanta, GA 30329
   (404) 320-3333
   (212) 382-2169 (National Media Office)

   A national organization providing information, patient services, and support for cancer patients.

3. Can Surmount

(Call the American Cancer Society for information.) An organization that offers information and support to cancer patients and their families. Local chapters.

4. I Can Cope

(Call the American Cancer Society for information.) Education and support for cancer patients and their families.

5. National Hospice Organization
(800) 658-8898

Nationwide and local hospice referrals.

Index